BASKETBALL'S
GREATEST STARS

BASKETBALL'S
GREATEST STARS

MICHAEL GRANGE

FIREFLY BOOKS

A FIREFLY BOOK

Published by Firefly Books Ltd. 2010

First printing

Publisher Cataloging-in-Publication Data (U.S.)
Grange, Michael.
    Basketball's greatest stars / Michael Grange.
[   ] p. : photos. (some col.) ;   cm.
Includes index.
Summary: A history of the National Basketball Association, illustrated through the profiles of its top players, past and present. Also includes the histories of 30 franchises and three essays about the game.
ISBN-13: 978-1-55407-637-6   ISBN-10: 1-55407-637-4
1. Basketball players.   2. National Basketball Association. I. Title.
796.323/64/0973 dc22   GV885.515.N37G736   2010

Library and Archives Canada Cataloguing in Publication
Grange, Michael
            Basketball's greatest stars / Michael Grange.
Includes index.
ISBN-13: 978-1-55407-637-6   ISBN-10: 1-55407-637-4
    1. National Basketball Association--Biography. 2. National Basketball Association--History. 3. Basketball players--United States--Biography. 4. Basketball--United States--History.
I. Title.
GV885.515.G73 2010   796.323092'2   C2010-901193-7

Published in the United States by
Firefly Books (U.S.) Inc.
P.O. Box 1338, Ellicott Station
Buffalo, New York 14205

Published in Canada by
Firefly Books Ltd.
66 Leek Crescent
Richmond Hill, Ontario L4B 1H1

Cover and interior design by Luna Design
Franchise profiles written by Derek Iwanuk

Printed in China

The publisher gratefully acknowledges the financial support for our publishing program by the Government of Canada through the Canada Book Fund as administered by the Department of Canadian Heritage.

LEGEND OF ABBREVIATED TERMS

G	Games
FG%	Field goal percentage
FT%	Free throw percentage
ORB	Offensive rebounds
DRB	Defensive rebounds
TRB	Total rebounds
AST	Assists
STL	Steals
BLK	Blocks
PTS	Points

Facing: Houston Rockets center Hakeem Olajuwon huddles with teammates prior to the start of Game 3 of the 1994 Finals. Houston beat the New York Knicks 93–89 to take a 2–1 series lead. The Knicks won the next two games and failed to close out the best-of-seven series, as Houston won the championship in Game 7 with a 90–84 victory at home.

Page 2: Shaquille O'Neal attempts to block Allen Iverson in Game 4 of the 2001 Finals. Los Angeles defeated Philadelphia 96–91 to take a 2–1 series lead. Iverson posted 35 points and Shaq swatted four balls to go along with his 30 points. The Lakers won the championship 4–1.

CONTENTS

Basketball's greatest rivalry:
Wilt Chamberlain defends
against Bill Russell in one of
the 142 games the two giants
battled against each other.

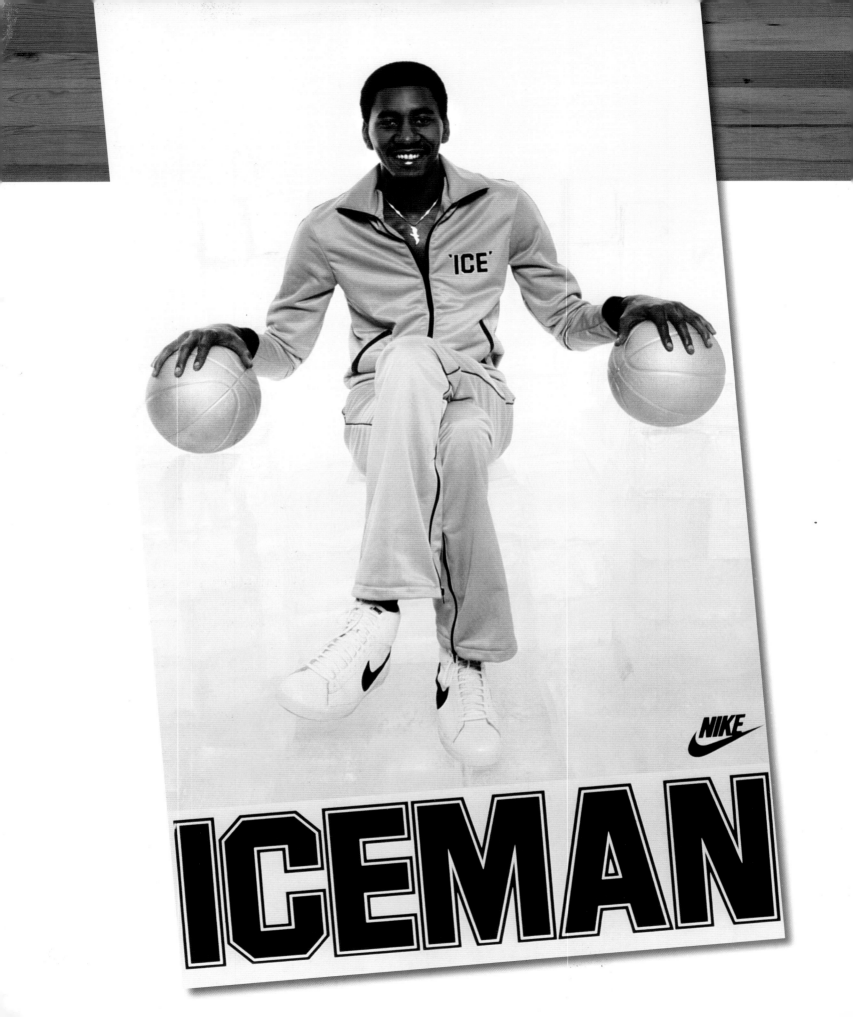

INTRODUCTION

Let's get this out front and center, this book is titled *Basketball's Greatest Stars*, and enclosed are profiles of 50 fantastic ball players: One-name icons like Kareem, Kobe, Magic and Bird. But we all know that there are more than 50 players, past and present, who rank among basketball's greatest, so by sheer mechanics, there are going to be some very good basketball players missing from this book.

George Gervin was a great star. He had a great nickname, "The Iceman." His Nike poster — him sitting cross-legged on a throne of ice blocks, palming a pair of silver basketballs — was one of my favourites in my early 1980s youth. But he's not in this book despite averaging 33.1 points per game on 52.8 percent shooting in 1979–80. I loved George Gervin. When I was kid I used to subscribe to a publication called *Basketball Digest*. It was a small format, black-and-white magazine with a glossy cover over basic newsprint. *Basketball Digest* seemed to write a lot about George Gervin and I was happy to read about his graceful swoops to the rim. But, Gervin is not in the book because he struggled to lead the very average San Antonio Spurs to greater success. The 1979–80 season might have been Gervin's best on paper, but the Spurs still only won 41 games and were one of the worst defensive teams in the NBA. If I was going to include one legendary scorer with some question marks about his ability to lead winning teams, well, my man was Dominique

During his 10-year NBA career after coming over to the league with the San Antonio Spurs in the 1976–77 ABA expansion, the Iceman led the NBA in points per game three years in a row (1977–78 to 1979–80), and again in 1981–82. His career NBA points-per-game mark of 26.2 places him eighth all-time.

Wilkins (see page 164). He defined the adage that it's better in the NBA to make errors of commission than errors of omission, and 'Nique was very committed — just look at his turnover totals! But he carried average-to-good teams to the cusp of being great and his game grew year-by-year, the rough edges being worn off by hard-earned wisdom gained through more than his share of mistakes. You have to respect that; or at least I do, so he's in the book.

It is *Basketball's Greatest Stars,* but perhaps it should be something like, *Basketball's Greatest Stars From Where I Sit* — either on press row at NBA games, reclining on the couch watching old game footage on NBA TV, or winding and rewinding some play by LeBron James (for whom my appreciation grows by the day thanks to the magic of digital cable, the advent of YouTube and the potential offered to deconstruct strokes of genius on wood). The problem in naming only 50 greats is that there is no system I'm capable of inventing that wouldn't involve some subjective analysis. Fore example, I've included Chris Paul in this book with a nod to the idea that in a very brief NBA career he's shown himself to be one of the best basketball players I've ever seen. But Deron Williams isn't in this book, and guess what? Deron Williams is a fantastic point guard and very well might be in a book like this someone else writes 10 years from now.

I watch basketball for a living, but writing a book like this takes me back to how I got into sports, and basketball.

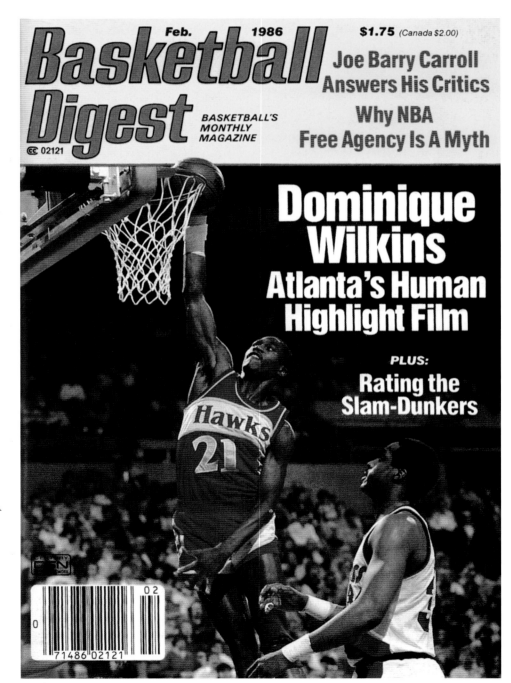

Feb. 1986 $1.75 (Canada $2.00)

Basketball Digest

BASKETBALL'S MONTHLY MAGAZINE

CE 02121

Joe Barry Carroll Answers His Critics

Why NBA Free Agency Is A Myth

Dominique Wilkins
Atlanta's Human Highlight Film

PLUS:

Rating the Slam-Dunkers

Growing up in Canada in the 1970s and 1980s, there was no NBA team to follow and only a handful of games to watch on television. I had *Basketball Digest* and a part-time librarian Mother, which was fortunate for me. She'd work on weekends, and when I was a little too young to be left at home on my own, she'd bring me to the library where I'd gravitate to the aisles of *Sports Illustrated* back issues. I'd pull them down and read them, cover-to-cover, year-by-year and decade-by-decade. I never really got to watch Dave Cowens play, but I read about him, and he read great — you could almost feel the floor burns. And then I'd see where other people rated him and I'd compare him statistically to some of his peers and then read even more about him, and somehow during that process, he became, to me, one of basketball's greatest stars.

I began covering the NBA shortly after the league expanded into Canada in 1995, and that helped inform me immeasurably. Not only were games available on television at all hours, but I was sitting courtside. You see some amazing things when you are that close. Charles Barkley was winding down his career about then, his span of time in the league arching from short-shorts to baggies. Watching him in person during his last tour with the Rockets I caught a flash of his thighs when his baggy shorts rode up as he was muscling under the glass. You don't forget things like that. Part of Barkley's appeal was that he was so physically dominant for his size. But when I caught a glimpse of those tree trunks he had for legs I realized: He was simply physically dominant no matter his size. There was no qualifier required to explain his feats on a basketball court. The man was a freight train powered by pistons unlike anything normally bestowed by nature, with an abundant amount of sublime skill to boot. Great player, great star: he's in the book. Similarly there's not that much debate about Scottie Pippen's credentials as one of the sport's legends. He's got rings, he's got the credibility bestowed on him by the likes of Michael Jordan and Phil Jackson. And I'll never forget watching him trap a ball handler just over mid-court at the sideline. I was sitting about three feet away. It was one of the first NBA games I'd ever covered, and it was like watching a great prey animal come across his supper. It was terrifying. Pippen was tracing the ball with both hands, and the ball handler — whose dribble was long since surrendered in a desperate attempt to plead for mercy — was waving the ball around looking for a teammate to pass to while trying reverse his pivot. Every move simply seemed to make the vice Pippen was applying tighter. By the time the ball handler called for timeout I felt compelled to check my shirt for blood spatters. You see something like that you're definitely putting Scottie Pippen in a book like this. Jordan? He would be in any book; but I was in Utah the night he pushed off on Bryon Russell and hit that jumper for the 1998 championship, and so it was with a special pleasure I put him in here, even if I wished he hadn't come back to play for the Wizards.

I could go on, but you get the picture. I hope you enjoy my take on the greatest to ever play the game.

Michael Grange

FOREWORD
Wayne Embry

You don't spend more than 50 years in the professional basketball business like I have and not learn a thing or two. And one thing I've definitely learned is that people love to compare players: Fathers comparing their heroes with the current stars their kids are watching, or people wondering if a quick little point guard who played in the 1950s could manage in today's NBA. Comparing players is a great way to start a conversation, I should know, I'm always getting asked those kinds of questions.

"Who was better, Russell or Chamberlain?" I'll get asked; I suppose I should have an answer. I played against both of them for most of my career, and Russell and I were teammates for two seasons. Let's just say they were both pretty damn good.

"But what about Kareem? Where does he rank?" Well, I have my opinions. It was me who traded him from the Milwaukee Bucks, where I was general manager, to the Los Angeles Lakers in 1975. People thought I was crazy, and I was. You can't trade Kareem and not set your team back. But he wanted to go and the Bucks needed to get some value in return. I did my best and lived to tell about it. It took a little while for the Bucks to regain their feet, but they won an average of 54 games a year from 1979–87, so it worked out pretty well.

I've been lucky to be around great players my entire career and after it too, and I feel fortunate to have some insight on matters like these. It is insight I kind of take for granted sometimes, but I realize that having it puts me on a pretty short list.

When LeBron James was set to break into the league, I was curious about the kid people kept telling me was special. "Michael Jordan and Magic Johnson rolled into one," they said, "the next Oscar Robertson."

Really? I played with Oscar for six years with the Cincinnati Royals and I always thought he was one of a kind. Later, during my years running the Cavaliers I'd gotten to see Jordan up close enough to know you didn't compare him to other players lightly, if at all. That man broke my heart

Wayne Embry as a Celtic in 1967–68: his only championship season. Embry chipped in a playoff average of 10 minutes, 3.7 points and 2.8 rebounds per game, as Boston took the title over Los Angeles. Embry was a Milwaukee Buck for his last season (1968–69) and retired to their front office, becoming the Bucks' GM in 1972, making him the first African American GM in North American professional sports.

too many times to count. But LeBron? Once I saw him play in high school, I was a believer. I don't know if he's going to be better than all the greats that came before him, friends and competitors of mine, but he sure has a chance, doesn't he?

In the last part of my career I've been working in Toronto as a special advisor to the Toronto Raptors, the NBA's only international franchise, and it's allowed me to see the stars that people might be talking about five decades from now. How will Steve Nash rank with the great point guards of my time when he's done? And what about Dwight Howard? Will he take his place beside Russell, Chamberlain and Kareem? In that respect it's been fun to meet people like Michael Grange, the basketball reporter for the *Globe and Mail* in Toronto. He'd be writing about LeBron and call me to talk about Oscar Robertson, or we'd be watching Howard work out before a game and we'd talk about Chamberlain. And now that he's asked me to write a forward for *Basketball's Greatest Stars*, I know why. All those comparisons will give basketball fans something to talk about.

Me, I don't really like to say one player is better than another; I've played with or against many great players, and scouted, signed or traded many more. But Mike? You can't blame him for comparing — that's what basketball fans do.

M⊕MENTS
That Shaped the NBA

The BAA and NBL Merge to Form the Modern NBA

Sometimes it's easy to forget that the NBA, with its history stretching back decades, is a relative newcomer among major North American team sports. Major League Baseball can trace its roots to the mid-19th century. The National Football League got rolling in the early 1920s and the National Hockey League has been awarding the Stanley Cup since 1926.

While basketball was a popular amateur sport that spread quickly through the YMCA, church basements and schools after it was invented in 1891 by Dr. James Naismith, it wasn't until the late 1940s that it found its professional feet. Prior to that, professional basketball was played mostly by barnstorming teams that traveled and played exhibitions in dance halls and concert venues. The Harlem Globetrotters got their start that way, as did the New York Renaissance. Leagues came and went, mostly on a regional basis.

The Basketball Association of America (BAA) was formed in 1946, with the first game being played in Toronto between the Toronto Huskies and the New York Knickerbockers. The league was inspired by owners of professional hockey teams in the Northeast who were looking for additional events to make use of their arenas. The first commissioner, Maurice Podoloff, had previously been the commissioner of the American Hockey League.

Bill Russell and Red Auerbach celebrate their eighth-straight NBA championship (9th in 10 seasons) with a game-seven, home-court victory, 95–93, over the Los Angeles Lakers on April 29, 1966. Auerbach's wheeling and dealing prior to the 1956 NBA draft enabled the Celtics to claim Russell (the second overall pick), creating the most dominant dynasty the sport has ever seen.

Maurice Podoloff, commissioner of the Basketball Association of America, is surrounded by (L-R) Ike Duffey, Anderson Packers (Indiana) owner; Leo Farris, National Basketball League president; Ned Irish, New York Knicks owner; and Walter Brown, Boston Celtics owner, to announce the merger of the BAA and NBL to form the NBA on August 3, 1949.

Before the BAA was the National Basketball League (NBL), which was founded in 1937. It was comprised mainly of small market and corporate teams in the Great Lakes area, with notable franchises that included the Oshkosh All-Stars, the Fort Wayne Zollner Pistons and later the Minneapolis Lakers that featured the great George Mikan.

The BAA teams, when playing in the Boston Garden and Madison Square Garden, drew meager crowds and sporadic media coverage, though the Finals games in Philadelphia drew encouraging numbers of fans. Meanwhile, the NBL teams played in smaller venues and smaller cities and also struggled to make a dent in the public consciousness.

After the 1947–48 season, Mikan's Lakers and the three other top NBL franchises — the Rochester Royals, Syracuse Nationals and Fort Wayne Pistons — joined the BAA to form the earliest incarnation of

the NBA, giving the new-look BAA not only the best markets and arenas, but most of the best players as well. The following summer, on August 3, 1949, the six remaining NBL teams joined the BAA and the enterprise was renamed the National Basketball Association, featuring three divisions and 17 teams playing a 66-game schedule. That first season, the Lakers defeated the Syracuse Nationals in six games of the best-of-seven Finals.

Breaking the Mold

Rules are made to be broken, reinvented, shaped, interpreted and occasionally followed. The rather straightforward game that Dr. Naismith invented featured only 13 rules, all of which have since been modified to a greater or lesser extent. One rule that exists pretty much as written originally called for the person inbounding the ball to take no more than five seconds to make a pass or else face loss of possession. Other rules have changed significantly. Naismith mandated that running with the ball would not be allowed; originally, players had to play the ball from where they stood, either shooting or passing before they could move again. Dribbling was eventually introduced in stages, taking its current definition in 1908; however, it didn't become a significant part of the game until the 1950s when manufacturing processes improved the balls, and playing surfaces became more consistent.

There are a number of rules and rule changes that could be considered vital to the sport's development, but among the rules that came into being after the NBA was founded and the game was taking shape some changes have had more impact than others.

The Widening of the Lane: The game's first dominant force was 6-foot-10, 250-pound George Mikan, who helped the Minneapolis Lakers to five titles in six seasons. So effective was Mikan that before the 1951–52 season, the league decided to widen the lane from 6 feet to 12, largely at the urging of New York Knicks' coach Joe Lapchick. The impact was immediate: While Mikan remained the league's biggest star, his scoring averaged dropped from 28.4 points a game to 23.8, as he could no longer set up a few feet from the basket for his famous hook shots. His shooting percentage fell from 42.8 percent to 38.9. With more room to operate, guards began to appear near the top of the scoring race for the first time. More than a decade later, another giant was playing havoc in the league. Wilt Chamberlain's romp through the basketball record books was most pronounced prior to the 1964–65 season when the lane was widened again, this time to 16 feet, its current width. Like Mikan, Chamberlain remained dominant, but his effectiveness was statistically reduced; for example, he never averaged more than 40 points a game again. Chamberlain finally gave up his scoring crown in 1966–67 to Rick Barry, a small forward, setting the tone for the modern NBA where perimeter players are the most dangerous offensive weapons on the floor.

The Shot Clock: Rare is the idea that gets implemented as envisioned and works as planned, permanently changing what was there before. The NBA's adoption of the 24-second shot clock is one of those rare gems. The idea had several fathers, but its champion was Danny Biasone, a bowling alley operator who also owned the Syracuse Nationals, one of the NBA's original franchises and the forerunner of the current Golden State Warriors. Frustrated by the degeneration of what should have been fast-flowing games into sluggish foul-and-stall contests, Biasone was looking for a solution. He heard that Howard Hobson, then coaching at Yale University, was advocating a 30-second clock for the college game, which would force the offensive team to shoot at the basket before the clock expired or be required to turn the ball over to the defense. For Biasone, it was an epiphany. The NBA was withering: The game had become a tactical gridlock where the team that was leading heading into the fourth quarter would hold the ball indefinitely, or until the other team fouled them. If the lead did happen to change hands, the new leader would begin stalling until another foul and on and on.

"Before the clock, there was no game at all," said Syracuse Nationals star Danny Schayes. "It would get into the second half, and the team that was ahead would just kill the ball, and then you'd have to foul. Then they would foul you, and the game would deteriorate. The game stunk! It was a march from one foul line to the other. Something had to be done." On November 22, 1950, the Fort Wayne Pistons defeated the Minneapolis Lakers 19–18 in the lowest scoring game in NBA history. Each team had only four baskets, and Fort Wayne outscored Minneapolis by 3–1 in the fourth quarter.

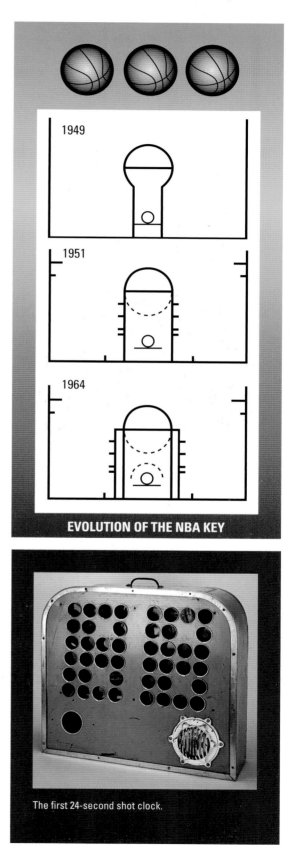

EVOLUTION OF THE NBA KEY

1949

1951

1964

The first 24-second shot clock.

Soon after, Biasone began lobbying for a shot clock. He and the Nationals' general manager Leo Ferris came up with the idea of a 24-second clock after looking at the number of shots taken in some of the league's higher scoring games. Finding that teams would combine for about 120 shots, they divided the number of seconds in a 48-minute game — 2,880 — by 120 and came up with 24 seconds as the right amount of time for a team to get a good shot off without the game stagnating. Its first test came on August 10, 1954, when some Nationals players and local Syracuse talent scrimmaged at Vocational High School in Syracuse, Biasone's alma mater, in front of the likes of Red Auerbach and other assembled NBA executives. The pace was quicker, scoring was up, and once they were able to find a manufacturer for the shot clocks, the rule was implemented. The payoff was immediate, as team scoring jumped from an average of 79.5 points a game to 93.1. Syracuse, fittingly, won the NBA title, using the clock to rally from 17 points behind in a dramatic championship game against Fort Wayne.

The Dave DeBusschere Trade

Dynasties have always defined the NBA, and most often their emergence can be traced to a deft player move. Would the Boston Celtics be the Celtics if Red Auerbach hadn't convinced Rochester to pass over Bill Russell as its first pick in 1956 when Russell was coming out of the University of San Francisco? The agreement was sealed when Auerbach convinced Celtics' owner Walter Brown to persuade Rochester owner Les Harrison to forgo taking Russell in return for Brown sending the Ice Capades (which he owned) to Rochester for a week. With Russell in the lineup as a rookie, Boston won their first NBA title and went

on to win 10 more in the next 12 years. The Los Angeles Lakers can trace the four championships they've won with Kobe Bryant to the decision Jerry West made to trade Vlade Divac — a proven NBA big man — to the Charlotte Hornets for Bryant, an 18-year-old who was trying to become the first perimeter player to jump from high school to the NBA.

But perhaps no trade set the stage for the NBA's future growth like the New York Knicks' decision to trade Howard Komives and Walt Bellamy to the Detroit Pistons for Dave DeBusschere on December 19, 1968. DeBusschere instantly became the missing piece in a championship puzzle. The bruising power forward allowed Willis Reed to move to center, while the departure of Komives opened up the point-guard spot for a promising second-year player named Walt Frazier. The Knicks reeled off 10 wins in a row on the way to the 1969 Eastern Conference Finals before losing to the Boston Celtics.

The 1969–70 season proved magical. The Knicks were playing their first full season in the new Madison Square Garden — a season punctuated with the Knicks' first NBA championship. They won it in a seventh game at home, with franchise cornerstone Willis Reed limping out of the tunnel to the roar of the crowd, and Madison Avenue darling Walt "Clyde" Frazier orchestrating the win with 36 points, 19 assists and 7 rebounds. They did it again in 1973, for their second title. The early 70s Knicks electrified the biggest media market in North America at a time when the ABA was trying to steal the NBA's market share, and basketball was still trying to gain traction alongside the other major league sports. The Dave DeBusschere trade made the Knicks, and the Knicks made it happen.

ABA–NBA Merger

The ABA never envisioned itself as a long-term rival to the NBA. Part of its pitch to prospective owners was that they could buy an ABA franchise for roughly half the going rate of an NBA club, and if they built a sturdy league, the then-10-team NBA would eventually have to merge with them, giving ABA owners a side door to respectability. The plan was a little lacking. By the time the ABA merged with the NBA in 1976, 27 other franchises — in some shape or form — had come and gone, their owners never realizing NBA riches. In the end, only four teams made the jump from the run 'n' gun league, and the owners of the San Antonio Spurs, Indiana Pacers, New Jersey Nets and Denver Nuggets each had to pay $3.2-million to the NBA for the right to join the league. They also had to forgo three years of television revenue among other penalties. It was, however, fun while it lasted. It was the ABA that introduced bikini-clad ball girls, the forerunners to the dance teams that are standard fare at every arena now. The league also introduced the three-point line and pioneered the possibility of teenagers making the jump from high school straight to pro basketball. By staging the first-ever slam dunk contest at the 1976 All-Star Game, the ABA set the stage for the NBA's All-Star event that has since morphed into a three-day weekend of activities and entertainment. Some of the best entertainment provided by the ABA was unintentional, such as when Marvin "Bad News" Barnes, the talented but troubled forward for the Spirits of St. Louis, balked boarding a plane that, because of a change in times zones, was scheduled to land earlier than when it took off. "I ain't going on no time machine," he said. "I ain't taking no flight that takes me back in time." Much of it went unseen as some of the best players in the sport's history — Julius Erving, Moses Malone, David Thompson, George Gervin, Artis Gilmore, Dan Issel and many more — cut their competitive teeth in the ABA, playing in front of sparse crowds without the benefit of television. The ABA's best players fit in well after the merger, playing leading roles on good teams, making the NBA better just by their presence. In the first season after the merger, the Portland Trail Blazers won the NBA championship with Maurice Lucas (whom they'd picked up in the ABA dispersal draft) as their leading scorer. They beat the Philadelphia 76ers in the Finals, a team stocked with ABA stars Julius Erving and George McGinnis. The Houston Rockets made the Eastern Conference Finals thanks to ABA star Moses Malone, and San Antonio and Denver, each with a roster heavily laced with ABA remainders, made the playoffs.

Appointment of David Stern

He's never scored a basket or been featured in a highlight reel, but David Joel Stern has had every bit as much to do with the success and growth of the NBA as Magic Johnson, Michael Jordan or LeBron James. In more than a quarter century as commissioner, Stern has fashioned a league

Julius Erving soars through the air with his much-copied foul-line takeoff dunk at the first-ever Slam Dunk Contest during the 1976 ABA All-Star Game in Denver, Colorado. The next dunk contest was at the 1984 NBA All-Star Game, also in Denver.

Dirk Nowitzki is presented the NBA MVP trophy by commissioner David Stern on May 15, 2007. Stern has been vital to the NBA's foreign growth. Nowitzki is the first European to win the MVP award.

NBA's general counsel and worked closely with then-commissioner Larry O'Brien to establish the NBA salary cap system for the 1984–85 season, the essential tenets of which remain in place. As a measure of the NBA's success under Stern, the salary cap figure in 1984–85 was $3.6 million per team. For 2009–10, it was $57.7 million.

Financially, there have been many success stories under Stern's stewardship. The league has expanded from 23 to 30 teams, nearly all playing in state-of-the-art arenas. And before he became commissioner, the NBA's television footprint was so small that the landmark 1980 NBA Finals featuring Julius Erving of the Philadelphia 76ers and Magic Johnson of the Los Angeles Lakers was shown only on a tape-delay basis. The league's current broadcasting deal is worth $930 million a year. Under Stern's guidance, the league has become international in scope, welcoming stars from Europe, South America and China, while the league's games are shown in more than 200 countries and broadcast in 43 languages.

But perhaps Stern's lasting legacy has been his ability to take challenges and turn them into triumphs. He presided over a lockout that resulted in the 1998–99 season being shortened to 50 games, but the league benefitted by gaining additional cost certainty for the owners and stability for the players. Stern also rose to the occasion when the infamous November 2004 brawl between the Indiana Pacers and Detroit Pistons at the Palace in Auburn Hills, Michigan, threatened to spoil the league's image. Stern came down hard and doled out 146 games in suspensions to nine players. Still concerned about the league's image he instituted a dress code for players the following season, taking aim at the so-called "gangster" or hip-hop styles favored by some players. Because the styles in question — baggy jeans and do-rags, for example — were popular among some black stars, critics suggested the change was racially motivated, but Stern was always able to weather the storm. The league he serves has benefitted from his long view and steady hand.

that is forward-looking and robust — as popular in China as in the United States — and he has placed himself on the short list of the best in a narrow field by navigating triumph and scandal with smarts and skill.

The New Jersey-raised son of a Manhattan delicatessen owner, Stern graduated from Rutgers in 1963 and Columbia Law School three years later. He joined the New York law firm of Proskauer Rose Goetz & Mendelsohn, became a partner at age 32, and took on the NBA as one of his clients. Nothing significant in the league has happened since without his fingerprints. While a lawyer working for the league, Stern was involved with the Oscar Robertson antitrust case, which resolved the issue of player free agency, and he helped to facilitate the merger with the ABA. In 1978 Stern left his law firm to become the

The Recuperative Powers of Michael Jordan

Even icons are fragile, prone to the weakness of flesh and bone. Would Michael Jordan be Michael Jordan if he hadn't been available to play nearly every game over his matchless career? From his breakout 1986–87 campaign, when he averaged 37.1 points a game to 1997–98 when he led the Bulls to their sixth NBA title, Jordan missed just seven regular season games other than his mid-career hiatus to play professional baseball. If, as comedian and actor Woody Allen said, 80 percent of success is showing up, Jordan was bound for greatness. The only exception to his near-perfect attendance record came during his sophomore NBA season when he missed 64 games. Three games into the year Jordan soared for a routine — for him — attack on the rim but landed flat-footed and awkwardly and felt a sharp pain in his left foot. Upon examination, it was revealed he'd fractured the navicular tarsal bone.

Greatness and health go hand-in-hand in the NBA. One of the most statistically amazing aspects of Wilt Chamberlain's statistically amazing 1961–62 season was that he averaged 48.5 minutes a game — he played

March 17, 1986: Michael Jordan goes hard to the rim in his second game back after returning from a broken foot which he injured on October 29, 1985. The Bulls lost to Atlanta 106–96.

Bryant Reeves puts down one of his 12 points on New Year's day 1998 against Philadelphia. Reeves' posted career highs in points per game (16.3) and assists per game (2.1) in the 1997–98 campaign.

every minute of regulation time in the 80-game season as well as every overtime minute. John Stockton and Karl Malone of the Utah Jazz became the most prolific duo in NBA history in part because they were almost never hurt.

After breaking his foot, Jordan's second season seemed over before it started. And foot injuries are not to be trifled with in the NBA. Bill Walton is widely considered one of the most talented and skilled centers to have ever played, but he only played 468 out of a possible 820 games in his star-crossed NBA career due to foot and ankle injuries that were often misdiagnosed or mistreated. Sam Bowie was a good enough prospect to be drafted ahead of Jordan by the Portland Trail Blazers in 1984, but injuries limited him to being a talented role player, never more. More recently Yao Ming of the Houston Rockets appears to be headed for a career compromised by foot problems.

As gifted as Jordan was as a player, he proved to be able to heal well, too. By late February, with the Bulls last in the Eastern Conference and seemingly out of playoff contention, Jordan was secretly playing pickup basketball at North Carolina to test his foot. Convinced that he was game-ready, Jordan began pressing Bulls' ownership and management about returning to finish the season. While medical opinions suggested that Jordan was only at a moderate risk of further injury, even that was too much for the powers-that-be, who all had a vested interest in making sure Jordan was healthy for the balance of his career, not a seemingly lost season. Jordan changed their minds, however, mainly by not changing his, and he returned to the court for the last 14 games of the season and lifted the Bulls to the playoffs. And just to prove that his foot was fine, he set an NBA playoff scoring record with 63 points in a double-overtime loss to the Boston Celtics in the first round of the playoffs. Jordan was back and league was healthier for it.

NBA Lockout

Bryant Reeves had his moments in his brief NBA career. In his third NBA season, playing for the then-Vancouver Grizzlies, the beefy seven-footer from tiny Gans, Oklahoma, averaged 16.3 points and 7.9 rebounds on 52.3 percent shooting. Respectable numbers for a young big man, even if he was playing for a team that had finished 19–63. But good enough to earn him a six-year, $65-million contract extension in the summer of 1997? Deserving or not, he got it. It was an enormous payday at the time — on average more than the likes of veteran Hall-of-Fame-bound centers

David Robinson and Hakeem Olajuwon were making — and it soon proved to be a bust, and as good an argument as any that NBA salaries had gotten out of control. When NBA owners locked out their players before the 1998–99 season, the reason most often cited was the six-year, $126-million contract extension signed by Kevin Garnett that same summer. And while it was the richest deal in team sports at the time, it made some sense — Garnett was a realistic candidate to be the best player of his generation. But paying $65 million for a role-playing big man on a 19-win team? That was too much. "It scares everybody: owners, fans, maybe even players," Milwaukee Bucks' owner Herb Kohl said when the big extensions were being handed out. "That kind of money creates an imbalance which is not healthy to our league and to our image with the fans."

The two sides came to terms in January and the league was able to cobble together a 50-game schedule. What was more significant was a new salary structure designed to save the owners from themselves. It was a deal generally considered a victory for the owners, as salaries were capped at between $9 million and $14 million, depending on years in the league; and a rookie pay scale was also introduced, with salaries tied to draft order. As if to prove the owners might just have had a case, Reeves returned from the lockout more than 40 pounds overweight and lost his starting position in the first year of his lucrative new contract. A back injury put him out of basketball in the middle of his seventh season, but not before his contract ran out.

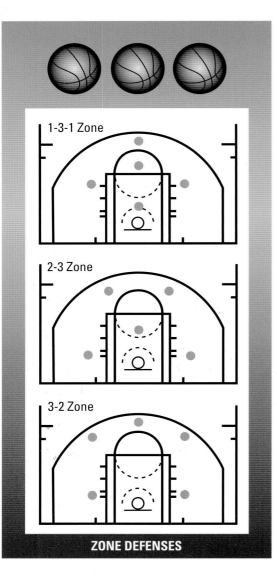

ZONE DEFENSES

1-3-1 Zone

2-3 Zone

3-2 Zone

Phoenix, 2001

Sustaining a true fan's interest is relatively easy. For whatever reason, the true fan loves the minutiae of the sport so much that even its flaws can be objects of interest. But when a sport is losing even its most ardent supporters, it's time for a change. You can make the case that there is no greater supporter of basketball than Jerry Colangelo. The son of immigrant Italian parents living in Chicago used the game to live the American dream. A star player at the University of Illinois, he graduated in 1962 and not so long after he worked for two years in the front office of the expansion Chicago Bulls before becoming the Phoenix Suns' first general manager in 1968, a position where he elevated himself to one of the game's most respected executives and, finally, an owner. His Suns teams were always in the playoff hunt and were known for a high-paced, free-flowing style of basketball.

In 2001 the NBA was in trouble. Television ratings were down nearly 50 percent since their peak during the final years of the Chicago Bulls' reign. At first it was easy to blame the fallout from Michael Jordan's retirement and the 1998 labor stoppage. But eventually it became clear that the game itself was a problem. In 1988–89, every NBA team except the lowly Miami Heat averaged more than 100 points per game. The league average was 109.2. Even the defensive-minded Detroit Pistons of the Bad Boys era averaged 106.6 points a night. But then the brakes came on and came on hard, as coaches like the New York Knicks' Pat Riley realized that by maximizing physical play on and off the ball — betting quite correctly that the referees can't call everything — scoring could be reduced drastically, a strategy that became a trend. In 1998–99 only the Sacramento Kings averaged more than 100 points per game and the league average had fallen to 91.6 points per game and fan interest fell with it. "I told [NBA commissioner] David Stern, 'When I get turned off and I'm a lifer, that's a real problem,'" said Colangelo. Stern's response was to authorize Colangelo to form a committee of other executives and former players and coaches to investigate the possibility of changes. They met in Phoenix in the spring of 2001, and the first order of business was to look at a video, comparing playing styles from the 60s, 70s, 80s and early 90s with the product currently on the floor.

"By having it all on one video, you could see our game evolving, or de-evolving, to be more accurate. It was obvious that we had to make some changes right away," said Colangelo.

For the 2001–02 season, the committee eliminated rules that made it illegal to play zone defense with an eye toward curbing isolation plays that had bogged down the game. The time allowed for teams to move the ball over the midcourt line was cut from 10 to 8 seconds to encourage more full-court pressure and running to counter that pressure. For the 2003–04 season, the committee took the next step and began outlawing all hand-checking on the perimeter, getting the league back closer to its roots and allowing the player with the ball to attack the defense with more speed and effectiveness, a change that encouraged teams to look for smaller, faster players rather than the lane-clogging thugs that were in vogue a decade earlier. Scoring climbed. In 2008–09 the league average hit 100 points per game again for the first time since 1995–96.

19-year-old LeBron James of St. Vincent-St. Mary's High School shouts to teammates at the Pangos Dream Classic game in Los Angeles in 2003. James was selected first overall by the Cleveland Cavaliers later that year.

LeBron James Meets Frankie Walker

Life can turn on the smallest things. Basketball history can, too. It's safe to assume that LeBron James was already a standout athlete by the time he was in the fourth grade. (Kids who are 6-foot-8 and 240 pounds by the time they finish high school have never been small for their age.) The speed and jumping ability that helped make James such a stunning NBA player are traits that can be improved with training, but not if they don't exist in some form in the first place. And James was probably a good kid — eager, coachable, approachable. You can assume all this because why else would the coaches of the East Dragons, his Pee-Wee football team in Akron, all consider taking him into their homes as a 9-year-old heading into fifth grade? That he needed a home is an essential part of the James biography. Born to 16-year-old Gloria James, the future NBA star was living in such an unstable environment that he had missed more than 80 days of school in the fourth grade. He and his mother had moved a dozen times in the previous three years, often enough that finding his way across town for school was sometimes a challenge left for another day. Frankie Walker coached James in Pee-Wee football and, as James writes in his autobiography, *Shooting Stars*, he recognized a young soul in need of help: "It looked to him like there was little joy in my life, as if I was older than my actual age and had already seen too much and been through too much … He saw someone who needed help." The Walkers were exactly what James needed and James lived with them and their three children throughout fifth grade and on-and-off through sixth grade until his mother was able to find a permanent home. The Walkers' discipline suited James well. Up at 6:45 a.m., or earlier if baths were needed, chores became part of his daily routine, as did attending school. "The Walkers laid a foundation for me," James writes. "A foundation I really had never experienced before. I got the stability I craved. They showed me living in a house in a family-style environment was the rule, the way most people lived their lives, not the exception … I loved being there. I loved being part of the flow that is family." James' talent was such that he would likely have received countless chances to make and remake his life anyway. But encountering Frankie Walker and his family at the time in his life he did meant that he has never needed a second chance to remake his life. One chance was enough.

Best of the BEST

Kevin Garnett protects the ball from Kobe Bryant while looking to set up a play on Christmas day, 2008. Both superstars burst onto the scene straight out of high school.

Abdul-Jabbar goes up for a skyhook against James Edwards of the Phoenix Suns in 1982–83. That season was the first of back-to-back Finals losses for the Lakers before winning it all in 1985 with Abdul-Jabbar taking playoff MVP honors.

KAREEM **ABDUL-JABBAR**

You could never say he wasn't intelligent, because his quiet dignity and relentless intellectual curiosity marked him as one of the most sophisticated athletes of his time.

You could never say he wasn't self-aware. In the years after his retirement he came to recognize that his aloofness and reluctance to embrace his fame — earned as the most accomplished and quite possibly the best player in NBA history — had isolated him within the sport.

But really, what was Kareem Abdul-Jabbar thinking?

While writing on his blog for the *Los Angeles Times* in 2008, the NBA's all-time leading scorer laid out a simple five-step guide that the average 50-something gym rat could theoretically follow to wow his friends with a skyhook, the signature sweeping move that Abdul-Jabbar brought with him to the NBA as an impactful rookie named Lew Alcindor in 1969.

It was a nice gesture, but Kareem trying to explain the skyhook to basketball mortals was like Michelangelo trying to explain the Sistene Chapel to a class of finger-painting first graders.

Some things are meant to be admired, not imitated.

No one had ever been so devastatingly effective with a hook shot before Abdul-Jabbar came into the NBA, and no one has been able to master his shot since. Kareem frustrated opponents with his signature shot for 20 seasons, leaving the game with six NBA titles; six Most Valuable Player awards; 19 All-Star

appearances and spots on the NBA's 35th and 50th anniversary teams.

"He got the skyhook to a point in his prime where it got to be like a layup for him," former Phoenix Suns' coach Cotton Fitzsimmons said of Abdul-Jabbar's famous shot. "But what really sticks in my mind is playing against him, you'd run an offensive set, use two or three screens, get a good shot, feel satisfied, then his team would have the ball, he'd catch it in the post and, with the grace of a ballet dancer, turn and shoot. What you worked 18, 20 seconds to get, he'd do in five."

The shot that Kareem made look so easy is actually much more difficult than he lets on, as the skyhook requires tremendous balance, timing and touch; something he exhibited every time he rolled his 7-foot-2 frame into the shot, finishing it with an ever-so-gentle flick of his wrist and a whispered goodbye from his fingertips.

"He's the most beautiful athlete in sports," said his Los Angeles Laker teammate Earvin "Magic" Johnson.

Abdul-Jabbar came into

Abdul-Jabbar of the Milwaukee Bucks and Dave Cowens of the Boston Celtics during the 1973–74 Finals. The Bucks lost in seven games.

the NBA as the No.1 pick by the Milwaukee Bucks in 1969 — they earned the selection in a coin toss with the Phoenix Suns, another expansion team — after leading UCLA to three straight NCAA championships and just as Bill Russell and Wilt Chamberlain were leaving center stage.

He became an instant star in Milwaukee, finishing second in the NBA in scoring (28.8 points per game) and third in rebounding (14.5 per game) as the previously woeful Bucks finished second in the Eastern Division with a 56–26 record. They added Hall-of-Fame guard Oscar Robertson to the lineup the next year, and Milwaukee became the 1971 NBA champions. That year, Abdul-Jabbar earned the first of his NBA-record six Most Valuable Player awards.

During his time in Milwaukee Abdul-Jabbar also gained a name for the shot he perfected while playing for John Wooden at UCLA in an era when the NCAA outlawed dunking, requiring big men to develop touch around the basket.

It was Bucks' announcer Eddie Doucette who coined a name for it. "I'd been watching him, and one night, it just hit me. It's so different than anybody else's hook. It's not a flat hook, a baby hook, a half hook, or a jump hook. It's a pure hook. And it does come out of the sky."

The Bucks championship in his second season was the highlight of what was a difficult decade for Abdul-Jabbar. On the floor he was without peer — he won five MVP awards in his first eight seasons — but he won only one title and was otherwise a man in conflict.

Born Ferdinand Lewis Alcindor Jr. in New York City in 1947, he converted from Catholicism to Islam in 1971 and changed his name from Lew Alcindor to Kareem Abdul-Jabbar — it means "noble, powerful servant." Becoming increasingly uncomfortable in the cozy confines of the Midwest, he eventually asked to be traded to either New York or Los Angeles.

- Drafted: 1st overall by the Milwaukee Bucks in 1969
- Milwaukee Bucks: 1969–75
- Los Angeles Lakers: 1975–89
- College: UCLA

"Kareem was very pleasant, but very subdued," said former Bucks owner Marvin Fishman. "He'd go eat by himself. He would sit in a Chinese restaurant with his back to everyone. He would eat his meal and go home. People thought he was standoffish, but no. He needed his privacy."

The decision to convert to Islam was reflective of another side of the player that became more apparent as his career went on — behind the aloof, distant stares was an active and searching mind.

One of his proudest keepsakes from his days as a high school star at New York's Power Memorial Academy is a photo that shows him in the background towering above reporters clustered around a table at which sat Martin Luther King Jr. Abdul-Jabbar had earned the press credential at a summer journalism workshop in 1964. "That's when I became a black historian. And that's still my gig," he said years later.

No kidding. In addition to leading the NBA in scoring, he leads in nonfiction titles, having written several highly regarded works of history. A regular *Sports Illustrated* cover subject, he's also been featured on the cover of *American Libraries.*

In the 1980s Abdul-Jabbar gained his greatest professional satisfaction. Teamed with the effervescent Magic Johnson, Abdul-Jabbar's dominance of the NBA's MVP balloting slowed, but he in turn became the bedrock of the Lakers' "Showtime" era that made eight NBA Finals appearances in 10 years, winning five championships.

Along the way, Abdul-Jabbar kept winning games with his skyhook and continued to build his statistical mountain. He played one year too long — at 42 he was a role player, the game having finally passed him by — but he could gain some satisfaction in having played long enough that the world he struggled to fit into as a young man had made room not only for his skyhook, but for him.

"The 80s made up for all the abuse I took during the 70s," he said, long after he left the game. "I outlived all my critics. By the time I retired, everybody saw me as a venerable institution. Things do change."

But his signature shot will stand the test of time.

CAREER HIGHLIGHTS

- Is the only NBA player in history to win 6 MVP awards and play in 19 NBA All-Star games
- Ranks first all-time in NBA history in points, minutes played, field-goals made and field-goals attempted
- Converted to Islam and changed his name from Lew Alcindor to Kareem Abdul-Jabbar in 1971
- Had numerous acting roles, including the role of Roger Murdoch in *Airplane*, and appeared as himself on many TV shows
- Won NBA Rookie of the Year award in 1969–70
- Averaged 34.8 PPG in 1971–72, which ranks as the 10th best single-season-scoring average in NBA history
- Played in 1,560 NBA games, which ranks second all-time
- Has written or co-written seven books

34

FORWARD

CHARLES **BARKLEY**

Barkley snags a rebound against the Chicago Bulls in Game 2 of the 1993 NBA Finals. The Bulls won 111–108; Barkley netted 42 points, his highest of the series.

Charles Barkley was right about one thing. He's no role model. How could he be? On court, off court, on television, in person — Barkley is one of a kind. But role model? Impossible. By the time he left Leeds, Alabama, the mold had long been broken.

As time has passed, the one-of-a-kind power forward with a penchant for saying what other people only think — except funnier — has had his image smoothed, even as the memories of his game have faded. He's the chubby, obnoxious uncle at the family barbecue now dispensing wisdom and opinion on television to NBA audiences who can't get enough. No one knows what he's going to say, but they can't stop listening and, most times, laughing.

"My basketball accomplishments speak for themselves," said Barkley, almost as well-known now in retirement as a say-anything broadcaster than as a do-it-all player. "My personality ... look, I've been good, I've been bad, I've been funny, I've been stupid, the same as everybody else. Mine is just in the limelight. Everyone knows I have a good heart. I'm a good person."

Raised by his mother and grandmother in Leeds, a small suburb just outside Birmingham, Alabama, Barkley hardly seemed poised for greatness, not as a 5-foot-10, 220-pound junior at Leeds High School who couldn't crack the starting lineup on the varsity. But he grew taller, if not slimmer, and headed into his senior season at 6-foot-4 — despite being listed at 6-foot-6 throughout his career, he never passed 6-foot-5 — and

led Leeds to a 26–3 season. Passed over by most of the big-name schools, he caught the eye of an assistant coach at Auburn University during the state championship tournament. The assistant told head coach Sonny Smith he'd just seen "a fat guy ... who can play like the wind."

He proved to be a dominant player, able to justify his occasional clashes with Smith by pointing to the Southeastern Conference Player of the Year Award he'd earned as a junior. His tendency to thumb his nose at authority cost him a spot on the 1984 Olympic team coached by no-nonsense Bob Knight; however his play at the tryouts attracted the NBA's attention. The 76ers picked him fifth in the draft, one of the strongest ever, with Hakeem Olajuwon, Sam Bowie, Michael Jordan and Sam Perkins selected ahead of Barkley.

The 76ers had concerns about his weight — he played at more than 290 pounds at times in college — so he slimmed down to 250 pounds as a professional and made an immediate impact on a veteran-laden Philadelphia club that featured Julius Erving, Moses Malone and Maurice Cheeks. That team went 58–24, but lost to the Boston Celtics in the Eastern Conference Finals, the first in what was a career of playoff disappointments for Barkley, who never won an NBA title, the one hole on his résumé.

In 1992, he had elevated to the peak of his considerable powers on the court, but after eight statistically astonishing seasons as the focus of the Philadelphia 76ers, where he routinely ranked among the top five in the NBA in scoring, rebounding and field-goal percentage, Barkley asked to be traded, frustrated by the club's lack of post-season success. The 76ers dealt him to the Phoenix Suns in July 1992.

With the pressure on, he delivered, winning the NBA's Most Valuable Player Award in 1992–93, leading the Suns to an NBA-best 62–20 record. In the playoffs he did even better, averaging 26.6 points and 13.6

rebounds, taking the Suns to the NBA Finals before the team finally bowed to Michael Jordan's Chicago Bulls in six games.

"It's just really difficult, you just hurt," he said afterwards, perhaps knowing it was the closest he would ever get to a championship.

Around this time, Barkley made what would become his landmark commercial for Nike: "I am not a role model," he said, glaring at the camera. "I am not paid to be a role model. I am paid to wreak havoc on the basketball court. Parents should be role models. Just because I can dunk a basketball, doesn't mean I should raise your kids." The Nike commercial became fodder for debate well outside the sports pages. Was he being disingenuous, knowing full well that as an NBA star he was a role model regardless? Did he merely reinforce what any good parent should know anyway — that famous athletes were flawed and complicated, and that the real responsibility for raising good citizens starts and ends at home?

- Drafted: 5th overall by the Philadelphia 76ers in 1984
- Philadelphia 76ers: 1984–92
- Phoenix Suns: 1992–96
- Houston Rockets: 1996–2000
- Jersey: #34; alternates: #32, #4
- College: Auburn

He was, at the very least, being himself. "I believe in expressing what you feel," he told the *New York Times Magazine*. "There are people who hide everything inside — and it's guys like that who kill whole families."

Keep in mind that by the time Barkley delivered his message he'd already been in trouble for spitting in the face of a little girl at courtside in 1991. (He had been aiming at a heckler near the girl, and subsequently apologized and befriended the girl and her family.) And later in 1997 he'd thrown a bothersome fan through a plate-glass window in an Orlando bar. He was fined $320, but never apologized, saying his only regret was that the bar was on the first floor.

Who knew what to make of this guy?

After four seasons with the Suns, he was traded to Houston, but found only disappointment there, too, as the Rockets never advanced past the Western Conference Finals with Barkley. For all his talent, some questioned whether it was Barkley himself who was the problem.

"Everybody knows Charles Barkley is a great guy," said Los Angeles Lakers guard Ron Harper, as Barkley's career wound down. "But every year, he's talking about winning a championship, and then he comes to training camp out of shape. That shows what kind of guy he is."

A more charitable view is that his prime overlapped with the best years of the Jordan era, making Barkley just one more Hall of Famer denied a ring by the best player in NBA history.

His career ended after 16 years when he ruptured a quadriceps tendon on a routine play early in the 1999–00 season. He eventually came back to play one more game, but knew the end of his career was at hand. He got off one more classic line: "Just what the country needs, another unemployed black man."

And then the clown prince of basketball returned to his hotel room and cried.

CAREER HIGHLIGHTS

- Was an NBA All-Star 11 times
- Had his own shoe line with Nike
- Shortest player in NBA history to lead the league in rebounds per game in a single season (14.6 in 1986–87)
- Famous for his controversial "I am not a role model" commercial
- One of only four players to have recorded 20,000 points, 10,000 rebounds and 4,000 assists in their career
- Has served as a TNT basketball analyst since 2000

Barkley goes for a dunk in the 1986–87 season. It was his first of three straight seasons leading the league in offensive rebounds.

Barry of the Golden State Warriors goes up against Wilt Chamberlain of the Philadelphia 76ers in 1973. The 1972–73 season marked Barry's return not only to the NBA, but to San Francisco — his original draft team.

G	FG%	FT%	ORB	DRB	TRB	AST	STL	BLK	PTS
794	.449	.900			6.5	5.1			23.2

24 FORWARD
RICK **BARRY**

It was so honest, it almost made you wince. Rick Barry was being asked his opinion in an interview and, as always, he gave it. The subject happened to be LeBron James, who had just led his upstart Cleveland Cavaliers to the NBA Finals for the first time in just his fourth season in the NBA in 2006. He was all of 22 years old. He was LeBron, a player for the ages.

But Barry wanted none of it.

"First of all, he has a major flaw in his shot that needs to be corrected," he boldly said. "There's no way — I mean, what are they teaching him? How could you have a player of his stature have a major flaw in his shot without someone working on it? How can a player of his stature and his ability not understand how to set his man up and use and read a screen properly? These are basic fundamentals of the game."

He didn't finish there, but the point had been made.

Thing is, perhaps no one on the planet is more qualified to critique the shortcomings of one of the world's best than Barry. He knows all about leading unlikely teams to unlikely places at an unlikely age.

Drafted second overall in 1965 by the now-defunct San Francisco Warriors, Barry was as precociously productive a player as any before him and since — and then he improved. He was named Rookie of the Year and earned a spot on the All-NBA team in his first season, averaging 25.7 points and 10.6 rebounds per game. And he was only 21.

At 22, just two years removed from leading the NCAA in scoring by averaging 37.4 points per game for the University of Miami Hurricanes, Barry put up 35.6 points on average for the Warriors in 1966–67 to lead the NBA in scoring, too. He took the Warriors to the NBA Finals against the powerhouse Philadelphia 76ers, and even though his team lost in six games, Barry set an NBA Finals record averaging 41 points a game. It stood until Michael Jordan broke it in 1993.

"This far in his career," said Bill Sharman, Barry's coach for his first two NBA seasons, "I would have to rank Rick as the greatest and most productive offensive forward ever to play the game ... He has to be the quickest 6–7 player the game of basketball has ever seen. He's awfully hard, if not impossible, to match up against defensively."

If it were only that simple. Rick Barry's shot may have been flawless, but he had his share of flaws. Fairly or not, by the time his career ended, he was known almost as much for his short-comings — his impatience with teammates, his sourpuss demeanor on the floor and his apparent willingness to jump teams when the money was right — as for his incredible all-around skills.

Barry sets up for a free throw in 1972–73. His granny-style shot earned him a lot of notoriety, as did his league leading 90.2% free-throw percentage that season.

After leading the Warriors to the Finals, Barry jumped to the rival American Basketball Association, lured by a richer contract — or at least that's one reason. The fact that his coach with the Oakland Oaks would be Bruce Hale, his father-in-law and former college coach, is lost sometimes recalling his history. Unfortunately for Barry, the courts ruled that he had to sit out the 1967–68 season, which added further to the perception that Barry epitomized the modern, money-hungry athlete.

By some accounts, stardom had changed Barry. As a rookie he played for $15,000 a year and rode buses to home games. Within a few short years, *Playgirl* wanted him to pose for the magazine and *Reader's Digest* named him one of the country's 10 sexiest men. His days of riding public transit were behind him.

"He bought a Porsche and went to another planet," his first wife, Pam Connolly,

said. "It was too much, too fast, too soon."

Not on the court, though: Barry handled everything that came at him. He led the ABA in scoring in 1968–69, averaging 34.1 points a game and earning first-team All-ABA honors despite a knee injury that limited him to 35 games and saw him miss the Oaks run to the ABA title. Still he became the only player to lead the NCAA, NBA and ABA in scoring.

Along with jumping leagues, Barry stood out also for his free-flowing, if sometimes tactless, comments. Asked why he objected to being traded to the Virginia Squires, Barry said, "I don't want my son coming home saying, 'Howdy, y'all.'"

He also became known for his antique free-throw shooting technique — the last player to shoot underhanded. It's a trait that drew its share of snickers, but surprisingly no imitators, even though Barry's 94.6 mark in 1978–79 stood as the highest in NBA history when he retired that

- Drafted: 2nd overall by the San Francisco Warriors in 1965
- San Francisco Warriors (NBA): 1965–67
- Oakland Oaks (ABA): 1968–69
- Washington Capitols (ABA): 1969–70
- New York Nets (ABA): 1970–72
- Golden State Warriors: 1972–78
- Houston Rockets: 1978–80
- Jersey: #24; alternates: #2, #4
- College: University of Miami

year, though it was broken by former Rockets teammate Calvin Murphy who converted 95.8 percent of his chances in 1980–81.

His basketball peak came in 1974–75. Back in the NBA with the Golden State Warriors (formerly his old team the San Francisco Warriors) he sparked one of the biggest upsets in league history. After finishing the regular season 48–34, the Warriors rolled through the playoffs and swept the favored Washington Bullets in the NBA Finals. Barry had a career year, finishing second in the NBA averaging 30.6 points per game and leading the league in steals with 2.85 per game. He also led all forwards in assists with 6.2 per game, reflective of the growth of his skills and handy proof that the Barry wasn't a bad guy to play with after all, his reputation as a difficult teammate — all eye rolls and "why didn't you catch that pass" grimaces — aside.

"It was always meant for the improvement of the team," said Warriors' teammate Jamaal Wilkes. "When you got to know him and saw how hard he was on himself, then you understood."

It's how Barry learned to play as a kid in Elizabeth, New Jersey. His father coached him and taught him early the right way to play the game. Barry never stopped expecting others — even LeBron James — to play the same way. And who could argue? It worked for him.

"My father was a perfectionist," Barry said. "So I became very demanding of myself, and I was very demanding of my teammates. If you screwed up, I said something to you. But it's a spur-of-the-moment thing. When it's over, it's over. I don't hold a grudge. That's what I needed to get me to succeed."

CAREER HIGHLIGHTS

- Only player in basketball history to lead the NCAA, ABA and NBA in scoring for a single season

- Was known for his "granny shot" (underhand) free throw style

- First NBA player to move from the NBA to the ABA (1968–69)

- Won the Rookie of the Year award in 1965–66

- Has an NBA career .900 free-throw percentage, which places him 3rd all-time

- Averaged 35.6 PPG in 1966–67 for the San Francisco Warriors, which ranks as the seventh-best single-season-scoring average in NBA history

G	FG%	FT%	ORB	DRB	TRB	AST	STL	BLK	PTS
846	.431	.780			13.5	4.3			27.4

ELGIN **BAYLOR**

Before Kobe, there was Michael. Before Michael, there was Julius. And before them all was Elgin Baylor. The NBA has been defined by eras and stars, but the precious few who could seemingly bend gravity to their will have always had a special place in the imagination of basketball fans.

Today people buy sneakers endorsed by stars who play in a style Baylor largely invented. But Baylor played from 1958 to 1971, prior to every game being televised and every moment preserved as a consumer touchstone.

What a shame.

At 6-foot-5 and 225 pounds, he could post-up Bill Russell, the Celtics' Hall of Fame center, and break down smaller guards off the dribble, making him the prototype for the slashing, dominant wing player that has defined the modern game.

"The way teams would play me, I would have to put the ball on the floor and go to the basket," Baylor said, trying to explain the inexplicable. "Once I got the ball, they would come up on me and double, sometimes triple [team]. So I'd have to take the ball to the hoop and, when you do that, you try to be creative. You just improvise. The defense dictates what kind of shot, and I was blessed to have good body control and do some things when I got in the air."

The record tells one story: In the 1960–61 season, Baylor averaged 34.8 points, 19.8 rebounds and 5.1 assists as a forward for the Los Angeles Lakers. The next season he averaged 38.3 points, 18.6 rebounds and 4.6

assists. He averaged 27.4 points, 13.5 rebounds and 4.3 assists for his career. One opponent compared guarding Baylor to "guarding a flood."

Baylor played 14 seasons, all with the Lakers, and was named an All-NBA First Team selection 10 times, an NBA All-Star 11 times and was inducted into the Naismith Memorial Hall of Fame in 1977, the first year he was eligible. Drafted first overall in 1958, he was the NBA Rookie of the Year and led the Lakers to the NBA Finals for the first time since the retirement of George Mikan. With Baylor in a starring role the Lakers franchise was able to make their move from Minneapolis to Los Angeles for the 1960–61 season where they became one of the NBA's iconic franchises.

He was, for his time, unique.

"Elgin was the leading creative force in basketball," his long-time Laker teammate Tommy Hawkins once said of Baylor. "He shot a greater variety of shots than anyone. It was half from practice and half instinctive. Elgin worked hard. He loved to play basketball and was always working on his shots. Elgin doesn't get the credit he deserves."

Baylor moves the ball against Sam Jones of the Boston Celtics in 1965–66. Baylor's Lakers would fall to the Celtics in seven games in the Finals that season.

Baylor's high-flying, acrobatic shot-making game foreshadowed the style many top stars have adopted since — a style that has nearly come to define the NBA's star culture. But there was substance to his style, and Baylor did his part to help the journeyman, too.

In 1963–64, Baylor was at the height of his powers and became an obvious inclusion for the NBA All-Star game in Boston, a landmark event scheduled to be televised on ABC for the first time. But the league was still establishing itself, and the welfare of the players often fell secondary to stability and profits of the owners.

The All-Stars voted 22–2 to strike. It was a moment fraught with tension, but the commitment of a star of Baylor's caliber gave the cause weight. At one point, Lakers' owner Bob Short arrived at the dressing room door and had a police officer pass word

to Baylor and teammate Jerry West that they had better play or suffer the consequences.

"Elgin sent back word with the same cop," recalled Tom Heinsohn, the Boston Celtics' players' union president at the time and future Hall of Famer. "He told him to tell Mr. Short to go [bleep] himself."

The union held its ground, won an instant concession on pensions and slowly became an equal partner in the growth of the NBA. The multi-media stars who have since made millions through guaranteed contracts, free agency and endorsement dollars owe Baylor a debt of gratitude.

His willingness to take a stand typified his persona as a superstar who carried himself like a regular guy. "Elgin was truly great. He was an unbelievably exceptional player, and a lot of it had to do with his desire to play the game at a very high level," said West, his Hall of Fame Laker teammate. "More importantly, Elgin was a great teammate, someone you enjoyed being around and competing with."

He was also a fun-loving team member, giving his teammates nicknames and joking with the team and media. Once when being interviewed on television after a game, Baylor received a gift certificate for a men's store from Lakers' broadcaster Chick Hearn. Baylor took it, looked at Hearn and handed it back. "Looks like you need this worse than I do," he said, leaving the loquacious Hearn silent for once.

Baylor built a career of relentless accomplishment, lacking only a signature moment. Playing in the Western Conference, he led the Lakers to eight NBA Finals, only to be turned back seven times by the mighty Celtics and once by the New York Knicks. A man of pride, he retired after just eight games in 1971–72, not wanting to hold his teammates back with his fading skills and balky knee. The Lakers won the title that year, and Baylor missed his moment again. His three seasons in the late 1970s as head coach of the New Orleans Jazz and his two decades as general manager of the Los Angeles Clippers (1986–2008) have likely only obscured his body of work even further.

No matter. Let the record show that Baylor played the game at a level equaled by only a handful in the history of the game, and he did it first. Leave it to those who followed his graceful path to be icons and legends and pop culture heroes. Elgin Baylor was a pioneer.

CAREER HIGHLIGHTS

- Is fourth all-time in career PPG average with 27.4

- Scored 71 points in a single game on Nov. 15, 1960, against the New York Knicks (a record for points in a game at that time — eighth best in NBA history)

- Scored an NBA Finals record 61 points on April 14, 1962 against the Boston Celtics

- Had 87 regular season games in which he scored at least 40 points

- Was an 11-time NBA All-Star

- Was the vice-president of basketball operations for the Los Angeles Clippers from 1986–2008

- Was the NBA Executive of the Year in 2006

- Drafted: 1st overall by the Minneapolis Lakers in 1958
- Minneapolis Lakers: 1958–60
- Los Angeles Lakers: 1960–72
- College: Seattle University

Baylor takes a jump shot against Walt Bellamy of the New York Knicks in the 1965–66 season. The two clubs split the season series with five wins apiece.

A marquee matchup: Bird and Magic Johnson work for space under the rim in 1983–84. Bird's Celtics beat Johnson's Lakers in seven games for the NBA crown. It was the first time the two stars met in the Finals.

LARRY BIRD

Every year the NBA gathers the best draft-eligible basketball players in the world and puts them through a battery of physical tests. Their body fat is measured. Their jumping ability is recorded. How fast are they? How strong?

It's understandable. Basketball is a game that honors athleticism in its rawest form.

But it's also worth noting that Larry Bird, quite possibly the best basketball player of his generation, would have scored miserably at every possible test. He wasn't a great leaper or bulging with muscles. He could run, but he wasn't winning medals at the track. He could hold his ground, but didn't have a weight-room chiseled physique. But somehow Bird managed three NBA championships, a trio of Most Valuable Player awards and a slew of statistically-magnificent seasons. If they ever figure out an objective measure for heart, passion, competitiveness, skill, seeing the play before it happens, poise under pressure and toughness, chances are Larry Bird would score rather well.

"I wasn't the quickest guy on the court, but I had a knack for getting to the basket with the ball," said Bird, whose highlight reel was long and littered with improbable shots, steals and seeing-eye passes, but short on dunks. "And I was always the first guy back on defense to stop a fast break, because I ran back, didn't jog, and I was always running to lead our fast break."

If he had one natural advantage it was his size. At 6-foot-10, 230 or so pounds, Bird was as big or bigger than nearly all the forwards he faced. And he was so smart and skilled that he could punish the smaller, quicker ones with his post game and fool the rest with his combination of shooting, passing and savvy. None of which would have mattered if he didn't have the confidence to do it all in the most pressure-filled moments.

They don't call him Larry Legend because he was good on a Tuesday night in Milwaukee — though he was brilliant on many, many Tuesday nights in Anytown, U.S.A. They call him Larry Legend because he was brilliant when the whole world watched.

"There are a lot of players in this league who play the game, but only a few who play in the final six minutes," says Earvin "Magic" Johnson, Bird's rival, foil and friend. "It's a different game then. Shots that guys will take in the rest of the game, they won't take here. Only a few will. Larry will."

At his peak in the mid-80s on his way to three consecutive MVP awards, Bird was the Celtics' logical option at the end of close games.

"The whole world knew who the ball was going to, but it's what you do with it once you get it," said Celtics' coach K.C. Jones. "Larry knew exactly what to do."

On one occasion, with Boston trailing the Seattle Supersonics by a point with three seconds remaining, Bird broke the huddle

Bird goes in for a layup over Sacramento's Otis Thorpe and Reggie Theus in 1986–87. The season marked Bird's last trip to the Finals.

and headed straight for the Sonics' Xavier McDaniel, who had been defending him. The story goes that Bird told McDaniel that he was going to get the ball, dribble left and shoot. He did, scored and won the game, just like he said he would.

"It just blew X's mind," Jones said. Arrogant? Maybe. But like just about everyone his age in southern Indiana, Bird grew up a St. Louis Cardinals fan, and it was Cardinals' icon Dizzy Dean who said, "It ain't bragging if you can back it up."

The bursts of on-court pride weren't consistent with Bird's low-key, off-court demeanor and his country-boy twang. He grew up in the most humble circumstances in tiny French Lick, Indiana, with an alcoholic father who had a hard time holding a job. Bird led his high school to a state championship as a senior, after which Indiana University's iconic head coach Bobby Knight recruited him to attend the basketball powerhouse. But the scale of the big campus

unnerved the small-town kid. The team didn't readily accept the rookie, and Knight wasn't the nurturing type. So Bird left school and took a job with the town, painting park benches and collecting garbage. He eventually enrolled at the poor sister in Indiana basketball, Indiana State, in 1975, the same year his father committed suicide.

What made Bird better, even more compelling than his skills and his willingness to use them, was that they were tested at the highest level, most memorably against Johnson, the equally-gifted Los Angeles Lakers' star. Their paths first crossed in the 1979 NCAA Finals when Johnson's Michigan State Spartans handed Bird's Indiana State Sycamores their first loss of the season in the highest rated college basketball game in television history. They entered the NBA together for the 1979–80 season. Bird won Rookie of the Year; Johnson led his Lakers to the NBA title, and that began a personal rivalry that defined the NBA for the next decade.

Bird earned his first championship in 1981, completing a remarkable turnaround for Boston, which had a record of 29–53 in 1978–79, the year before he arrived. But the sweetest of his three titles came in 1984 when the Lakers and the Celtics — Bird and Magic — squared off in the Finals for the first time.

- Drafted: 6th overall by the Boston Celtics in 1978
- Boston Celtics: 1979–92
- College: Indiana State University

The Lakers won the first game and should have won Game 2, but a costly turnover allowed the Celtics to tie the game and then win in overtime. After the Celtics were thumped 137–104 in Game 3, Bird took charge in the pivotal fourth game, scoring the winning basket in overtime in Los Angeles. Game 5 was played in 97-degree heat in the old Boston Garden, and Lakers' coach Pat Riley compared it to playing in hell. Referee Hugh Evans had to leave the game at halftime, suffering from dehydration. As for Bird, the guy who didn't jump that well or sprint that fast and was missing those washboard abs? The heat didn't bother him. "Hell, what's the fuss? We used to play in conditions like that back home all summer," said Bird, who scored 34 points and grabbed 17 rebounds as Boston won putting them up 3–2 in the series. The Lakers took Game 6, 119–108, but Boston prevailed in Game 7 with Bird earning the series' MVP.

It was just another great moment in a stunning career that ended with Bird too injured to keep playing, undone by excruciating back pain. Fittingly, his last moment on the court came at the 1992 Olympics when he and Magic were teammates on the gold-medal winning "Dream Team." The rivals had become friends and enjoyed one last moment in the sun together.

You can measure Larry Bird all you want, but the true measure of respect the man and the player had earned came in 2002 when Johnson was inducted into the Naismith Basketball Hall of Fame.

He chose Bird to introduce him.

CAREER HIGHLIGHTS

- Two-time Finals MVP

- Was a 12-time NBA All-Star

- Was a three-time NBA Three-Point Shootout Winner

- Fifth all-time in career triple-doubles with 59

- Scored a career high 60 points on March 12, 1985 against the Atlanta Hawks

- Averaged a career high 29.9 PPG in 1987–88

24
GUARD

KOBE **BRYANT**

You could make a movie about Kobe Bryant: the child star who made it to Hollywood, tarnished his early success by clashing with authority, endured a grave, personal crisis and ultimately found redemption in the form of a 2008 MVP award and the 2009 NBA title. You could start with a scene at the Inglewood YMCA on a typically sunny California day in the late spring of 1996.

On hand was Jerry West, the Los Angeles Lakers' general manager, there at the behest of agent Arn Tellem, to see Bryant, then a 17-year-old from the Philadelphia area, bidding to become the first perimeter player to make the jump to the NBA straight from high school.

Count West among the NBA skeptics, but he was quickly impressed by the 6-foot-6 ball of high-flying energy.

"I went to the Inglewood YMCA," West said, "and here's this bright-eyed, cheerful, bubbly, exuberant young man, ready to show us his wares. I had seen high-school film of him, but you can't tell how competitive a player is on film. I watched him and I thought, 'Oh, my gosh, this guy's not too bad for a young guy.' It was obvious he had very, very unique talent, something I hadn't seen in a person of that age. And he didn't want to stop [working out]. He wanted to keep going and going and going. It was really eye-popping to watch."

Intrigued by what he saw, West invited Bryant to work out again, but this time brought along 40-year-old Michael Cooper. Though recently retired, the 6-foot-6 blade was not far removed from being the man Larry

Bird called the best defender he ever played against. Bryant destroyed him. West was sold.

"Oh, my gosh," West recalls thinking, "this kid's got to be the best player in the draft. How can we get this guy?"

And so it began. West arranged for the then Charlotte Hornets to select Bryant with the 13th pick in exchange for veteran Laker center Vlade Divac, and it soon became apparent to NBA insiders and fans alike that Bryant was a special player. This was, after all, the kid who broke Wilt Chamberlain's Southeastern Pennsylvania all-time, schoolboy record while leading Lower Merion High School to three state titles.

Bryant became the youngest player ever to start an NBA game on January 28, 1997, at age 18 years, five months and five days. In some ways it culminated the journey for the only son of Joe "Jellybean" Bryant, a talented NBA journeyman who finished his career in Italy, where the future superstar spent his formative years shaping the competitive personality that has never wilted, despite a journey of 11 professional seasons and four NBA titles. He always had it. Playing on his father's team one year was Brian Shaw, a first-round pick of the Boston Celtics playing overseas due to a contract dispute. An 11-year-old Bryant constantly badgered Shaw to play one-on-one. Shaw agreed to play H-O-R-S-E, and regrets it.

Kobe shoots a free throw in a 102–96 win over the Phoenix Suns on March 12, 2010. Kobe went 6 for 9 from the stripe with a double-double on the night.

Kobe throws down a highlight-reel dunk on the New Jersey Nets in 1999–00, the Lakers' first championship season since 1987–88.

CAREER HIGHLIGHTS

- Scored 60 or more points in a game five times in his career
- Won back-to-back scoring titles in 2005–06 and 2006–07
- Averaged a career high 35.4 PPG in 2005–06, which is the eighth best average in NBA history
- He had four consecutive games of 50 points or more from March 16–23, 2007
- *Sporting News'* NBA Athlete of the Decade for the 2000s
- Won the NBA Slam Dunk Contest in 1997
- Holds the NBA record for most three-point field goals made in one game with 12. The record is shared with Donyell Marshall
- Youngest player to score 20,000 points at 29 years and 122 days

"To this day Kobe claims he beat me," says Shaw, eventually a Laker teammate of Bryant's and then a Lakers' assistant coach. "I'm like, right, [I'm really trying to beat] an 11-year-old kid. But he's serious." But even then it was the will Bryant displayed that stood out. "His dad was a good player, but he was the opposite of Kobe, real laid-back," Shaw adds. "Kobe was out there challenging grown men to play one-on-one, and he really thought he could win."

Bryant never lacked confidence. He ended his promising rookie season by shooting three airballs in the closing minute in the deciding game of the Western Conference Semifinals as the Lakers lost to the Utah Jazz. He was not yet the player he would become.

"In practice, he would dribble-dribble-dribble through the whole team, nobody could stop him, but that's not basketball," West says. "He had a lot to learn."

He learned — sometimes the hard way, but he learned. He was an All-Star Game starter in his second season, made third-team, All-NBA his third season and has been an

All-NBA selection every year since while earning All-NBA defensive recognition every year but 2004–05. He became the youngest player in the league to win three NBA titles as he played an able Robin to Shaquille O'Neal's Batman during the Lakers' run from 1999 to 2002. But it was Bryant who started the three-peat with his 25-point, 11-rebound, 7-assist, 4-block game in Game 7 of the Western Conference Finals against the Portland Trail Blazers.

If the plot of our movie has a low-point, it comes after that, where Bryant's feuding with O'Neal leads to the breakup of the Lakers. O'Neal is traded to Miami, and left to his own devices Bryant proves himself one of the most prolific scoring machines in NBA history, highlighted by an 81-point explosion against the Toronto Raptors on January 22, 2006. It became the second-highest, single-game total in league history, surpassed only by Chamberlain's legendary 100-point night in 1962.

"It's just kind of seeing, 'This is what we need at this moment. Can I deliver?'" Bryant said later of his history-making outburst, which came in a game the Lakers were trailing by 18 points in the third quarter. "I was able to deliver."

But Bryant did it all on a team that no longer factored among the NBA's elite. O'Neal was traded following the Lakers' loss to the Detroit Pistons in the 2004 NBA Finals and the question became: Could Bryant lead a team to an NBA title by himself? His image had already taken a hit off the floor in the wake of his being charged with sexual assault by a hotel employee in Colorado in July 2003, although the charges were dropped and a civil suit settled out of court.

The answer, of course, is a resounding "Yes!" With the addition of Pau Gasol midway through the 2007–08 season, the Lakers surged, only to fall short in the NBA Finals against the Boston Celtics, with Bryant taking his share of the blame. In spite of this, he won his first NBA Most Valuable Player award, gaining recognition not only for his typically stellar numbers — he averaged 28.3 points, 6.3 rebounds and 5.4 assists — but for the way he lifted his teammates to new heights.

In that light, and in the context of the unwritten screenplay, the 2008–09 season was Bryant's moment of redemption, beginning with his role on the gold-medal-winning Team USA at the Beijing Olympics, to the Lakers' league-best 65–17 regular season en route to his flawless performance in the NBA Finals, He averaged 32.4 points, 7.4 assists and 5.6 rebounds in the Lakers' 4–1 victory over the Orlando Magic.

Bryant, the child prodigy, could now walk with legends. With four NBA championships by age 30, he's on pace to match or surpass the five titles of Lakers' great, Magic Johnson, or the six won by Michael Jordan — his idol and the player with whom he's most often compared.

"I just don't have to hear that criticism, that idiotic criticism anymore.

- Drafted: 13th overall by the Charlotte Hornets in 1996
- Los Angeles Lakers: 1996–
- Jersey: #24; alternate: #8
- College: Lower Merion High

That's the biggest thing. I don't have to hear that stuff anymore," he said, moments after the Lakers clinched the title against Orlando. "It felt like a big old monkey was off my back. It felt so good to be able to have this moment … to be here and to reflect back on the season and everything that you've been through. It's top of the list, man."

A happy ending made in Hollywood.

13
CENTER

WILT CHAMBERLAIN

The debate about who is the best basketball player of all time will always include Wilt Chamberlain. How could it not?

His list of achievements is the Mount Everest of sports, a rare summit approached only by the likes of Babe Ruth or Lance Armstrong or Michael Phelps or Secretariat — those who have dominated their competition so completely that no one remembers the runner-ups.

The greatest basketball player of all time? It's a subjective argument, but it's worth noting that Chamberlain was responsible for the NBA changing four different rules to offset his advantages, including widening the lane from 12 to 16 feet (so he would have to start possessions farther from the basket), and preventing the foul shooter from breaking the plane of the line before the ball hit the rim as Chamberlain, a notoriously poor free-throw shooter, would occasionally jump from the stripe and lay the ball in or dunk it.

"They can say all the things they want to say, but there's only one guy they ever made rules to stop from doing what he could do better than anyone else, and that's yours truly," Chamberlain said.

Or, as Larry Bird once put it: "Let me tell you something. At one time, they were saying that I was the greatest. And before me, it was Magic who was the greatest. And now it's Michael's turn. But open up the record book and it will be obvious who the greatest is."

Born in Philadelphia in 1936, Chamberlain became perhaps the first nationally-famous high school star. The 7-foot-1, 300-pound giant's first love was track and field, and he excelled in the long-jump, high-jump, shot put and the quarter-mile. He played three seasons at the University of Kansas, left school early to play a year for the Harlem Globetrotters, and eventually was drafted No.1 overall by the Philadelphia Warriors in 1959.

He played from 1959 to 1973 and retired as the game's all-time leading scorer and all-time leading rebounder, with averages of 30.1 points per game — second-best all-time — and 22.9 rebounds, the best mark in NBA history.

His 31,419 career points has remained the fourth-highest total in NBA history more than three decades since he last dropped in one of his patented finger-rolls from above the rim. His rebounding total of 23,924 may never be broken, given that Bill Russell, who retired in 1969, is the only other player to top 20,000 rebounds. Moses Malone, who is third on the list with 17,884 boards, retired in 1995. Chamberlain scored 100 points in a single game on March 2, 1962. It took 44 years for another player to top 80, something Kobe Bryant managed when he dropped 81 in 2006. He once had 55 rebounds in a game, while playing against Russell no less, another NBA record that will likely stand for all time. He averaged 50.4 points in the 1961–62 season. The second-highest average is 37.09, posted by Michael Jordan in 1986–87. He's the

Wilt Chamberlain battles for a rebound against Jerry Lucas and Phil Jackson of the New York Knicks. It was Chamberlain's last season.

- Drafted: by the Philadelphia Warriors in 1959 (territorial selection)
- Philadelphia Warriors: 1959–62
- San Francisco Warriors: 1962–65
- Philadelphia 76ers: 1965–68
- Los Angeles Lakers: 1968–73
- College: University of Kansas

Chamberlain stuffs Tom Sanders in 1966–67. The 76ers beat the Celtics in the Eastern Division Finals that season and won the NBA Finals over the San Francisco Warriors — Chamberlain's first.

only center in NBA history to lead the league in assists, which he did in 1967–68. No one had ever averaged 30 points for a season when Chamberlain joined the NBA in 1959–60. Chamberlain averaged 37.6 as a rookie.

"He almost was embarrassed to a point," said Al Attles, who played with Chamberlain during his epic 1961–62 season. "He once told me if he knew stats were going to become such a big deal, he might have done more. But he'd sometimes hold back, not be as aggressive as he could because he didn't want to embarrass anyone. He'd hardly ever dunk. It was all so easy for him."

Take his legendary 100-point night against the New York Knicks in Hershey, Pennsylvania, on March 2, 1962. It surpassed the NBA record of 78 points he set three months before. He topped 70 points three times that season, and in the three games previous to the record he scored 67, 65 and 61 points.

A big, lumbering center? Not

CAREER HIGHLIGHTS

- Averaged at least 18 rebounds per game in every year of his 18-year career

- Scored at least 60 points in a game 32 times

- Won NBA MVP only four times; he did not win MVP the year he averaged 50.4 PPG

- Averaged an NBA record 27.2 rebounds per game in 1960–61

- Holds five of the top 10 all-time single-season PPG averages (averaged at least 36 PPG five times in his career)

- Was selected to 13 All-Star games

- He's the only player to record 2,000 rebounds in a single season, which he accomplished twice (1960–61 and 1961–62)

- Only player to score 4,000 points in a single season (4,029 in 1960–61)

- Grabbed a record 55 rebounds in a single game against the Boston Celtics on November 24, 1960

- Grabbed at least 40 rebounds in a single game 15 times

Chamberlain. "Coach [Bill] Sharman would have us run sprints, baseline to baseline," said Flynn Robinson, a Laker teammate. "Wilt would win them every time. How many centers today can do that?"

He showed his athletic versatility after retiring by playing professional volleyball. He was good at tennis and racquetball. He ran the Honolulu Marathon. There was credible discussion of Chamberlain making an NBA comeback in his fifties.

A man of his size was a revelation when he began playing professionally. He was often six inches taller than the men covering him. A man of his strength, quickness and acumen would still be a revelation 40 years later.

The only frayed corner of Chamberlain's considerable legacy is that he didn't have the body of championships to match his individual records. He won four Most Valuable Player awards, but only two NBA championships. The success of Bill Russell's Celtics during the Chamberlain years is a handy reference point. Boston won 11 championships in 13 years beginning in 1956–57, with Russell anchoring the paint. Boston won the NBA title in each of Chamberlain's first seven seasons, eliminating Wilt's team from the playoffs in five of them. Chamberlain's teams met Russell's Celtics in the playoffs eight times and won only once. Chamberlain's poor free-throw shooting — he shot just 51.1 percent for his career — cost his team late in close games as the game's best offensive option would shy away from the ball. Similarly, his remarkable record of never fouling out of a game may have hurt him too, as the statistics-conscious Chamberain's desire to keep his streak alive would affect how he would play defensively at key moments. Couple those traits with a habit of rubbing coaches and teammates the wrong way on occasion and it's not clear that Chamberlain's considerable talents were always used to maximum effect, at least as far as winning was concerned.

But it's only because his gifts were so extraordinary that the expectations were so high.

"Wilt was my greatest opponent," Russell said of his rivalry with Chamberlain. "It's not even close. Wilt was the greatest offensive player I have ever seen. Because his talent and skills were so superhuman, his play forced me to play at my highest level."

In 1966–67, Chamberlain found himself part of an impressive Philadelphia lineup featuring the likes of Hall of Famers Chet Walker, Hal Greer and Billy Cunningham and coached by Alex Hannum, whom he had meshed well with previously in San Francisco. With sufficient secondary scoring, Chamberlain focused on defense, rebounding and passing and led the 76ers to a 68–13 record, the best in NBA history at the time. More significantly, Chamberlain's 76ers crushed the hated Celtics 4–1 in the Eastern Conference Finals, before downing San Francisco in the Finals for Chamberlain's first NBA title.

His second championship came in 1971–72 when he played for the Los Angeles Lakers, who acquired him in a trade in 1968. He helped the Lakers to a 69–13 record in 1971–72, including an NBA record 33-game win streak. His roles on two of the best teams in NBA history suggest that Chamberlain could be a pretty good team player when he made it a priority. But this is sure: he was a giant of his sport and of all sports.

Chamberlain died in 1998 at age 63 of heart failure, and they built a statue in his hometown to remember him. It was, appropriately, larger than life, measuring 18 feet tall and weighing 7,000 pounds.

The only question is, was it big enough?

G	FG%	FT%	ORB	DRB	TRB	AST	STL	BLK	PTS
924	.375	.803			5.2	7.5			18.4

BOB COUSY

When Chris Paul crosses over his man, drags the help defense with him and drops the ball behind him so his teammate can have the easy layup, he is paying tribute to Bob Cousy. It's the same when Steve Nash looks right and passes left, hitting his teammate for a dunk, or when Jason Kidd grabs a defensive rebound and sprints for the other end of the floor, leading the herd. They are all bowing to Bob Cousy, the NBA point guard who did it first.

For 13 years, Cousy, the ball-handling wizard who introduced the fast break to the NBA, led the Boston Celtics. He shaped their transition game and turnaround from a fledgling NBA franchise with a record of just 22–46 the year before his arrival into an enduring dynasty, lifting basketball from its flat-footed, plodding origins in the process.

He was once asked who taught him to play the point, arguably the most important position in the game.

"Honestly? Nobody," said Cousy, who translated his ability to create chances for others into six NBA championships, earned a place on the NBA's 25th, 35th and 50th anniversary teams, and was inducted into the Naismith Basketball Hall of Fame. "I just played. The defense tells you what you must do every time down the floor. For me, it was easy. Maybe that's because I have a vivid imagination. The simple formula is still the same: you react to what the defense does."

Eight straight years he led the NBA in assists, but being the first of his kind did not come easily. Born in 1928, by his own admission he grew up a "ghetto kid" in New York City, taking up basketball in part as relief from his unhappy home life. He was the son of working-class French immigrants who learned English as a second language as his parents argued and struggled to make their way.

He was cut twice from his high school team, but a broken right arm at age 13 made the difference. Forced to play exclusively with his left hand, he became nearly ambidextrous, earning him notice and later a spot on the varsity. As a senior, he led the city in scoring.

But the game wasn't ready for him or his style. He earned a scholarship at the College of the Holy Cross but found himself struggling for playing time because the coach didn't trust Cousy's seemingly flashy game. He eventually became a three-time All-American, but when it came to turning professional in the earliest days of the NBA, the Boston Celtics passed on the local college star.

"I don't give a damn about sentiment or names," Celtics' coach and general manager Red Auerbach said at the time.

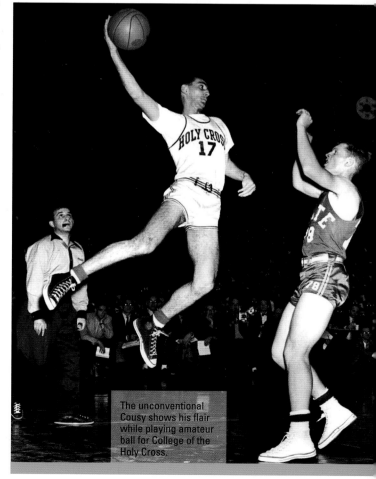

The unconventional Cousy shows his flair while playing amateur ball for College of the Holy Cross.

CAREER HIGHLIGHTS

- Dished out 28 assists against the Minneapolis Lakers on February 27, 1959, including an NBA record 19 in one half

- Had a cameo in the 1993 basketball film *Blue Chips*

- Was a 13-time NBA All-Star and a two-time NBA All-Star Game MVP

- Coached the Cincinnati Royals from 1969–73 and played seven games for the team in 1969–70

- Was named to the All-NBA First Team 10 times

He wanted a big man, not a 6-foot-1 guard.

"The only thing that counts with me is ability, and Cousy still hasn't proven to me he's got ability," Auerbach added. "I'm not interested in drafting someone just because he happens to be a local yokel."

The Celtics took him anyway, the last pick in the dispersal draft after the Chicago Stags folded. Thus started one of the most compelling partnerships in sports history — except no one knew it yet.

Auerbach still hadn't embraced Cousy's stylish approach. Cousy's teammates didn't know what to make of it, either. Cousy passed to teammates who were running, which was novel at the time, and predictably some of those passes ended up as turnovers. Auerbach addressed it with his rookie guard.

"He could very easily have told me to go to hell, or complained to the writers, or blamed all his problems on the other guys," Auerbach said in Bill Reynolds' biography, *Cousy: His Life, Career, and the Birth of Big-Time Basketball.* "He could have made my job unbearable and disrupted the team at the same time. But he didn't. He looked at me and asked, 'What am I doing wrong?' Right then, I

knew I had a superstar on my hands."

But credit Auerbach for realizing what he had and letting Cousy run the show. Boston had only six plays and their fast break, but were the highest-scoring team of their era — and it was Cousy who made it work.

"I couldn't have played for someone who orchestrated my moves from the bench," Cousy said later. "Even I didn't know what I was going to do."

With Cousy in charge, the Celtics broke quickly up the floor.

"Cousy's true basketball genius showed when he had the ball in a transition situation," Reynolds wrote. "He had an intuitive sense of where everyone was on the court, thanks to his exceptional peripheral vision, the fact that he could look straight ahead and still see almost 180 degrees ... He knew he could give the ball to [forward Tom] Heinsohn on the wing, because Heinsohn could both catch a hard pass and put the ball on the floor. He knew not to throw [forward Jim] Loscutoff the same pass, since his hands were not as good as Heinsohn's and he wasn't skilled enough to put the ball on the floor and take it to the basket, even if he caught it."

Cousy did behind-the-back passes with purpose, claiming the flash was secondary.

"I'm actually a conservative guy," said Cousy. "The problem was that I was the only one [playing with flair] at the time. Every 12-year-old is doing what I did [50] years ago. The style was instinctive to me. I did what I had to do to win."

He made an impact off the court as well, using his star power to bravely become the founding president of the NBA's Players Association in 1954. He quickly befriended Chuck Cooper, the Celtics rookie who was the first black player to play in the NBA, once riding home with him on an overnight train from an exhibition game in the South when the Celtics' hotel wouldn't provide his teammate with a room.

For all of Cousy's magic, the Celtics disappointed in the playoffs in his first six years, but won the NBA championship in 1957 when Auerbach added Bill Russell, Heinsohn and K.C. Jones. Cousy won the NBA's MVP that year and went on to lead Boston to five more titles before he retired in 1963.

Once a player the team didn't want, playing a style no one appreciated, Cousy became the face of the franchise, an innovator who changed the game.

- Drafted: 3rd overall by the Tri-Cities Blackhawks in 1950
- Boston Celtics: 1950–63
- Cincinnati Royals: 1969–70
- Jersey: #14; alternates: #19
- College: College of the Holy Cross

Cousy makes a leaping bounce pass while being double teamed by Jerry West and Elgin Baylor in the early 1960s.

Duncan strips Pau Gasol of the ball in a 103–101 overtime win on November 4, 2002. Duncan would go on to claim his second consecutive NBA MVP award that season.

TIM DUNCAN

It's a saying parents have been repeating to their children forever: "Good, better, best/Never let it rest/Until your good is better and your better is your best."

San Antonio Spurs star center Tim Duncan's mother, Ione, used to say it to her son and his older sisters when they were growing up in the house their father built in the U.S. Virgin Islands. The theme of constant, incremental, improvement was like a mantra for the Duncan family.

For the children, the application came in the swimming pool, where thousands of training laps go into each second of progress. Duncan's older sister followed it all the way to the 1988 Olympic Games, and her younger brother was on his way as a top age-group swimmer with his own Olympic dreams.

Duncan's mother might also have told him that life is what happens when you're making plans, however, as he never realized his goal of swimming for gold, the dream swept away by a pair of tragedies. The first was Hurricane Hugo, the massive storm that touched down September 17, 1989, and ravaged the tiny island Duncan grew up on. The storm caused an estimated $2 billion in damage and devastated 90 percent of the buildings on the island, among them the pool where Duncan trained. He tried gamely to continue his training by swimming in the ocean, but between tricky currents and sharks, it proved a challenge. Then, six months later, the day before his 14th birthday, Duncan's mother — the person who drove him to swim practice and volunteered at meets — died of breast cancer.

With no pool and his mother gone, Duncan turned to a new hobby, basketball, and used his mother's mantra all over again, applying a swimmer's work ethic to his new sport. He utilized every drill his brother-in-law, Ricky Lowery, who had played at a small college in the United States, could devise. Duncan was tall, with long arms and huge hands, so he clearly had the physical attributes conducive to basketball, but he had a passionate drive, too. Shaquille O'Neal nicknamed Duncan "The Big Fundamental" because he has had an old man's game since he broke into the NBA. He's been an old soul for a lot longer.

"I've been grown-up for a long time," he said. "I went through that with my mom, and I grew to where I understood life and death and everything in between. It does make you realize your own mortality and the mortality of the people around you."

Duncan will never be accused of using his time unwisely. Just four years after turning to basketball, he was offered a scholarship at Wake Forest University and earned a psychology degree. He rejected the idea to leave early to turn pro because he promised his mother he'd complete his education, and

Duncan shoots over top of Hornets center Emeka Okafor on January 18, 2010, a 97–90 Spurs victory.

the time at Wake Forest allowed him to work on his fundamentals. He left as one of the best players in the history of the tradition-rich Atlantic Coast Conference — named three times as NCAA Defensive Player of the Year and a unanimous selection as NCAA Player of the Year as a senior.

• Drafted: 1st overall by the San Antonio Spurs in 1997
• San Antonio Spurs: 1997–
• College: Wake Forest University

"To Timmy, every minute on the sidelines was a minute of practice lost," Wake Forest head coach Dave Odom said.

"Everything I do is basic, and that doesn't sell," Duncan says of his game, which consists of using both hands inside, precision footwork and thoughtful help on defense. "I don't have the icing. My icing is, I just want to win."

The payoff came in 1997 when Duncan became *the* choice to be taken first overall in the NBA draft. The Spurs won the draft lottery after compiling a 20–62 record in 1996–97, when incumbent superstar David Robinson was injured for all but six games. Duncan's arrival and Robinson's return to health sparked San Antonio to a 35-win improvement in 1997–98, with Duncan dominating as a rookie, averaging 21.1 points, 11.9 rebounds, and 2.5 blocked shots a game on 54.9 percent shooting. He earned a place on the All-NBA First Team and was the obvious Rookie of the Year.

A season later, Duncan led the Spurs to their first NBA title and earned his first Finals MVP award. By his third season, he had formally supplanted Robinson as the Spurs' franchise player. "It was a tough thing for me when the offense started going through Tim," says Robinson. "But it was the right thing to do."

All along Duncan's numbers were both steady and excellent, almost always improving in the postseason. For his career, Duncan has averaged 23.3 points and 12.6 rebounds in 160 playoff games, often saving his best for the most important games, impressing everyone but himself. In the deciding game of the 2003 Finals, he came within two

rebounds of posting the first quadruple-double in NBA playoff history, as the Spurs eliminated the New Jersey Nets in six games. Duncan averaged 24.1 points, 17 rebounds, 5.2 blocks and 6.6 assists for the series. Jason Kidd, the Nets point guard, told Duncan he was the best player on the planet. Duncan's reaction? "That's cool."

Nearly every year at the NBA All-Star Game, the scene was the same when O'Neal and Duncan were on the Western Conference team. On one side of the hotel ballroom where the media swarm to interview players would be O'Neal, always with a throng six deep waiting to hear what he might say. On the other side would be Duncan, every inch a champion, but hardly a sound-bite machine. He might have half-a-dozen reporters listening, probably six more than he would like.

"He's the ultimate team player," said Larry Brown, who saw Duncan at his best when the Spurs beat his Detroit Pistons in the seven-game 2004 NBA Finals, with Duncan earning his third Finals MVP award. "He's incredible; his teammates love him. I would love my son to have him as his role model."

As a role model, Duncan would stand for teamwork, humility, sacrifice and a constant striving for improvement — and loyalty, too. In an era when players have skipped franchises and fan bases like stones on a flat lake, Duncan has played his entire career in the Spurs black and silver.

In his first 12 seasons he won four NBA titles, two MVP awards, three Finals MVP awards, 12 All-NBA selections, including nine First-Team mentions and seven All-Defensive First-Team selections. With Duncan as a constant, the Spurs became one of the NBA's consummate modern franchises — able to surround Duncan with players that excel while he leads by example.

"Your superstar always sets the tone for your team. It's not the coach or the other players; it's your superstar," says Spurs' owner Peter Holt. "So what we see year after year is when we have a new player coming in and he walks into the gym in August and there's Tim Duncan working out hard, that impacts them. Tim does a lot of things by his own book, but it's the right book."

The title is an obvious one: *Good, Better, Best: The Tim Duncan Story.*

CAREER HIGHLIGHTS

• Has averaged at least 10 rebounds per game in all 13 years of his NBA career
• Has 2,235 blocks which puts him 11 all-time in NBA history
• Has 682 point-rebound double-doubles in his career, which is third all-time
• Averaged a career high 25.5 PPG in 2001–02
• A 12-time NBA All-Star
• A nine-time All NBA First Team selection
• An eight-time NBA All-Defensive First Team selection

G	FG%	FT%	ORB	DRB	TRB	AST	STL	BLK	PTS
836	.507	.777	2.5	4.2	6.7	3.9	1.8	1.5	22.0

JULIUS **ERVING**

Professional basketball was ailing. Teams were losing money. Talent was split between two leagues: the more established National Basketball Association and the upstart American Basketball Association. The game itself was fighting an image problem as the sport was deemed "too black" and too riddled with drug problems to be fully accepted by the mainstream. A game of style, grace, athleticism, power and skill was hobbled by its reputation. In the arc of the sport's history, the early-to-mid-70s will go down as the period when basketball was certainly being checked for vital signs, if not actually put on life support.

Enter the Doctor, as in Dr. J — Julius Winfield Erving II — a uniquely gifted athlete and a person who dispensed precisely the medicine the game needed in generous doses of mastery, dignity, class and excitement.

"You'd have to use key words like electrifying, revolutionary," said Orlando Magic senior vice president Pat Williams, who brought Erving to the Philadelphia 76ers in 1976 after the ABA–NBA merger. "There's never been anybody quite like him."

In Erving's wake, Larry Bird and Magic Johnson made the NBA strong and vibrant; Michael Jordan made it an entertainment colossus. But the man they called "The Doctor" was the player who jolted the game back to life.

A late bloomer who was off the radar at the University of Massachusetts, the 6-foot-7 forward made his name during the latter stages of the ABA, defining the rebel league with his majestic flights, the signature red-white-and-blue ball a grapefruit in his outstretched hands.

Dr. J goes under the hoop for the layup against the Utah Stars. Erving's Nets defeated the Stars 4 games to 1, claiming their first ABA championship in 1972–73.

Erving jams the ball against the Denver Nuggets in the mid-1970s. Erving's basketball rights were sold by New York Nets owner Roy Boe in 1976 to the Philadelphia 76ers for $3 million.

As a rookie with the Virginia Squires in the 1971–72 season, Erving averaged 27.3 points and 15.7 rebounds. He was voted Rookie of the Year and named to the All-ABA Second Team. He quickly gained confidence using a style of play that would come to define him. Driving on 6-foot-9 Dan Issel and 7-foot-2 Artis Gilmore of the Kentucky Colonels in his first ABA game, Erving remembers he "went in between both of them and just hung there and waited for them to come down. Then I dunked on them so hard I fell on my back. Just doing that made me confident to go after anyone, anytime, anywhere without any fear."

He spent five seasons in the ABA with the Squires and then the New Jersey Nets, winning three scoring titles, three Most Valuable Player awards and two league championships. In one of the league's last great moments, Erving won professional basketball's first-ever slam dunk championship at the 1976 ABA All-Star Game. He used his signature running leap from the foul line, a dunk that today's stars still pay homage to.

CAREER HIGHLIGHTS

- Was an All-Star in every year of his 16-year basketball career
- He was 11-time NBA All-Star and five-time ABA All-Star
- He's the father of professional tennis player Alexandra Stevenson
- One of only a handful of players to have their jersey number retired by two teams: His number 32 with the New Jersey Nets and his number 6 with the Philadelphia 76ers
- Was a three-time ABA MVP and a one-time NBA MVP
- Was a two-time NBA All-Star Game MVP (1977 and 1983)
- Averaged at least 20 PPG in nine straight seasons from the 1976–77 season to the 1984–85 season
- Was selected to the All-NBA First Team five times

Many argue Erving inspired the NBA to finally integrate four ABA teams into the fold for the 1976–77 season, desperate to have the buzz Dr. J generated.

"There was an extraordinary attractiveness to the greatest stars in the ABA, and none of them shone more brightly than Julius Erving," said NBA commissioner David Stern. "Certainly, the anticipation of his arrival in the NBA enhanced the 1976 expansion and admission of the four teams. There was a sense of, 'Who is this guy that everyone says is so much better than everyone else? Let's see him against the NBA players.' Lo and behold, he was as great against the NBA players as he was in the ABA."

- Drafted: 12th overall by the Milwaukee Bucks in 1972
- Virginia Squires: 1971–73
- New York Nets: 1973–76
- Philadelphia 76ers: 1976–87
- Jersey: #6; alternates: #32
- College: University of Massachusetts Amherst

Born on February 22, 1950, in Roosevelt, New York, Erving was a talented high school player, but at 6-foot-3, nothing too special. The major college basketball powers passed over him and he ended up at the University of Massachusetts. Although he grew to 6-foot-7 once he started college, the 26.3 points and 20.2 rebounds he averaged over his sophomore and junior seasons were dismissed as the product of a good player competing in a weak league. He didn't get a sense of where he stood until he got a late invitation to a tryout in Colorado for a pre-Olympic team that would tour the Soviet Union. To the surprise of everyone, but perhaps to Erving most of all, he dominated the camp, giving himself an inkling that his game might travel well. "There were a lot of guys walking around Colorado Springs with newspaper clippings saying they were the best in the country," Erving said. "When I played them, I'd kill them. It sank in that being an All-American is a product of media hype."

In 1976, in one of the shrewdest moves in NBA history, Phildelphia 76ers' general manager Pat Williams purchased the rights to Erving for a $3-million payment to the cash-strapped Nets and signed Erving to a $3-million contract. Erving quickly proved worthy of the buzz building around him. He averaged 21.6 points and 8.5 rebounds for the season and led the 76ers to a 2–0 lead in the NBA Finals before losing four straight to the Portland Trail Blazers. As it became clear that he was every bit as capable of dominating in the NBA as he had in the ABA, the 76ers slowly built their team around him. And they were finally rewarded: After five seasons of playoff frustration, they rolled to an NBA title in 1983.

Erving retired after the 1986–87 season at age 37, still an exceptional player but not the athletic marvel who had marked his early professional seasons. By the time he stopped making house calls, Dr. J became one of only five players in professional basketball history to amass 30,000 points. He had an NBA Most Valuable Player award to go with the trophies he won in the ABA and he was an obvious choice for the NBA's 50th anniversary team in 1996, not to mention the Naismith Basketball Hall of Fame. But his on-court heroics were almost secondary to his status as the game's transcendent star. Posters of him in mid-flight were fixtures on the walls of teenagers across North America, his off-court popularity cemented by his air of measured, yet accessible, cool.

For a sport in need of an image boost, Erving was just what the doctor ordered.

WALT **FRAZIER**

He was a frustrated, under-used rookie on a still-emerging team, but even then he had a sense of style. So, to comfort himself, Walt Frazier bought a hat in every NBA city. In Baltimore one day, it was a classic fedora, similar to the one Warren Beatty was wearing while lighting up the screen in the hit 1967 movie *Bonnie and Clyde*. A persona was born.

It was a New York Knicks' trainer who gave the rookie with the hat the nickname "Clyde," but it fit and it stuck, and Walt "Clyde" Frazier grew into it quite nicely. He ended the 1967–68 season on the NBA's All-Rookie Team and by his second season, the improving Knicks made the 6-foot-4, 205-pounder their point guard. He proved deserving, with a no-nonsense calmness that belied a fierce competitive spirit and team-first attitude. The Knicks capped off the magical 1969–70 season with an unlikely Game 7 victory over Wilt Chamberlain and the Los Angeles Lakers in the Finals. Frazier finished with an epic 36-point, 19-assist, 5-steal performance in the deciding game, and the guard known far and wide as Clyde had arrived in Times Square as a star.

His style — he followed up the hats with mink coats, alligator shoes and a Rolls Royce, among other touches — made him a legend in the City that Never Sleeps. His play with the Knicks made him a touchstone for one of the NBA's iconic franchises and one of the most respected players in league history.

He was the king of cool.

"I was young, living in Manhattan and playing for the Knicks," Frazier said after his career. "It was a great time."

His style got the attention, but his game — deadly mid-range shooting, lockdown defense and cool in the clutch — earned him the respect.

"He was the greatest athlete I ever played with," said Willis Reed, the Knicks' Hall of Fame center who teamed with Frazier to bring the 1970 and 1973 championships to New York. "He was a phenomenal player, very unselfish, could do anything."

It is telling that, on a team that included future presidential candidate Bill Bradley, two future NBA general managers (Reed and Dave DeBusschere), a future university professor in Dick Barnett, and Phil Jackson (who emerged as one of the winningest coaches in NBA history), Frazier was the floor leader for head coach Red Holzman.

Born in 1945 in Atlanta, Frazier came upon his leadership skills early. "I was the oldest of nine kids," he said. "I was in charge. I grew up in a leadership role." Frazier was first to practice and last to leave,

Frazier goes up tall for the one-handed four-footer in the Eastern Conference Finals. The Knicks took the series 4–3 enroute to their second champioship.

Frazier drives past the Bucks' Oscar Robertson in the 1974–75 season. The Knicks dropped the season series to the Bucks 3–1.

leading by his example.

He also became known for his on-court cool, another habit he developed from an early age. "I used to be a hothead. But when I was in the eighth grade, my coach called me over and said, 'Son, don't lose your head. Your brain is in it.' I never forgot that." Over 13 seasons, 10 in the white-hot spotlight of New York and three injury-plagued years in Cleveland, he never received a technical foul.

As bright as Frazier's light shone in the 70s with the Knicks, his success wasn't inevitable. He was a two-sport star in high school and had a dream of playing football for a living, but recognized that black quarterbacks were hardly welcome in the professional ranks at the time. Because Georgia was off the beaten track for basketball during the early 1960s, most of the interest in Frazier came from traditional black universities. Happenstance saw him end up

- Drafted: 5th overall by the New York Knickerbockers in 1967
- New York Knicks: 1967–77
- Cleveland Cavaliers: 1977–80
- Jersey: #10; alternate: #11
- College: Southern Illinois University

CAREER HIGHLIGHTS

- NBA All-Star Game MVP in 1974–75
- A seven-time NBA All-Star
- One of the first NBA players to endorse a signature shoe, the Clyde, manufactured by Puma
- Works as a color commentator for the New York Knicks on MSG network
- Averaged a career high 23.2 PPG for the New York Knicks in 1971–72
- Named to seven NBA All-Defensive First Teams

at Southern Illinois University, a small Division II school, and even there Frazier faced challenges. An All-American his first two seasons, he was ruled academically ineligible as a junior, his angry coach limiting him to practicing only three days a week with the varsity and only on defense, but Frazier turned it into an advantage.

"I'm a very pragmatic person," Frazier said. "I knew it was my fault. I thought, 'what better way to get back at the coach but to master defense and wreak havoc on the offense?'… I created so many problems that the coach would say, 'Frazier, go sit down.'"

In his last year at SIU, Frazier led the Salukis to the National Invitation Tournament championship in Madison Square Garden, earning Most Valuable Player honors along the way, and was welcomed by the Knicks as the No. 5 pick in the 1967 draft.

The Knicks were poised to begin a basketball renaissance. In 1969, they lost a hard-fought series to the Boston Celtics and vowed to not let it happen again. They exploded in 1969–70, and inspired the city with a then-NBA record 18-game winning streak on their way to an NBA-best 62–20 regular season.

Proof of Frazier's cool in the clutch came in Game 7 of the Knicks' championship series win against the Los Angeles Lakers in 1970. It is famous in NBA annals because it's the game that team captain Willis Reed limped from the Knicks' dressing room moments before the tip, after missing most of Game 5 and all of Game 6 with a leg injury. The Garden fans went crazy and were rewarded when a hobbled Reed, playing with pain-killing injections, scored the game's first two baskets. But it was Frazier who won the game for New York with his all-time performance, outscoring every player on the floor.

Frazier admitted later that he was initially frustrated that the highlight of his playing career was over-shadowed by Reed's dramatic moment. But as his career progressed, Frazier's brilliance was often over-shadowed. Sometimes it was his own doing, given that his dedication to fashion and night life sometimes earned him more notice than his steady, galvanizing play.

But he's hardly one to harbor regrets. He capped off his fourth straight All-NBA First Team selection with another championship in 1973, this time earned while playing alongside Earl "The Pearl" Monroe, his old rival from the Baltimore Bullets. "He was fire, I was ice," said Frazier. Once more, the Knicks were winners and the toast of New York, with their point guard again raising his game in the playoffs, averaging 21.9 points, 7.3 rebounds and 6.2 assists on 51.4 percent shooting during the Knicks' run to the championship.

That was Frazier's way. His career numbers were impressive — 18.9 points, 5.9 rebounds and 6.1 assists in 13 seasons — as a result, he was a six-time All-NBA selection and seven-time All-Star while being named to the NBA's All-Defensive First Team seven straight seasons. But Frazier was even better in the playoffs. In his 93 playoff appearances as a Knick, he averaged 20.7 points per game, 7.2 rebounds and 6.4 assists on 51.1 percent shooting, all the while playing some of the best defense the league has ever known.

The man could sure dress, but put him in a game with everything on the line and the man they called Clyde came through in style.

G	FG%	FT%	ORB	DRB	TRB	AST	STL	BLK	PTS
1124	.497	.785	2.5	8.3	10.8	4.2	1.3	1.6	19.8

KEVIN GARNETT

From the moment Kevin Garnett burst onto the scene in the NBA with the Minnesota Timberwolves in 1995, it was clear he was going to stand for something. As a 19-year-old making the leap straight from high school to the pros — the first time in 20 years anyone had tried — he stood for either the degradation of the game or the opening of the floodgates for one of the biggest talent rushes the NBA has ever seen.

And as he developed into one of the most diverse talents the league has ever known — a seven-footer who could play all five positions at both ends of the floor — observers had to invent new ways to categorize him. He stood for a new brand of player.

"What is Garnett?" longtime coach and broadcaster Hubie Brown once wondered. "I don't know what he is. I'd hate to say he's just a power forward. He plays small forward. At the end of the game, he plays point guard on critical possessions. He does so many things and he does them well."

He is the only player in NBA history, for example, to average at least 20 points, 10 rebounds and 5 assists a season for six straight years. Only four players in league history have led their team in points, rebounds, assists, steals and blocks since 1973–74, and Garnett

Kevin Garnett guards Pau Gasol in Game 5 of the 2008 NBA Finals. Boston lost the game but won the series in Game 6 at home.

is one of them. He did it in 2002–03 with a line of 23 points, 13.4 rebounds, 6 assists, 1.6 blocks and 1.6 steals per game, joining Dave Cowens, Scottie Pippen and Tracy McGrady in the record books. His all-around dominance earned Garnett his due in 2004 when he was named MVP after averaging 24.2 points, 13.9 rebounds, 5 assists, 2.2 blocks and 1.5 steals for Minnesota en route to a franchise-best 58 wins.

Before the 1997–98 season, the Timberwolves signed the sophomore player to the then biggest contract in team sports — a six-year extension for $126 million. Overnight Garnett became a symbol of what might happen if owners didn't curb their compulsion to spend. The popular line of thought was that the owners locked the players out at the start of the 1998–99 season — a

Kevin Garnett in his Timberwolves days goes for a reverse layup against the Dallas Mavericks in Game 2 of the Western Conference Quarterfinals of the 2002 playoffs.

labor stoppage that resulted in the creation of the modern NBA salary-cap system — because of Garnett's deal.

But who would have guessed when it was all said and done, Kevin Garnett, nicknamed "Da Kid," and "The Big Ticket," would stand for old-school basketball values? Or that he would win over even the crustiest throwback with his passion and professionalism before he even won his first NBA title?

Garnett was traded to Boston in 2007 and it was their that Celtics' great Bill Russell — to whose game Garnett's was often compared — saw the way Garnett revived the Boston franchise with his team-first play and fever-pitch defense. Russell offered the ultimate tribute in an interview broadcast during the 2008 playoffs.

"I think you're going to win at least two or three championships here," Russell told Garnett. "And if you don't … I'll share one of mine with you. This is a friendship thing I'm talking about … you have no idea how proud I am of you. I couldn't be more proud of you than I am of my own kids."

By any measure the Celtics' gamble — dealing seven players to Minnesota to get Garnett in the summer of 2007, the biggest trade for one player in NBA history at the time — immediately proved successful. Teamed with incumbent star Paul Pierce and newly arrived shooting guard Ray Allen, Boston exploded out of the gate. The same team that lost a franchise-record 18 straight games on their way to a 24–58 mark in 2006–07 improved to 66–16 the following season, a record 42-win jump. With the best supporting cast of his career, Garnett's offensive numbers fell off slightly but his impact was otherwise stunning.

"The best quality is that he owns up to his mistakes, because stars rarely do," Celtics' head coach Doc Rivers said. "When he turns around in a film session and says, 'Damn it, that's my fault,' then what's [rookie] Glen

Davis going to do? Everyone falls in line and that makes your job a treat."

With Garnett's infusion of energy, skill and know-how, Boston became one of the best defensive teams of this era, for which Garnett was recognized as the Defensive Player of the Year in 2008. It culminated with a dramatic NBA Finals showdown against Kobe Bryant and the Los Angeles Lakers that Boston won in six games. Paul Pierce was the deserving Finals MVP, but Garnett brought the franchise back to glory in 2007–08.

It was redemption for him. For all his numbers and the respect Garnett earned, playoff success had largely eluded him. Eight times he brought the Timberwolves to the postseason and seven times they lost in the first round. He stepped up his game in 2003–04 when he won his

- Drafted: 5th overall by the Minnesota Timberwolves in 1995
- Minnesota Timberwolves: 1995–2007
- Boston Celtics: 2007–
- High School: Farragut Academy in Chicago

Most Valuable Player award while teaming with the battle-scarred veterans Sam Cassell and Latrell Sprewell to advance to the Western Conference Finals, but even that promise was short-lived, the team undone by contract problems and injuries. The lone star on a declining franchise, momentum gathered to trade Garnett. Some pointed to his team's playoff struggles and questioned whether he was part of the problem — a notion he put to rest in Boston.

"People got bored with 23 points, 12 rebounds and 6 assists. Got bored with that and they wanted more," said Sam Mitchell, one of Garnett's mentors during his early days in Minnesota. "You take those numbers and plug them in on any team and see what you get. Take those numbers and plug them in with Ray Allen and Paul Pierce and see what you get."

What do you get? At least one championship and a Celtic for life. Just ask Bill Russell.

CAREER HIGHLIGHTS

- Averaged at least 20 points and 10 rebounds per game in nine-straight seasons from 1998–2007
- Won an Olympic Gold Medal with the U.S. Men's Basketball Team in Sydney in 2000
- A 13-time NBA All-Star
- Has been named to the NBA All-Defensive First Team eight times
- Led the NBA in rebounds per game four years in a row from 2003–06

G	FG%	FT%	ORB	DRB	TRB	AST	STL	BLK	PTS
1270	.439	.815			6.3	4.8			20.8

17

FORWARD

JOHN HAVLICEK

The vast majority of basketball players aspiring to become professionals would be happy to have one NBA career. Boston Celtics' great, John Havlicek, had three — or at least one stellar career divided into three distinct periods.

And they were all outstanding.

The lynchpin of a powerhouse group at Ohio State University, Havlicek was the last player taken in the first round of the 1962 draft when the Celtics selected him. Given that he wasn't even considered the best player on the Buckeyes — that designation went to Jerry Lucas, chosen first overall that year —

expectations were low for the 6-foot-5 forward. That said, Havlicek established himself as a brilliant athlete who was All-State in baseball and football growing up in Bridgeport, Ohio. The Cleveland Browns drafted him as a wide receiver the same year the Celtics drafted him; he made it to Cleveland's final cuts before he began his run with the Celtics.

But stepping into a star-laden Celtics lineup, who were coming off their fourth-straight NBA championship, Havlicek quickly figured out what he could bring: a dose of kinetic energy off the bench.

Checking into the game against the other teams' tiring starters or its second unit, Havlicek helped the Celtics push the pace even faster, developing his reputation as a tireless hustler and defender who never seemed to stop.

"He was the greatest conditioned athlete I ever saw," said Celtics' architect Red Auerbach, who also described Havlicek as "the guts of the team."

His frenetic, restless style wasn't an obvious ticket to the NBA's 35th and 50th Anniversary Teams or the Naismith Hall of Fame, or a 16-year career during which he scored 26,395 points, was named to the First or Second All-NBA Team 11 times and won eight NBA titles.

He didn't initially impress Bob Cousy, the quintessential point guard of the early Celtics' dynasty, who called Havlicek "a non-shooter who would probably burn himself out."

Cousy was wrong on both counts. Havlicek's energy off the bench as the NBA's prototypical sixth man sparked the veteran Celtic team to a fifth straight title in 1963; the rookie chipping in 14.3 points per game. After a summer working on his shooting, he helped the Celtics to another title in 1964 while leading the team in scoring with 19.9 points per game.

Havlicek became the dominant figure at the tail end of the Bill Russell era, leading the aging team to two straight

John Havlicek leads the drive against the Phoenix Suns in the 1976 Finals. Boston took the championship 4–2.

John Havlicek works against Herm Gilliam of the Atlanta Hawks in 1972–73, his second of four-straight seasons where he garnered both First Team All-NBA and All-Defense honors.

championships — the last two of Russell's career. In the 1968 playoffs, Havlicek averaged 25.9 points, 8.6 rebounds and 7.5 assists and followed up in 1969 by averaging 25.4 points, 9.9 rebounds and 5.6 assists. Havlicek averaged more than 45 minutes a game on those postseason runs.

- Drafted: 1st overall by the Boston Celtics in 1962
- Boston Celtics: 1962–78
- College: Ohio State University

But perhaps the best was yet to come for Havlicek. Following Russell's retirement after the 1968–69 season, Boston struggled as they tried to rebuild, but Havlicek had the best statistical seasons of his career. In 1971, he was named First Team All-NBA for the first time in his career, an honor he earned for the next three seasons. Boston slowly began to accumulate a new generation of talent, including the likes of Dave Cowens at center and Jo Jo White at guard. But it was Havlicek, in his third phase, that led the Celtics to titles in 1974 and 1976 — this after a shoulder injury in the 1973 Eastern Conference Finals that likely cost Boston a spot in the NBA Finals and spoiled what had been a franchise-best 68–14 regular-season record.

The win in 1974 represented perhaps the most poignant of Havlicek's eight titles. Five years after Russell's retirement and a season removed from having a likely title snatched away by his injury, Havlicek's customary stoicism dissolved after he earned the Finals' MVP award, averaging 27.1 points, 6.4 rebounds and 6.0 assists for the playoffs. The 33-year-old Havlicek kissed and hugged his way around the dressing room following Boston's dramatic Game 7 win over Kareem Abdul-Jabbar and the Milwaukee Bucks, saying: "Thanks for doing this for me … this is the greatest one."

Even at that stage, Havlicek wasn't done. Another legend-making moment came during the second overtime period of Game 5 of the 1976 NBA Finals — a contest some consider the best game ever played. Havlicek's running bank shot with seconds left in the second

overtime appeared to win the game for Boston. The crowd at the old Garden spilled onto the floor, but it turned out the Phoenix Suns' Paul Westphal had called a timeout with a second remaining to play, setting up a 20-foot prayer shot by teammate Gar Heard to force a third overtime. The Celtics finally won, in large measure thanks to a then 35-year-old Havlicek whose tank never seemed to hit empty.

Playing so many important games over so many years, Havlicek regularly found himself at the center of the action. For example, he's immortalized in Celtics' lore for the steal that sealed Game 7 of the 1965 Eastern Conference Finals against Wilt Chamberlain and rival Philadelphia 76ers. The Celtics led by just one point when Bill Russell's entry pass hit one of the wires that supported the basket in that era, giving Philadelphia the ball and five seconds to score the winning basket.

"Russell said that these goat horns are growing about an inch a second on the top of my head … someone please bail me out," Havlicek recalled.

Who better than Havlicek? With Hal Greer inbounding, everyone figured his first option was Chamberlain. But Russell denied the easy entry pass and Havlicek played just off the high-scoring Chet Walker, counting down the time in his head before Greer had to inbound the ball. When he got to three, he looked up and saw Greer looking to Walker.

"I had a feeling [Greer] was going to go to Walker instead of feeding Chamberlain, so I gambled," said Havlicek.

He was right and tipped the pass to teammate Sam Jones, who dribbled out the clock as gravel-voiced Celtics' announcer Johnny Most immortalized the moment and Havlicek for a generation of Celtics fans:

"Havlicek steals it! Over to Sam Jones! Havlicek stole the ball! It's all over! Johnny Havlicek is being mobbed by the fans. It's all over! Johnny Havlicek stole the ball! Oh, boy, what a play by Havlicek at the end of this ball game!"

Some argue "Havlicek stole the ball" is the most famous moment in NBA history, which may be true.

But for John Havlicek it was just one big moment in a career full of them.

CAREER HIGHLIGHTS

- Was the NBA Finals MVP in 1974
- Eleventh on the NBA all-time scoring list with 26,395 points
- Nickname was "Hondo," which was inspired by the John Wayne character in the movie of the same name
- Was a 13-time N
- Averaged a   8.9 PPG in 1970–71
- Was nam   NBA First Team four times
- Was named to the NBA All-Defensive First Team five times

LeBRON JAMES

No player has come into the NBA with more hype than LeBron James.

He was just 18 years old when he stepped onto the floor in Sacramento's raucous ARCO Arena to make his NBA debut with the Cleveland Cavaliers, but he'd had enough attention — good and bad — for someone twice his age.

In the 11th grade, he appeared on the cover of *Sports Illustrated* with the headline "The Chosen One," a title he liked enough to have tattooed across his back. As a high school senior, his games were nationally televised, getting record ratings. Shaquille O'Neal came to watch him play and Kobe Bryant gave him shoes. He worked out with Michael Jordan. When his mother secured a bank loan to buy him a $50,000 vehicle for his 18th birthday, it became a national controversy regarding his high school and college eligibility and corruption in amateur sports. His senior season was nearly scrapped when it was discovered a local sporting goods store had given him a pair of expensive "throwback" jerseys. He was suspended, but the suspension was overturned amid more controversy. The Cleveland Cavaliers were fined $150,000 by the NBA for having James work out with them. Adidas and Nike courted him to burnish their brands, a battle Nike won by paying James $90 million to wear their shoes before he'd ever played an NBA game.

So how did the No. 1 pick of the 2003 draft do when it was finally time to play? Sometimes you have to believe the hype. With all eyes on him James delivered, manag___ points, 9 assists and 6 rebounds ag___ ___mento on

James gets set for Game 2 of the 2008 Eastern Conference Quaterfinals against the Washington Wizards with his now ubiquitous pre-game chalk routine.

opening night, followed by a 21-point, 12-rebound, 8-assist game in Phoenix. The Cavs lost both games, but there was no longer any choice but to recognize someone special had landed in the NBA.

"I love the spotlight," James said after his heady debut. "It's not pressure for me. I'm just being myself."

What does it mean for LeBron James when he said "just being himself"? It's in progress, given he finished his seventh NBA season before his ___hday.

___ can start with a package of physical ability that is shocking. He's ___oo___ and perhaps as heavy as 270 pounds of chiseled muscle. He came into the NBA with a 44-inch leap and can cover the 94-foot court in 9 or 10 rapid strides, journeys that usually end up in arena-shaking dunks, sending opponents

- Drafted: 1st overall by the Cleveland Cavaliers in 2003
- Cleveland Cavaliers: 2003—
- High School: Saint Vincent-Saint Mary in Akron, Ohio

James in the 2009–10 season where he averaged 29.7 points per game and recorded 31 double-doubles and four tripple-doubles.

tumbling like bowling pins. "As big as he is, you hope he just doesn't run you over and give you a concussion," veteran small forward Stephen Jackson said of encountering James in full flight.

But the physical tools are just the start of it.

The comparisons for James among the pantheon of NBA greats usually start at Michael Jordan for James' athleticism and ability to score at will; Magic Johnson for his size and court savvy; and Oscar Robertson, perhaps the only player before James with a similar combination of abilities.

But one aspect that makes James even more unusual is an apparent need to be part of a team. First yes, but first among equals. It's not always a common trait among the best of the best.

"One thing I like about being around him is he never separates himself from the team," said Joe Smith, an NBA veteran who played parts of two seasons with James. "That's rare. Some guys feed into certain things and separate themselves in the locker room, on the bus or on the plane. LeBron is not that type of guy on or off the court. That's why I appreciate playing alongside him, and why a lot of guys kind of cling to him because of his status and how he treats people."

Best-ever teammate?

"It's not like I take pride in it or practice it or something," James says. "That's just who I am … I've always had a good relationship with my teammates because of who I am personally."

His background sheds some light on his approach. He grew up a shy, uncertain kid in the tough part of Akron, Ohio, a working-class city south of Cleveland. Raised alone by his struggling teenaged mother, Gloria James, the Cavaliers' star missed 80 days of school in the fourth grade and moved six or more times. A local youth-football coach, Frank Walker, took notice and offered to have James live with his family. The routine agreed with James — he had a perfect attendance record in fifth grade and was never worse than a B student after he moved into a subsidized housing unit with his mother for sixth grade; a home at last. Around this time he connected with a youth-basketball team coached by the father of one

of his friends, Dru Joyce. James became the star of one of the best Amateur Athletic Union (AAU) teams in the United States, but he loved the structure and stability his basketball family gave him. The core of that AAU team enrolled in St. Vincent–St. Mary High School in Akron and made its Fighting Irish the best high school team in the United States. Even as his star exploded, James has never forgotten his past as shown in a powerful documentary, *More Than a Game*, about the team's high school days. It debuted in September 2008 at the Toronto International Film Festival. When the lights came up, the 1,200 people in the theater gave the film a standing ovation. James and his friends gathered in a sobbing embrace.

From those roots James' ascent in the NBA has been unwavering, with no end in sight. He was Rookie of the Year in 2003–04, averaging 20.9 points, 5.9 assists and 5.5 rebounds a game. In his second season, he averaged 27.2 points, 7.2 assists and 7.4 rebounds and earned All-NBA honors for the first time and All-League recognition, something he would repeat the next four seasons. He lifted the Cavaliers from 17 wins to 35 wins as a rookie, to 50 wins and an NBA Finals appearance by his fourth season and then a league-best 66 wins in 2008–09. The transcendent performances are already part of his NBA legend: The fifth game of the 2007 Conference Finals against the Detroit Pistons when James scored 48 points, including 29 of the Cavaliers' final 30 in a double-overtime win; the 45-point explosion in Game 7 of the 2008 Eastern Conference Finals in a duel with Paul Pierce of the Boston Celtics, albeit in a Cavaliers' loss.

Cleveland lost in the 2009 Eastern Conference Finals to Dwight Howard and the Orlando Magic, but James' playoff run only underlined why he won the Most Valuable Player that season. He averaged 35.3 points, 9.1 rebounds and 7.3 assists for Cleveland.

An otherwise magical season ended in a note of controversy when James left the court without shaking hands with the Magic team or speaking with the media. The criticism was fast and harsh. But James never backed down. "Shaking hands is not a big deal to me," he said later. "It's not being a sore loser, it's moving on. Sometimes people want you to accept losing and I'll never accept losing."

As the sport's brightest star just heading into his prime, he may not have to very often.

CAREER HIGHLIGHTS

- A Six–time NBA All-Star
- A two-time NBA All-Star Game MVP
- Led the NBA in scoring in 2007–08 averaging 30.0 PPG
- Scored an NBA playoff record of 25 consecutive points against the Detroit Pistons on May 31, 2007
- Youngest player (19 years and 88 days) to score 40 points in a game. He scored 41 points against the New Jersey Nets on March 27, 2004
- Won an Olympic Gold Medal with the U.S. Men's Basketball Team in Beijing in 2008
- Two-time NBA MVP (2008–09 and 2009–10)

Magic drives the basket against
Russ Schoene and Sedale Threatt
of the Seattle SuperSonics in 1989.
Magic's Lakers swept Seattle in the
Western Conference Semifinals.

G	FG%	FT%	ORB	DRB	TRB	AST	STL	BLK	PTS
906	.520	.848	1.8	5.5	7.2	11.2	1.9	0.4	19.5

EARVIN JOHNSON

For basketball fans, it was their "Kennedy" moment: A place in time when they knew where they were and how they felt — simply, universally, sad.

On November 7, 1991, Earvin "Magic" Johnson, perhaps the most beloved player in National Basketball Association history, leaned into a microphone at a press conference in Los Angeles and announced he was retiring from basketball because he'd contracted the human immunodeficiency virus that could lead to AIDS.

It was as if a bright comet streaking across the sky had been snuffed out. Time stopped.

Johnson's Los Angeles Lakers teammates, told moments before, dissolved in tears. So did those watching across the world. Everyone, it seemed, was devastated at the news: One of the most exciting athletes and vibrant personalities the game had ever known was suddenly dealing with a death sentence.

Everyone, it seemed, except the man himself.

"I'm going to go on," Johnson said in a calm, steady voice, perhaps the only dry-eyed person in the room. "I'm going to beat this, and I'm going to have fun."

It takes a certain strength of character to face the possibility of death with the same attitude that you approach life. And for someone acquiring HIV in the early 1990s, it certainly seemed like death was a likely outcome. But going on, taking on obstacles and having fun doing it was what Johnson had been known for until that point. Why change?

It was the "have fun" aspect of his personality that generated so much of the goodwill Johnson enjoyed in his career. His smile could light up an arena. His enthusiasm could lift a team.

It sustained him as he averaged 19.2 points, 11.2 assists and 7.8 rebounds over 13 seasons while being named to the All-NBA First Team nine times, the NBA's 50th Anniversary Team and the Naismith Basketball Hall of Fame. Magic is widely regarded as the best point guard in basketball history. Only Oscar Robertson recorded more triple-doubles than the 138 Johnson had in his NBA career.

But it was his attitude that became as much his calling card as his game. He was happy to play. He enjoyed his teammates. And he loved to win.

"I don't think there will ever be another 6-foot-9 point guard who smiles while he humiliates you," said long-time Laker teammate James Worthy.

Born August 14, 1959, in Lansing, Michigan, Johnson received his nickname after tallying 36 points, 16 rebounds and 16 assists in a high school game as a 15-year-old. A local sportswriter dubbed him "Magic" and it stuck. He became a celebrity leading his hometown Michigan State Spartans to an NCAA championship in 1979, beating Larry Bird's undefeated Indiana State Sycamores. The match-up pitting the two best players in college basketball — the flashy black kid against the fundamentally sound country boy from Indiana — became the most-watched

Magic catching his breath during a game in the mid-1980s. From 1982–83 to 1990–91 Magic earned nine straight First-Team All-NBA berths.

NCAA game in television history. Johnson shone the brightest, scoring 24 points, 7 rebounds and 5 assists, and being named the Final Four MVP.

With Bird landing in Boston with the Celtics and Johnson drafted No.1 overall by the Los Angeles Lakers, their rivalry lifted the NBA to new heights of popularity, and the two became close friends, bound by mutual respect.

"The first thing I would do every morning was look at the box scores to see what Magic did," said Bird. "I didn't care about anything else."

Johnson had the size of a power forward, the ball-handling skills of a slashing wing and the pass-first demeanor of a pure point guard. The NBA had never seen anything like him and may never again. His rookie season (1979–80) saw him help the Lakers to a 60–22 record while revitalizing All-Star center Kareem Abdul-Jabbar, who won his sixth and final Most Valuable Player award with Johnson's help. But it was Johnson who carved his own place in NBA history that year in Game 6 of the NBA Finals against the Philadelphia 76ers.

With Kareem out due to injury, Lakers coach Paul Westhead started Johnson at center and the 20-year-old rookie responded with 42 points, 15 rebounds and 7 assists, and the Lakers clinched the NBA title.

"We all thought he was a movie-star player, but we found out he wears a hard hat," said Westhead. "It's like finding a great orthopedic surgeon who can also operate a bulldozer."

What position did he play? All and none.

"Well, I played center, a little forward, some guard," said Johnson. "I tried to think up a name for it, but the best I came up with was C-F-G Rover."

It was the beginning of a remarkable decade for Johnson, the Lakers and the NBA, but not without hiccups. In his second

- Drafted: 1st overall by the Los Angeles Lakers in 1979
- Los Angeles Lakers: 1979–91 and 1995–96
- College: Michigan State University

season, Johnson injured his knee, missed 45 games and was the goat when he shot an airball at the buzzer in an upset loss in the first round of the playoffs against the Houston Rockets. In 1981–82, Johnson's reputation took a hit when he clashed with Westhead and the coach was fired, replaced by Pat Riley. Johnson was booed for the first time in his career and wasn't voted in as a starter at the All-Star Game, but when the Lakers won their second championship in three seasons, the page turned.

Johnson's game continued to grow. As Abdul-Jabbar aged and eventually retired, Johnson put up some of the best scoring numbers of his career. He won the first of three Most Valuable Player awards after the 1986–87 season, averaging a career-high 23.9 points per game to go along with 12.2 assists and 6.3 rebounds. His 11.2 assist-per-game average is the highest in NBA history, and his 10,141 career assists place him second only to John Stockton.

"There have been times when he has thrown passes and I wasn't sure where he was going," said Laker teammate Michael Cooper. "Then one of our guys catches the ball and scores and I run back up the floor convinced that he must've thrown it through somebody."

His career ended too early. After the HIV diagnosis, he at first retired on his doctor's advice to conserve his strength while battling the frightening virus. Later, the concerns of his fellow players kept him away from the court, though he was voted in by the fans as a starter for the 1992 All-Star Game. He earned MVP honors and was surrounded at the buzzer by well-wishing players from both sides. "The first game ever called on account of hugs," said Johnson.

There was a brief stint coaching and a 32-game comeback at the end of the 1995–96 season, which was more about the then 36-year-old legend retiring on his own terms.

There's no question he has lived life that way. He came out swinging against his diagnosis and has shown no signs of slowing down. The same energy and personality he had on the floor has translated into business, and he now stands as one of sport's most successful entrepreneurs. He's healthy, by all indications, and he can still light up a room.

"Every time I see him," says Bird, his rival and friend, "I'm happier."

CAREER HIGHLIGHTS
- Was a 12-time NBA All-Star
- Won five NBA championships with the Lakers
- One of only four players to have recorded 10,000 assists in a career
- Averaged an NBA record 11.2 assists per game
- Had 24 assists on May 15, 1984, which is an NBA Playoffs single-game assists record that he shares with John Stockton
- Led the NBA in assists per game four times, including a career-high 13.1 in 1983–84

G	FG%	FT%	ORB	DRB	TRB	AST	STL	BLK	PTS
1072	.497	.835	1.6	4.7	6.2	5.3	2.3	0.8	30.1

MICHAEL JORDAN

Michael Jeffrey Jordan crafted an athletic career that left him not only universally acknowledged as the best basketball player ever, but an icon across sports and across culture — a one-name adjective for competitive excellence: Jordan.

His ability to raise his game when the stakes were highest is legendary, and perhaps best explained by how he performed with comparatively nothing on the line.

One of hundreds of examples came on a bland winter afternoon against the lowly Toronto Raptors, a struggling expansion team. It was a nothing NBA game, just one of the 1,072 works of art Jordan orchestrated over his career. He was 35 years old and widely expected to retire at the end of the 1997–98 season. He could have been excused for winding down. Instead, playing in front of 33,216 people in a converted baseball stadium, Jordan led the Bulls to an early lead and then back from the brink when the upstart Raptors pushed the Bulls. He hit the game-winning jumper with 5.9 seconds left, to the delight of the *home* crowd, happier to have their own Jordan story than a plain old win.

"I play my best when I please myself first," Jordan said afterward. "I appreciate the fans. It's amazing how many people that you can touch."

Amazing indeed. At 6-foot-6 and about 215 pounds, he was the prototype for the modern perimeter player. He was fundamentally sound, having played three seasons for Dean Smith at the University of North Carolina, yet he played the game with

With 6.9 seconds to play, Jordan hoists the series' winning shot against the Utah Jazz in Game 6 of the 1998 Finals.

a flair and an imagination that no one since has quite mastered — nor could they, given Jordan's stunning physical gifts: leaping ability and body control good enough to win dunk contests; massive hands that allowed him to control the ball like a grapefruit; the perfect combination of size and speed for a shooting guard.

But all that ability combined with an iron competitive will and a surgeon's precision? Taken together it was an unstoppable force.

Boston Celtics' star Larry Bird wasn't prone to overstatement, but he captured Jordan for a generation of fans just beginning to glimpse his brilliance when he relived the experience of trying — and failing — to contain Jordan as he went about scoring 63 points in a first-round playoff game (an NBA record) at the end of Jordan's second season. "That was God disguised as Michael Jordan," said Bird.

Jordan dominating playoff games became a recurring theme: He won six NBA championships and was the Finals' Most Valuable Player all six times.

Whether the grandest stage or a mid-season afternoon game against a league also-ran, they all meant the same to Jordan. He played hard all the time,

CAREER HIGHLIGHTS

• Led the league in scoring 10 times, including seven seasons in a row from 1986–87 to 1992–93

• Averaged 37.1 PPG in 1986–87, which is the fourth-highest regular-season-scoring average in NBA history

• Was a two-time NBA Slam Dunk Contest winner

• Was a 14-time NBA All-Star

• He played for the Birmingham Barons, a Chicago White Sox farm team, in 1994 and batted .202 with 3 HRs, 51 RBIs and 30 SBs

• Scored at least 60 points in a game five times, including an NBA Playoffs record 63 in 1986

• Second all-time in career steals with 2,514

but brought something extra when it mattered most: the seven three-pointers against the Portland Trail Blazers in Game 1 of the 1992 Finals; the buzzer-beater jump shot, what became known as The Shot, and a leaping, fist-pumping celebration after breaking the Cleveland Cavaliers' hearts in a deciding Game 5 of the opening round of the Eastern Conference Finals in 1989; the 38 points he scored against the Utah Jazz in Game 5 of the 1997 NBA Finals while ill with the flu; the 55 points he laid on the New York Knicks in Madison Square Garden on March 28, 1995, in his fifth game after returning to basketball following his one-year hiatus he took to try his hand at professional baseball.

Jordan's signature moment might have been the move he made on hapless Bryon Russell of the Utah Jazz on the last possession in Game 6 of the 1998 NBA Finals. He faked Russell right, used his left hand to push Russell a little further right while at the same time regaining his balance, creating a wide-open look at the series-winning basket and then nailing it. Strictly speaking, it may have been

an offensive foul, but it was so crafty and timely it should only be applauded for its flawless execution and evidence that Jordan was as savvy as he was talented.

"How should Jordan be remembered?" Jazz coach Jerry Sloan was asked afterwards. "As the greatest who ever played the game."

Who did Jordan not touch? He became the gold standard for athletes who aspire to use their gifts to build a commercial brand. In 1998, *Fortune* magazine did a cover story on Jordan's impact on companies like Nike, Coca-Cola and McDonald's, not to mention the NBA and the Chicago Bulls. It estimated the "Jordan Effect" on the economy to be worth about $10 billion at the time — and rising.

Appreciating Jordan was easier than explaining him. It wasn't talent alone that created the meteor that burned brightly across the NBA sky from 1984 to 2003, a period in which he posted the highest all-time scoring average with 30.1 points per game, and placed third in all-time points scored with 32,292. He was talent and dedication and drive in a single package and easily earned his way onto 14 All-Star teams, 10 All-NBA first teams and nine All-NBA defensive first teams. He was also named the league's MVP five times.

Imagine what he might have done had he not retired in his prime to play a season of professional baseball? Or sat out three seasons before his late-career comeback with the Washington Wizards, when he made the jump from the owners' suite to the floor? By his standards, his last two seasons were hardly memorable, unless you consider that at age 39 and in his last NBA season he averaged 20 points, 6.1 rebounds and 3.8 assists. It wasn't Jordanesque production, but it was certainly All-Star worthy. And that season he played all 82 games for the Wizards, their drive for the playoffs just falling short. He became the highest scoring 40-year-old in NBA history when he dropped 43 on the New Jersey Nets a week after his birthday in February 2003, including the winning basket.

Where did it all come from? He was a good player going into Laney High School in Wilmington, North Carolina, where Jordan's family moved shortly after he was born in Brooklyn, New York, on February 17, 1963. But he was no LeBron James, who had a national reputation before he finished high school. Jordan was, famously, cut when he tried out for the varsity team in Grade 10, but slights like that and the countless backyard battles he had with talented older brother Larry, by all accounts an athletic marvel who stood only 5-foot-7, honed a unique level of competitiveness that never wavered, even as he became one of the richest, most accomplished athletes of his era.

"I play to win, whether during practice or a real game," he said. "And I will not let anything get in the way of me and my competitive enthusiasm to win."

When he signed his first NBA contract, it included a "love of the game" clause that allowed him to play basketball any time he wanted. When he neared the peak of his fame, filming *Space Jam*, he insisted that a regulation basketball court be built on the set so he could get his games in with the other NBA players who appeared in the movie. When he retired the first and second times, he couldn't help but return to play.

Anyone lucky enough to see him at the height of his power, playing for everything or nothing at all, wished he never had to go.

- Drafted: 3rd overall by the Chicago Bulls in 1984
- Chicago Bulls: 1984–93 and 1994–98
- Washington Wizards: 2001–03
- Jersey: #23; alternates: #45
- College: University of North Carolina

Jordan drives around John Starks of the New York Knicks in Game 3 of the 1993 Eastern Conference Semifinals. Chicago took the series in six games on their way to a third straight championship.

Malone drives under Shaquille
O'Neal in Game 4 of the 1997
Western Conference Semifinals.
Malone led all players with 42 points
in the 110–95 Jazz win.

G	FG%	FT%	ORB	DRB	TRB	AST	STL	BLK	PTS
1476	.516	.742	2.4	7.7	10.1	3.6	1.4	0.8	25.0

KARL **MALONE**

He was built like a slab of granite and his game was a bedrock of consistency.

Karl Malone made the "power" of the power-forward position the hallmark of his game over the course of his 19 NBA seasons, all but one spent with the Utah Jazz. He bulked up when basketball was still a game for skinny guys. He proved the value of year-round conditioning, missing just four games due to injury during his first 18 years in the league.

He proved that sheer willpower can turn an overlooked talent into a player so routinely excellent that his place in the game's history is beside the likes of Chamberlain, Jordan and Russell — the best of the best.

"Karl Malone's lesson is that … you can work on your body, you can work on your shooting, you can work on your defense," said Jerry Sloan, Malone's longtime coach in Utah. "You can do all those things and make yourself better."

A fitness fanatic since his freshman year at Louisiana Tech, Malone never stopped training, adding pounds of muscle to an already impressive 6-foot-9 frame. If the Jazz were on the road, he'd find a gym and do his lifting. At home he had a $100,000 fitness gym installed in his basement. During the summers, he'd work out twice a day in the heat at his ranch in Arkansas. He played at 260 or more pounds during his career, none of it fat.

"I don't do it for fun," Malone once said of his obsessive approach. "And I don't do it for glory. I do it because it's necessary. I feel that my strength and endurance give me an advantage, and I want to keep that advantage."

Malone goes strong to the hoop against the Miami Heat on January 8, 1996, netting 32 on the night and 2,106 for the season (second in the NBA).

His other advantage was his burning competitive spirit. Nicknamed "The Mailman" because he always delivered, his intensity manifested itself in league-leading technical foul totals and a tendency to collide hard with opposing guards who dared challenge him in the paint or anywhere else for that matter. He earned a reputation as one of the dirtiest players in the NBA.

"I make my fouls worth it," said Malone, "but I don't go after anybody."

Anyone who admired a game being played like it mattered — something Malone did in all of his 1,476 appearances, good for fourth on the all-time list — had to appreciate his fiery temperament.

"There's no way I consider him a dirty player," Chicago Bulls' head coach Phil Jackson said of Malone. "He's physical, throws his body around and does play the enforcer role on that team. But that's not the same thing as being dirty. The main thing a coach asks from his players is to be competitive every minute. And Karl Malone is."

In one of the great mysteries of the NBA draft process, Malone was taken 13th overall by Utah in 1985, despite lifting unheralded Louisiana Tech to within a basket of the Elite Eight in his last year and averaging 18.7 points and 9.3 rebounds for his career. It was all just more fuel for Malone's unquenchable fire.

- Drafted: 13th overall by the Utah Jazz in 1985
- Utah Jazz: 1985–2003
- Los Angeles Lakers: 2003–04
- Jersey: #32; alternates: #11
- College: Louisiana Tech University

"All the doubters out there, I never forgot them. And I never will," Malone said. "If I walk into an arena with 19,000 fans, and 18,999 are cheering for me, I hear that one boo. That is what keeps me hungry. I'm never satisfied where I'm at."

While a player of Malone's gifts and drive would have been a star wherever he played, landing in Utah assured his ascension to the game's pantheon. Already there was another overlooked college player, a short, wiry point

guard named John Stockton whom Utah drafted 16th in 1984. The two were opposites in size and personality, but the crafty, feisty point guard and the thundering power forward went together like butter on toast on the court.

By the time Malone retired after 19 seasons — his final year played without Stockton on the Los Angeles Lakers — he placed second in scoring in NBA history with 36,928 points. He averaged 25 points and 10.1 rebounds for his career and set NBA records with eleven 2,000-point seasons, most defensive rebounds in a career, and most free throws attempted and made. He won the NBA's Most Valuable Player award in 1996–97 at the age of 33, when he averaged 27.4 points and 9.9 rebounds on 55 percent shooting and the Jazz posted a franchise-best 64–18. He won MVP honors again in 1998-99 when he averaged 23.8 points, 9.4 rebounds and 4.1 assists for a Jazz team that went 37–13 in a season that started late because of a labor dispute. It was a season where a lot of his peers were out of shape when the lockout ended. Not Malone.

As for Stockton, he played 18 years with Malone and finished as the NBA's career leader in assists, the vast majority of those to the Mailman, which is why the Jazz built a pair of matching bronze statues in honor of the two men at the intersection of John Stockton Drive and Karl Malone Drive in Salt Lake City.

Did Malone make Stockton or did Stockton make Malone? For anyone who watched them execute thousands of pick-and-roll plays with surgical precision, it hardly mattered. The results spoke for themselves.

"There's a country saying, 'You can't have the chicken without the egg,'" Malone said. "I don't know. Is John the chicken or the egg? That's why you can't gauge what we mean to each other."

There is one hole in Malone's résumé, otherwise a body of work like almost no other in NBA history. His relentless effort and consistent greatness never produced an NBA title. He led the Jazz to eight 50-win seasons and three 60-win seasons and had them on pace for a fourth in the lockout-shortened 1998 season. His playoff production was equally impressive, but the two times he made it to the NBA Finals he ran into Michael Jordan and the Chicago Bulls.

For such a willful player, it was the one goal he couldn't cobble out of more work and a bigger effort. And, ironically, when he did leave Utah as a free agent and took a bargain-basement contract to play with the Lakers in a bid to cap off his career with a ring, his body finally gave way at age 40. A knee injury caused him to miss 40 games — more than he'd missed in his entire career to that point — and hobbled him during his third NBA Finals appearance in which the Lakers lost to the Detroit Pistons.

Despite demand for services, Malone was done. His mother Shirley died before his final season in Los Angeles. She had raised him and seven siblings alone, working two and three jobs, her work ethic the "bedrock religion" she passed on to her son. With his mother gone, Malone's fire finally began to cool, and he didn't want to play that way. He announced his retirement on what would have been her birthday.

"Championships and all those things aside, he was a championship guy," Sloan, his old coach, said. "A lot of guys won championships. But not many put as much work into it as he did."

CAREER HIGHLIGHTS

- Scored a career-high 61 points in only 33 minutes on January 27, 1990, against the Milwaukee Bucks
- Was a 14-time NBA All-Star
- Was an 11-time All-NBA First Team selection
- Won two Olympic gold medals for the U.S. Men's Basketball Team in 1992 and 1996
- Was the co-MVP of the NBA All-Star Game in 1993 with his teammate John Stockton
- Has 779 career point-rebound double-doubles, which is first all-time (this statistic accurate since 1986–87)
- Was on 14 All-NBA teams
- Averaged at least 20 PPG in 17 of his 19 years in the NBA

MOSES MALONE

He was a man of action, not words, so there's some irony that Moses Malone is perhaps best known for something he said.

As the steamroller that was the 1982–83 Philadelphia 76ers neared the NBA playoffs, reporters asked the logical question of Malone: What was his prediction for the postseason?

"Fo, fo, fo," he said in his clipped, rural Virginian accent. Translated it was "four, four, four," a clean sweep of the playoffs.

History — and the 76ers championship rings — would prove Malone wrong. After sweeping the opening seven-game series against the New York Knicks, Philadelphia dropped Game 4 in the second round to the Milwaukee Bucks before finishing them off in Game 5 and then sweeping the Los Angeles Lakers.

The rings, then, were inscribed "Fo, fi, fo." Close enough.

In 1981–82, Malone was a restricted free agent coming off his second MVP award after averaging 31.1 points and 14.7 rebounds for the Houston Rockets. Philadelphia pursued him with the richest deal in league history at the time: a six-year, $13-million contract. The 76ers were convinced Houston wouldn't match it and they were correct, eventually settling for journeyman center Caldwell Jones and a draft pick in return.

What no one doubted is that almost from the moment the 76ers made the move to acquire Malone, the franchise's fortunes would change. Everyone knew it. The predictions came fast and furious. The 76ers

were instant favorites to win the NBA championship that had eluded them since Julius Erving arrived from the ABA for the 1976–77 season, despite three trips in that time to the NBA Finals and two more to the Eastern Conference Finals.

As if to put any doubts to rest, the lineup featuring Malone, Erving, Bobby Jones, Maurice Cheeks and Andrew Toney overwhelmed the league, coming out of the gate 50–7, threatening to make good on Malone's preseason prediction that Philadelphia would become the first NBA team to win 70 games. Instead, they finished 65–17 and then became the only NBA team to lose just one game on the way to the championship, proving that superstars can be good teammates, too.

"He was quoted as saying when he got here, it was Dr. J's show, but now it's going to be a better show," Erving said. "Moses was phenomenal, and he was the high hat we were waiting for."

The feeling was mutual.

"It was an honor to play with Doc," Malone said. "I watched him play with the Virginia Squires [of the ABA], and he was my favorite player. And to be his teammate was just great."

Philadelphia's Malone gets set to take one of his 11,090 NBA free throws, of which he made 8,531 (second all-time).

Malone's grinding, relentless inside game complemented Erving's elegance. It was easy for him to defer to Erving and his new teammates. Erving's game was low maintenance and so was Malone. He perfected a lunch-bucket approach in which he generated his own offense by coming up with the misses of others and even some of his own, famously tapping the ball to himself until he could come up with it in good position to score. It may have looked ordinary, but the results were spectacular.

"It's an honor to think people consider me a great player," Malone said when he learned he was being inducted into the Naismith Hall of Fame in 2001. "I never considered myself a great player. I considered myself a hard worker."

The tireless effort paid dividends. Malone played 19 NBA seasons, accumulating 29,580 points and 17,834 rebounds, ranking third in rebounding and fourth in scoring. Only Wilt Chamberlain ranked higher in both categories. Malone owns the NBA records for offensive rebounds in a game, season and career. He made superstar money and posted

CAREER HIGHLIGHTS

- Averaged at least 20 points and 10 rebounds per game in 11 straight seasons (1978–88)

- Became the first player to lead the league in rebounds 5 years in a row (1980–84)

- Is the father of Michael Malone, a professional football player who played for the Miami Dolphins in 2007

- Played 21 seasons in the ABA/NBA combined, which is more than any other player in the history of both leagues

- Is the only player in NBA history to average at least 20 points and 10 rebounds per game for four different teams

- Was a 12-time NBA All-Star and a one-time ABA All-Star

superstar statistics, but did it all with his hard-hat on, bulling his 6-foot-10, 250 pounds through the paint, trying to make each miss his own.

His former teammate, Mike Dunleavy, once asked him about his approach. "Suppose there are 100 rebounds in a game," Malone told him, "I'm going after all 100, and 15 will fall into my hands."

"Pretty simple, but true," Dunleavy said years later. "Moses wasn't the greatest athlete in the league. He didn't have huge hands, and he wasn't a great leaper. But he worked so hard. His effort was off the charts, proving if you try your hardest all the time, there's no telling where you might end up. You'll surprise yourself sometimes."

Malone was one of the most sought-after high school basketball players in the United States. In his three seasons at Petersburg High School, the basketball team had a record of 67–3, including two undefeated seasons, a 50-game winning streak and two state championships. He agreed to attend the University of Maryland but couldn't resist when the Utah Stars of the ABA offered a million dollars if

- Drafted: N/A
- Utah Stars (ABA): 1974–75
- Spirits of St. Louis (ABA): 1975–76
- Buffalo Braves: 1976–77
- Houston Rockets: 1976–82
- Philadelphia 76ers: 1982–86 and 1993–94
- Washington Bullets: 1986–88
- Atlanta Hawks: 1988–91
- Milwaukee: 1991–93
- San Antonio: 1994–95
- Jersey: #2; alternates: #24, #22, #13, #20, #21, #4 and #8
- High School: Petersburg in Petersburg, Virginia

he would turn professional out of high school. Then a skinny teenager, Malone averaged 18.8 points and 14.6 rebounds as a rookie playing against men, something no high school player had done so successfully before and didn't happen again until the likes of Kevin Garnett and Kobe Bryant and others did it two decades later.

He didn't miss a beat when he finally made the NBA, being retrieved in the dispersal draft by Portland and then traded to Buffalo and then Houston. He made his first bold playoff prediction when he led the 40–42 Rockets to the 1980-81 NBA Finals, saying that he could take four guys from the playground and beat the Boston Celtics. Not quite. Boston won the series 4–2, but not because Malone didn't back up his boast. He averaged 26.8 points and 14.5 rebounds for the playoffs.

And while his championship season in Philadelphia was undoubtedly his career high point, it wasn't the end. Already a nine-year professional basketball veteran by then, Malone played 12 more seasons and earned five more All-Star nominations, churning out 20-point and 10-rebound nights without making a highlight reel dunk or bringing anyone out of their seats.

It was his way. He just went to work and didn't stop until the job was done.

Houston's Malone goes for a layup against the New Jersey Nets in the late 1970s. Malone spent six seasons in Houston, his longest stay on any team, having played for nine teams and two leagues over 21 seasons.

99 CENTER

GEORGE MIKAN

Every sport has its giants. And then there's George Mikan.

He was an original. He was dominant. And he was huge, figuratively and literally.

In his six seasons before retirement (spanning the Basketball Association of America's last season, 1948–49, and the NBA's first five seasons, 1949–54), Mikan won five championships. He was first or second in league scoring for all but one of those seasons, and was a top-three rebounder over the same period. Without any debate it was Mikan — Mr. Basketball — who was the best player on the best team in the infancy of the professional game.

"In our time, George was Michael Jordan, Magic Johnson and Larry Bird rolled into one," Laker teammate Vern Mikkelsen once put it.

To illustrate this, the Lakers came to New York to play one night and the marquee at Madison Square Garden read: Geo Mikan vs. the Knicks.

"I went into the locker room, sat down, took off my glasses … and started to change into my uniform," Mikan said. "I finished getting dressed, put my glasses back on and the other guys were still sitting there in their street clothes. They looked at me and said, 'OK, big shot. You're supposed to play them. So go out and play them.' They razzed me for a long time. Really, it was both thrilling and embarrassing to see your name on the Madison Square Garden marquee."

Viewed after a half century of basketball history has passed, Mikan's role in the evolution of the sport seems a natural part of a continuum. He was the game's first highly skilled and really big center at 6-foot-10 and 250 pounds. He gave way to Bill Russell and Wilt Chamberlain, who in turn linked eras with Kareem Abdul-Jabbar, setting the standard for Hakeem Olajuwon, Shaquille O'Neal and Tim Duncan, all the way to burgeoning Orlando Magic star Dwight Howard.

Missing in that version of events is the reality that until Mikan came along, basketball belonged to smaller players, favoring quick dribblers and set shooters. The idea of building your offense around a big man was untested.

"The only big men before Mikan were grotesque, freaky looking guys," said Bud Grant, a reserve on those great Lakers teams and later an iconic coach of the Minnesota Vikings in the NFL. "Mikan was not that way at all. He stood up straight with those broad shoulders and ran the floor."

Mikan's success with the Lakers meant that "going big" became a proven formula for NBA success.

"He showed the world a big man could be an

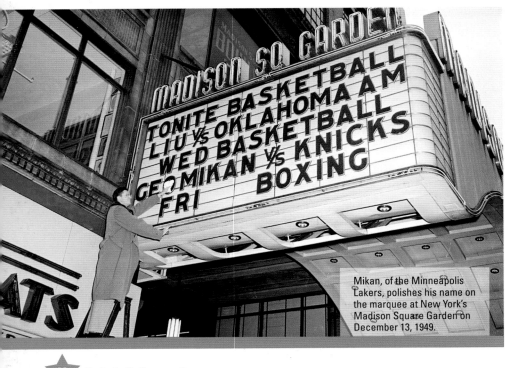

Mikan, of the Minneapolis Lakers, polishes his name on the marquee at New York's Madison Square Garden on December 13, 1949.

A rookie Mikan beats Lee Knorek to drop in one of his 18 baskets in a 101–74 win over the New York Knicks at Madison Square Garden on February 22, 1949.

athlete," said Chamberlain, who along with Mikan was selected as one of the 50 greatest players in NBA history. "He showed a big man was not just a freak, not just a gook, not just some big guy who could hardly walk and chew gum at the same time. He was a splendid athlete. He was the first true superstar of the league."

- Drafted: N/A
- Minneapolis Lakers: 1948–56
- College: DePaul University

It almost never happened. Born in 1924, Mikan grew up playing basketball using a homemade basket hung on the garage of a house behind his father's tavern in Joliet, Illinois, but to no great effect, even given his height. He was cut by his high school team, and instead of a career in professional sports he aimed toward the priesthood, though he eventually enrolled at DePaul University to study law. As a big Catholic who loved hoops, he couldn't resist the urge to try out for Notre Dame. Tryouts for college teams were the norm then and he took his shot over the Christmas break only to be cut there, too.

"I guess they just didn't think I had it," Mikan recalled of the Notre Dame experience. "It just about broke my heart."

But he received another chance. Ray Meyer, an assistant coach at Notre Dame, had watched Mikan's tryout. By chance Meyer ended up hired as the head coach at DePaul, where Mikan trudged back to finish his freshman year. Meyer worked with Mikan and introduced a range of novel techniques to boost his skill and coordination. He had him skip rope for quickness and play defense against guards for agility. He even enrolled him in dance lessons to improve his footwork and had him hit a speed bag to improve his hands. Meyer also had his prize pupil shoot 100 hook shots with his back to the basket with his right hand and 100 rolling to his left. Mikan became so proficient at both that to this day the routine is known as the Mikan Drill.

"That first season, Mikan improved from

game to game, like a flower blooming," Meyer said.

Mikan was twice the College Player of the Year and three times All-American. He led his Blue Demons to the 1945 NCAA title, just as the pro game started to find its feet. Mikan started pro ball with the Chicago Gears of the National Basketball League in 1946 and led them to a title that year. He ended up with the Minneapolis Lakers of the NBL in 1946–47 and stayed with them as they merged with the Basketball Association of America, which formed the modern NBA in 1949–50. Mikan's teams won because no opposition player could match him. In his first eight professional seasons, Mikan's teams won seven championships, including four of the first five NBA titles. He was big and played like it.

"George had a great killer instinct," said Boston Celtics' contemporary Bob Cousy. "He was no gentle giant."

The imprint he left on the sport is immeasurable. In college, he routinely tapped out shots on their way into the basket because the goaltending rule hadn't been invented. Before Mikan, it never occurred to anyone that a rule like goaltending would be needed. When he started playing professionally, the lane measured only six feet wide, meaning Mikan was in range for his hook shot the moment he posted up. As a result the lane was widened to 12 feet, on the way to the current 16-foot width. In a 1950 game, the Fort Wayne Pistons jumped out to an early 19–18 lead and then held the ball for the rest of the game rather than have it go back to Mikan, winning the lowest-scoring game in NBA history. That led to the introduction of the 24-second shot clock in 1954–55.

Mikan retired in 1954, aside from a brief comeback in the 1955–56 season, but his impact didn't stop there. In his absence the Lakers struggled and their popularity waned, prompting their move to Los Angeles for the 1960-61 season. A lawyer by training, Mikan became the inaugural commissioner of the ABA and invented the iconic red-white-and-blue ball. He later helped lead a successful campaign to bring the NBA back to Minnesota.

He was a giant of the game.

The first one.

CAREER HIGHLIGHTS

- Scored a career-high 61 points in a game against the Rochester Royals on January 20, 1952. The rest of his team scored a combined 30 points

- Was the first commissioner of the ABA

- Led the league in points per game three times including a career-high 28.4 PPG in 1950–51

- Was a four-time NBA All-Star

HAKEEM **OLAJUWON**

If there is one thing that let Hakeem Olajuwon know everything would be different, it was his new shoes. Only a few hours into his new life in the United States and still years away from realizing his basketball destiny as one of the five best centers in NBA history, Olajuwon was asked by a trainer at the University of Houston what size shoe he wore.

"I told him 14 was my usual size," said Olajuwon. "I was shocked that he produced a brand-new pair. It wasn't something you could find in Nigeria."

He had only been playing basketball seriously for a few months, having first taken up the game as a 17-year-old in Lagos, Nigeria, upon the urging and nagging of his friends. But as a 6-foot-10 firecracker of athletic potential, it didn't take long for the basketball world to find him.

Within weeks he was included on the Nigerian national team. An American, Christopher Pond, was coaching the Central African Republic and convinced the raw teenager that his talent would be best shaped playing in the United States. Pond had a relationship with the University of Houston, and in September Olajuwon found himself in the Cougars' training room preparing to play a pick-up game with his new teammates and picking through more shoes than he'd ever seen in his life.

He tried on the 14s the trainer brought him, but they were tight.

"I was going to take off a pair of socks and [the trainer] said, 'No, let's try 15,'" Olajuwon recalled. "Those were tight, too. He

Olajuwon drives to the basket against Phoenix's Joe Kleine during the 1994 Western Conference Semifinals. Olajuwon and the Rockets would win the Finals, giving Houston its first NBA title.

got 16s. I could not believe all of these brand-new shoes. I put them on and they fit. For the first time ever, I would play basketball without pain in my feet. It was always a distraction when I was running and jumping. But this was comfortable. I thought, 'Oh, man! They're in trouble out there on the court.'"

Yes, indeed. Olajuwon led the Cougars to three straight Final Four appearances, beginning in 1982 as a charter member of the basketball fraternity "Phi Slama Jama."

While still developing as a player, Olajuwon's potential tantalized the NBA, and the hometown Houston Rockets selected him first overall in the

CAREER HIGHLIGHTS

- A 12-time NBA All-Star

- Ranks eighth on the NBA all-time scoring list with 26,946 points scored

- One of only four players to have recorded a quadruple-double, which happened on March 29, 1990 against the Milwaukee Bucks. He had 18 points, 16 rebounds, 10 assists and 11 blocks.

- Averaged at least 20 points and 10 rebounds per game in the first 12 years of his career

- Averaged at least 2.0 blocks per game 15 years in a row, including a career-high 4.6 in 1989–90

- Is a six-time All-NBA First Team selection and five-time NBA All-Defensive First Team selection

- Was a two-time Defensive Player of the Year in 1993 and 1994

1984 draft, taken ahead of Michael Jordan, whom the Chicago Bulls picked third overall.

Hakeem was good enought that no one has ever seriously questioned the Rockets' decision to take him ahead of Jordan. He helped the Rockets advance to the NBA Finals in 1986 in just his second season, proving his playoff mettle early on by averaging 26.9 points and 11.8 rebounds during Houston's surprising run, ended by the powerhouse Boston Celtics. Olajuwon demonstrated his worth during a magical stretch when he led the Rockets to consecutive NBA titles in 1994 and 1995. It coincided with Jordan's retirement to pursue professional baseball, and during which Olajuwon established himself as the best basketball player in the world.

The Golden Age for the center position will always be the mid-1960s when Bill Russell and Wilt Chamberlain and a cast of talented understudies clashed every week it seemed. But what to make of the era with Olajuwon at his peak?

When the Rockets won their consecutive championships, Patrick Ewing of the New York

Knicks and David Robinson of the San Antonio Spurs, both voted to the NBA's 50th anniversary team and both members of the Naismith Basketball Hall of Fame, were in their prime. Shaquille O'Neal, the next great big man and another member of the 50th Anniversary Team, was just approaching his best, but had already become a formidable force.

Olajuwon dominated them all. Over the first 12 years of his NBA career, the lithe and explosive Nigerian showed his amazing consistency as a regular-season performer, averaging at least 20 points and 10 rebounds, usually significantly more. He did it in a unique manner, reflecting an elite athlete who grew up excelling at team handball and soccer before taking up basketball. His footwork and movement skills were the envy of most guards. "I had a different basis for sports than the American players," he said. "Maybe it put me behind at the start of basketball, but I think it gave me a different view of the angles and the moves and the things I could do. I never thought, 'That's not a basketball move.' I just did it."

He received a crash course with the help of another Rockets' legend, Moses Malone. Olajuwon played against Malone during the off-season while still at the University of Houston, and it was during those games that he perfected his Dream Shake, a soccer-based move with endless dizzying permutations.

"There was nothing he couldn't do," said his Rocket teammate Mario Elie. "He'd make athletic moves that no man his size has ever made."

And to think Olajuon might have been most effective as a defender. When he retired in 2002, he earned All-NBA honors 12 times, ranked 8th in career scoring and 11th in career rebounding, but he was also the NBA's all-time leading shot-blocker and was named to the NBA's All-Defensive Team nine times.

"It amazes me that people continue to take it to the basket against him," Scott Brooks, a Rocket teammate, once said. "They must not watch TV."

Olajuwon routinely led all NBA centers in steals and is the only player in NBA history to have more than 200 blocks and 200 steals in the same season.

It all came together during the Rockets' championship runs. In the 1994 NBA Finals against Ewing's New York Knicks, Olajuwon ruled the paint against his old Georgetown rival, outscoring him in every game of the series, averaging 26.9 points per game and sinking 50.0 percent of his shots compared to Ewing's 18.9 points per game on 36.3 percent shooting. In 1995 the Rockets faced the San Antonio Spurs, the top-seeded team in the West led by regular-season MVP Robinson, but it didn't pose a problem. Olajuwon was at his best, averaging 35.3 points, 12.5 rebounds, 5.0 assists, 4.1 blocks and 1.3 steals over six games, compared with Robinson, who averaged 23.8 points, 11.3 rebounds, 2.7 assists and 1.5 steals.

"I really felt like I could keep him under control, play well and defend him," said Robinson. "I was in my prime defensively. But I didn't stop him very well … he just controlled the series."

In the Finals stood a blossoming Shaquille O'Neal, all 7-foot-1, 315 pounds of him. But it was Olajuwon who played like a giant, averaging 32.8 points and 11.5 rebounds in the four-game sweep over Shaq and his Orlando Magic teammates.

It was a fitting high point to a career full of highlights.

"When you write the story, it's like a fairy tale," said Olajuwon, who retired in 2002 and entered the Hall of Fame in 2008.

They didn't call him Hakeem "The Dream" for no reason.

- Drafted: 1st overall by the Houston Rockets: 1984–2001
- Toronto Raptors: 2001–02
- College: University of Houston

Olajuwon tries to block a shot by Patrick Ewing during a 1990 game in New York. Olajuwon led the NBA in blocked shots during the 1989–90 and 1990–91 seasons.

33

CENTER

SHAQUILLE O'NEAL

The biggest, strongest man to ever play in the NBA had just reached the top of the mountain that everyone had told him he had to climb to reach his destiny. His Los Angeles Lakers, the team of Mikan, Chamberlain and Abdul-Jabbar, had just won the 2000 NBA title.

The confetti was flying, the trophy was shining, but the big man was crying.

How odd it seemed, that Shaquille O'Neal, the NBA's joking giant, was sobbing in triumph. O'Neal, the most anticipated big man to come into the league in nearly 30 years, flat out dominated the series. He was the unanimous choice for Finals MVP after ringing up 41

points in the series-clinching Game 6 against Indiana. Overall, he averaged a monstrous 38.0 points and 16.7 rebounds in the Finals, a series that capped off a playoff run in which he played the best ball of his career, averaging 30.7 points and 15.4 rebounds per game while shooting 56.6 percent, this after a season in which he'd been a near-unanimous choice for Most Valuable Player.

But instead of celebrating, O'Neal was crying.

"A lot of people think I was probably happy," he said. "No, I wasn't happy. I was getting my revenge on the critics. All [the] people who said …'Shaq couldn't do this, Shaq couldn't do that.' Well, I did it. I proved you wrong, now what you gonna say? That's why I cried."

With great talent comes great expectations, and few NBA players have come into the league with greater expectations thrust upon them than the man known simply as Shaq. The expectations started, of course, with his incredible size. The league had its share of seven-footers, but never a seven-footer built like a linebacker — a 350-pound slab of muscle who could spin, cut, run and jump. The league had never seen that. No one had.

He wasn't just big. O'Neal was athletic too, with the lightest size-twenty-something feet to have ever walked the earth, it might be safe to say.

"If you could construct a basketball player physically, Shaq would be the model," said Jerry West, the Lakers' executive who engineered the 1996 trade that delivered O'Neal to Los Angeles from Orlando, paving the way for three Lakers' championships. "He has this great size and incredible strength, but on top of that he has unbelievable balance, incredible footwork, and a great sense of where he is on the court."

An unusual man deserves an unusual story. O'Neal's happened on a U.S. Army base in what was then East Germany. Dale Brown, legendary coach of the Louisiana State University Tigers, was conducting a coaching clinic. A big, earnest guy standing about 6-foot-5 began quizzing Brown on training techniques. "I asked him how long he'd

O'Neal dribbles past Hakeem Olajuwon of the Houston Rockets during a game on November 14, 1997. Shaq contributed 24 points to the Lakers' 113–103 win.

A lean-looking O'Neal dunks against the San Antonio Spurs during a 1993 game in Orlando, Florida.

been in the service," Brown recalled later. "He said, 'I'm only 13.' I looked at his feet. They were size 17. I said, 'I would love to meet your father.'"

O'Neal was living in Germany with his stepfather, Phil Harrison, a career army man. O'Neal eventually moved back to the United States and starred in Texas high school before enrolling at LSU, where he dominated for three seasons. He declared himself for the 1992 NBA draft and Orlando selected him first overall.

"The NBA ain't ready for this kid. This is like Wilt coming into the league," said then-Indiana Pacers' general manager Donnie Walsh.

Boston Celtics' Hall of Fame center Robert Parrish experienced O'Neal's strength and skill during the exhibition season. "The strongest I've played against since Artis

- Drafted: 1st overall by the Orlando Magic in 1992
- Orlando Magic: 1992–96
- Los Angeles Lakers: 1996–2004
- Miami Heat: 2004–08
- Phoenix Suns: 2008–09
- Cleveland Cavaliers: 2009–
- Jersey: #33; alternates: #34, #32
- College: Louisiana State

CAREER HIGHLIGHTS

- Led the NBA in field-goal percentage 10 times in his career
- Won an Olympic gold medal with the U.S. Men's Basketball Team in 1996
- Has appeared in numerous movies such as *Blue Chips* and *Kazaam*
- Holds the NCAA record for most blocks in a single game with 17
- Averaged at least 20 PPG in 14 straight seasons from 1992–93 to 2005–06, including a career-high 29.7 PPG in 1999–00
- Is a 15-time NBA All-Star
- Selected to the All-NBA First Team eight times
- Scored a career-high 61 points on March 6, 2000, against the Los Angeles Clippers

Gilmore," Parish said, referring to the former ABA and NBA star long considered the strongest player to have ever played in the NBA. "And he's more agile than Artis. That's a scary thought. When he gets polished, he's gonna be two hands full."

O'Neal was huge and he was good, averaging 23.9 points, 13.9 rebounds and 3.5 blocked shots while shooting 56.2 percent as a rookie. He made the All-Star Game, won Rookie of the Year honors and kept everyone smiling along the way.

The nicknames, for example, mostly bestowed on him by himself: "The Big Diesel" was self-explanatory, but later on came "The Big Aristotle" for his learned ways and "The Big Cactus" when he played a season-and-a-half in the desert for the Phoenix Suns. He made some forgettable movies and branched out into music, recording several rap albums with varying success.

"I did six," he once said of his recording career. "Two platinum, two gold and two double-wood." This sense of playfulness added to his popularity.

"Kids like me because they see themselves in me," he once said. "I don't speak with a Harvard-type vocabulary. I only wear suits when I need to. I don't talk about stuff I haven't gone through. I am just me. They like rims, I like rims. They like rap music, I like rap music. They like platinum, I like platinum."

But after eight years in the league, O'Neal didn't have an NBA title or an MVP award. The Magic made the Finals in his second season, but were swept by the Houston Rockets and O'Neal was outplayed by Houston's Hakeem Olajuwon. In fact O'Neal's teams had shown themselves to be relatively easy outs in the postseason, swept five times in his first eight years, and eliminated 4–1 on another occasion.

Coupled with his never-improving foul shooting, which hovered around 50 percent for his career and made him a liability late in games; injuries that cost him significant playing time; his off-court interests and his tendency to fall out with his teammates, critics had plenty of ammunition when they wanted to call out O'Neal.

That changed in the 1999–2000. A healthy O'Neal played 79 games, led the league in scoring, placed second in rebounding and led in blocked shots, while setting a career-high in assists. He finished only one vote shy of being named the NBA's first unanimous MVP. Two titles — and two more Finals MVP awards — followed, before two years of playoff disappointments and conflicts between O'Neal and Kobe Bryant forced the Lakers to trade O'Neal to Miami. O'Neal gained some measure of revenge when he helped the Heat to the 2005–06 title, his fourth.

But even after his 17th season in the NBA, by which time he'd become the NBA's fifth all-time leading scorer and 15th-leading rebounder, his legacy was still being shaped. The Heat traded him to Phoenix in February 2008, and the Suns lost in the first round of the playoffs and failed to qualify the following season. In June 2009, O'Neal was traded to Cleveland and "The Big Pierogi" became one of his nicknames. He was expected to do for LeBron James what he'd done for Bryant in Los Angeles and Dwyane Wade in Miami: win an NBA title.

"I'm still here. I'm a force to be reckoned with," he said, flashing his smile. "… I'm still the Shogun."

And forever Shaq.

G	FG%	FT%	ORB	DRB	TRB	AST	STL	BLK	PTS
792	.436	.761			16.2	3.0			26.3

BOB **PETTIT**

You know you're good when they invent a new position for you.

Before Bob Pettit arrived in the NBA with the Milwaukee Hawks as a stringy bundle of relentless energy, only three positions existed on a team: center, forward and guard.

But the 6-foot-9, 215-pound Petitt changed that. Tough enough inside to play center but skilled enough outside to play forward, Pettit became the NBA's first power forward. It was a label invented for him and which became part basketball's lexicon.

In addition to his work on the glass and in the paint, a product of his unrelenting hustle and surprising strength, he was in some ways most dangerous when he drifted out to 18 and 20 feet to loft the consistent jumper he perfected on a homemade hoop in his yard growing up in Baton Rouge, Louisiana.

Although Pettit retired from the NBA in 1965, there have been few, if any, better than the league's original power forward.

"In those days, teams worked on blocking guys out, especially Bob, because he was such a great offensive rebounder," said long-time Hawk teammate Al Ferrari. "He would get blocked out maybe five, six times in a row, but he never stopped coming. And on that next time, he'd get a rebound and score an important basket."

Frank Ramsey, the Boston Celtics forward who played against Pettit for most of his career, including four NBA Finals, summed it up quite succinctly: "Couldn't nobody guard him."

After leading the Louisiana State University Tigers to a pair of SEC titles along with an NCAA Final Four appearance in 1953, Pettit entered the NBA in 1954 as the second overall pick of the Milwaukee Hawks. He was voted Rookie of the Year after averaging 20.4 points and 13.2 rebounds per game, and selected First Team All-NBA. He played in the All-Star Game that year and every year until he retired, four times receiving the Most Valuable Player award. Though bothered by knee problems in his final season, he was still good enough to be named to the All-NBA Second Team.

Pettit owned his position like few others. He retired as the NBA's leading all-time scorer with 20,880 points and currently stands 28th overall. Five decades later, his average of 26.3 points per game stands seventh on the NBA's career all-time list and his 16.2 rebounds per game trails only Wilt Chamberlain and Bill Russell in the record books.

All in all, a pretty impressive résumé for a skinny kid not good enough to play any other high school sports and who was cut from the varsity basketball team in the ninth and tenth grades. But those setbacks simply played into what may have been Pettit's most significant talent: a tireless determination to improve.

"I can't stress how important the mental

Pettit in his LSU uniform on February 23, 1954. He was drafted by the Milwaukee Hawks and won the Rookie of the Year Award later in the year.

approach to the game is," Pettit said. "As a sophomore in high school, my ambition was to win a letter by the time I was a senior. Ten years later, my ambition was to be the best basketball player in the world. You set goals for yourself, you reach them, you ratchet them up."

On April 12, 1958, Pettit reached his most ambitious goal as he led the St. Louis Hawks — formerly of Milwaukee — to the NBA Finals for the second straight year. Once again, they faced the Boston Celtics, who had beaten them for the title the season before in seven games, including a 125–123 double-overtime loss in the deciding contest, one of the most dramatic games in NBA playoff history.

The next time around, St. Louis caught a break when Celtic center Bill Russell sprained his ankle in Game 3 and missed the rest of

the series. In a tight Game 6 and facing the possibility of having to play Game 7 on the road in Boston, Pettit didn't want to waste the opportunity.

"He said, 'Coach, just give me the ball,'" said Ferrari.

In the closing six minutes, Pettit scored 19 of his team's final 21 points, including a dramatic tip-in with just seconds remaining that won the game for the Hawks. He scored a total of 50 points in the deciding game of the NBA Finals, a feat that has never been matched.

The Hawks' championship and Pettit's playoff performance, combined with being awarded the NBA's MVP that season, confirmed Pettit's superstar status — if he wasn't the best player in the world at that moment, he was on a very short list.

- Drafted: 2nd overall by the Milwaukee Hawks in 1954
- Milwaukee Hawks: 1954–55
- St. Louis Hawks: 1955–65
- College: Louisiana State University

"That was the best game I ever played," said Pettit of his Game 6 dominance. "Especially because of what it meant."

Pettit didn't rest on his laurels. By that time, he had embraced off-season weight training, quite possibly the first NBA player to do so. It was a bold move in an era when the common wisdom was that added size would compromise quickness and agility. But it worked for Pettit. He bulked himself up to 245 pounds by the end of his career.

"A big part of my game was offensive rebounding, and that came down to timing, getting position near the basket, and strength," he said. "The more I worked with the weights, the more I began to 'think strong,' especially in my hands, a rebounding key."

The Hawks had no idea their franchise player had bulked up. "I showed up at camp, told the story to my owner, and he threw a fit," Pettit said. "He thought I'd get muscle-bound, thought I was endangering my career.

"I don't know of any other player at the time who worked seriously with the weights. All I can tell you is I went into the NBA at 215 and came out 245."

His list of accomplishments grew accordingly. His only disappointment was that the Hawks won only one NBA title. But perhaps just as remarkable was Pettit's after-basketball life. With his knee aching and his skills slipping ever so slightly, he walked away from the game at age 32 and into the business community in New Orleans and never looked back.

"I'm very fortunate because I can say I've enjoyed my life after basketball as much as my life in it," Pettit said. "I don't know that a lot of former athletes can say that. I always wanted to come home, hunt, fish, a little golf, go home at night, put my pajamas on and read a book. Some people might need a little more, but that's an enjoyable life to me."

CAREER HIGHLIGHTS

- 11-time NBA All-Star
- Two-time NBA MVP
- Four-time NBA All-Star MVP
- 10-time NBA First-Team selection
- Was the NBA scoring champion in 1955–56 and 1958–59
- Averaged a career-high 31.1 points per game in 1961–62
- One of only five players in NBA history to average at least 20 rebounds per game in a single season (20.3 RPG in 1960–61)

Pettit leaps to make a
one-handed shot over Dick
Ricketts of the Cincinnati
Royals during a game on
December 10, 1957.

Robertson goes for a layup during a game in the early 1970s. Traded to the Bucks by the Cincinnati Royals, Robertson helped lead the team to the championship in 1971.

OSCAR **ROBERTSON**

Some people accept their circumstances. Some won't stop until they change them.

Count Oscar Robertson among the latter group. He was given great gifts: At 6-foot-5 and over 220 pounds, he had the size of some power forwards of his era. But he also had the skill and athleticism of a point guard — a position he dominated, creating the template for the likes of Magic Johnson and LeBron James, big men who use the whole floor to create their art.

His passion to develop those gifts was guided by a steely will to better himself and others through his skills. If playing basketball involved being able to shoot, pass, rebound, handle the ball, see the court and lead a team, Robertson made it a point to excel in every facet of the game. The debate about the best basketball player of his and subsequent generations will always include his name. When the debate turns to the most complete player, Robertson's name will usually end it.

"He is so great he scares me," Boston Celtics coach Red Auerbach once said of Robertson, who played 10 seasons for the Cincinnati Royals beginning in 1960–61, before spending the last four yeas of his career with the Milwaukee Bucks, with whom he won the NBA championship in 1971.

"Oscar was the only one who could control a game from the guard position," said Zelmo Beaty, a former St. Louis Hawks center. "Anything he wanted to do, nobody could stop him. He was head and shoulders above everyone."

For a player who is a Hall of Famer and a member of the NBA's 50th Anniversary Team,

Robertson drives past Jim Price of the LA Lakers during a 1973 game.

statistics typically only tell part of any story, but in Robertson's case they tell it loudly. In 1961–62, Robertson's second year in the NBA, he averaged 30.8 points, 12.5 rebounds and 11.4 assists for the season. That made him the only player in NBA history to average double-digit totals in three statistical categories — a so-called "triple-double" — for an entire season. It was no anomaly. In his rookie year with the Royals in 1960–61, he averaged 30.5 points, 10.1 rebounds and 9.7 assists. The former No.1 overall pick followed up his stellar second season by averaging 28.3 points, 10.4 rebounds and 9.5 assists in year three. In his fourth season (1963–64), he averaged 31.4 points, 9.9 rebounds and 11 assists. When you add up the numbers and divide them over his 309 games, Robertson's averages for his first four seasons come out to 30.2 points, 10.7 rebounds and 10.4 assists — four years of triple-doubles when no one else has done it once, before or since. For his career, Robertson racked up 181 games with at least 10 points, 10 rebounds and 10 assists. As of 2009–10, the next highest total on the list was Magic Johnson's 138. Impressive yes, but perhaps proof that Robertson's records — like Wilt Chamberlain's — will never be broken.

"It belongs with DiMaggio's [56-game] hitting streak, with any record that's ever been set," said Jason Kidd, only the third player to top 100 triple-doubles for his career. "Unless there's somebody close to doing it again, I think that would be the only way people could really appreciate it. That's the only opportunity we'd have to quite understand what Oscar did. I don't think he gets enough recognition for what he did achieve."

No one, not even Robertson, recognized his achievement. The term "triple-double" didn't become part of the NBA lexicon until the mid-1980s when Johnson was racking

them up with some regularity for the Los Angeles Lakers and a Lakers' public relations director coined the term to summarize Johnson's all-around excellence.

"I never heard anything about the triple-double season until [after my career]," Robertson said. "I don't remember ever looking down at a stat sheet and noticing that all the figures were doubles. Fact is, I never looked at a stat sheet."

Over time he came to appreciate his achievement and what it represented. "[It's] more an idea than an average," he wrote in his autobiography, *The Big O.* "The idea of excellence in all phases of the game."

Playing for Cincinnati, the only thing missing from Robertson's résumé was an NBA title. He turned the sad-sack Royals into a winning franchise, but they never advanced past the Eastern Conference Finals in his 10 seasons. His fortune changed when Cincinnati traded him to the Milwaukee Bucks in 1970. He teamed up with Lew Alcindor, who later changed his name to Kareem Abdul-Jabbar, already a dominant force in just his second season.

Surrounded by the best talent of his career, Robertson dialed his game down, averaging career-lows across the board as the

- **Drafted:** 1st overall by the Cincinnati Royals in 1960 (territorial selection)
- **Cincinnati Royals:** 1960–70
- **Milwaukee Bucks:** 1970–74
- **Jersey:** #14; alternate: #1
- **College:** University of Cincinnati

Bucks romped to a 66–16 record and swept the Baltimore Bullets in the NBA Finals. The Bucks averaged more than 60 wins for the next three seasons, but never won a title again. Robertson's impact was perhaps best measured by his retirement before the 1974–75 season; without him, the Bucks slipped to just 38 wins.

His accomplishments on the court, considerable as they were, form just one part of his legacy. He served as the president of the NBA Players Association from 1965 to 1974, and in 1970 became part of one of the most important court cases in NBA history — the so-called Oscar Robertson suit. That suit won NBA players the right to free agency among other benefits, and for a time placed NBA players as the highest paid athletes among the four major North American sports.

It was just more trail blazing for Robertson in a career that was full of him making his own way. He led Crispus Attucks High School to the Indiana state title in 1955, a first for an all-black school in the state, and he became the first black to play basketball at the University of Cincinnati, where he was the College Player of the Year for three straight seasons. His career accomplishments culminated in his becoming one of the inaugural inductees in the National Collegiate Basketball Hall of Fame in 2006.

While he believes his union activity alienated him from the NBA upon his retirement, he thrived in business. He also received acclaim for donating one of his kidneys to his middle daughter, who required a kidney transplant in 1997. Robertson subsequently became a spokesman for organ donation.

"I'm not a hero, I'm a father," he shrugged.

CAREER HIGHLIGHTS

- The only player in NBA history to average a triple-double for a season — averaging 30.8 points, 11.4 assists and 12.5 rebounds per game in 1961–62 for the Cincinnati Royals

- His nickname was "The Big O"

- Won the NBA MVP in 1964

- 12-time NBA All-Star

- Fifth all-time in career assists with 9,887

- Fourth all-time in assists per game average at 9.5

- Led the NBA in assists six times

G	FG%	FT%	ORB	DRB	TRB	AST	STL	BLK	PTS
963	.440	.561			22.5	4.3			15.1

BILL RUSSELL

For anyone there, it stood out as a moment of clarity even in the superficial hubbub that is the NBA's All-Star Weekend. It was a reminder that all the glitz and glamour were just window dressing for those truly interested in being great.

The league that Bill Russell helped build is about a lot of things — flash, cash, celebrity and entertainment among them. But Russell stood for none of that.

Above all, he stood for winning.

Everything but winning matters when the NBA gathers for its mid-season celebration, but for a few moments on All-Star Saturday Night on February 2009, NBA commissioner David Stern cut through it all when he announced that Russell, the spine of the Boston Celtics dynasty that won 11 NBA championships between 1957–69, including eight in a row — which in some ways created the foundation for all that has followed — would be honored with an award long overdue.

"Each year the Finals MVP is given to an exceptional, extraordinary player based on his performance on the grandest stage in all of basketball, the Finals," said Stern. "Who better to name this prestigious award for than one of the greatest players of all time and the ultimate champion? Accordingly, it is my pleasure to announce … this award will henceforth be named for Bill Russell, a true legend of the game. The award will be called the Bill Russell NBA Finals Most Valuable Player Award."

Russell should have cackled — his trademark giggle as much a part of his reputation as his scholarly gray beard. Or perhaps he might have harrumphed at even the idea of an individual award, given that every fiber of his being as an athlete had been about the importance of the team over the individual.

Instead, his eyes welled up and he paused, almost too overwhelmed to speak. His wife, Marilyn, had just passed away. His friend, Red Auerbach, the architect of the Celtics' dynasty, had died the year before.

"I wanted to thank my teammates because we played a team game quite well," he said, then paused. "I accept this for my team, and my team included our coach, Red Auerbach, and all my teammates over the years. This is one of my proudest moments in basketball because I determined early in my career the only important statistic in basketball is the final score. And so I dedicated my career to playing, to make sure as often as possible we were always on the positive side of the final score."

No one made the goal so simple, and no one accomplished it better than William Fenton Russell, born in 1934 in Louisiana and raised in a tough section of Oakland, California. He began playing basketball at an early age, but wasn't particularly successful, getting cut from the team in junior high school and nearly cut again in high school. He was awkward and lacked scoring touch, but he was tall and athletic and savvy. Only nearby University of San Francisco offered him a scholarship, and Russell embraced it, seeing the sport as a way to emerge from trying economic circumstances.

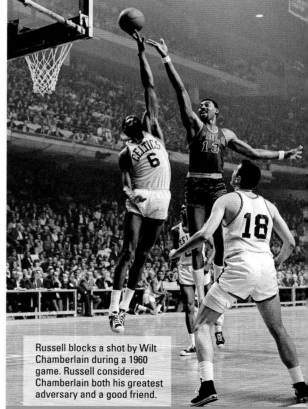

Russell blocks a shot by Wilt Chamberlain during a 1960 game. Russell considered Chamberlain both his greatest adversary and a good friend.

Russell shoots a hook shot during a 1967 game against New York. Although he was a selective shooter with a respectable field-goal percentage, Russell was not considered a skilled offensive player.

He became a trailblazer on and off the court. An exceptional athlete who competed in track and field while at USF, running the quarter-mile in 49.6 seconds and topping 6-foot-9 in the high jump, his intellect also set him apart. At a time when defenders were taught to stick with the players they guarded and never leave their feet, Russell used his incredible agility and instincts for the game to move from side to side and harass penetrating guards or block shots from the weak side. It was revolutionary for the time, and early on his coaches resisted, but Russell stuck with it and USF benefitted, winning 55 straight games at one point and two national championships.

In Boston, Auerbach had put together a team good enough to make it to the NBA playoffs, but lacked defense and rebounding. He wanted Russell, but had to pull some deft moves to get him in the draft. First Auerbach traded two future Hall of Famers (Ed Macauley, and Cliff Hagen) to St. Louis for the rights to the No. 2 pick. He then had Celtics owner, Walter Brown, extract a promise from the owner of the Rochester Royals — who held the first pick — to pass on Russell in return for getting the Ice Capades (which Brown owned) at his arena for a week. Amazingly it worked and Boston got Russell's rights as the Hawks selected him second overall in 1956.

After winning the gold medal at the 1956 Olympics, Russell joined the Celtics and delivered, averaging 14.7 points and 19.8 rebounds and leading Boston to its first title. An ankle injury hampered Russell in the Finals the following year and the Celtics lost to the St. Louis Hawks, bolstered by their Celtics additions a year earlier, but then Boston reeled off eight straight titles and 11 in 13 years, with Russell the cornerstone.

Auerbach retired from coaching prior to the 1966–67 season to concentrate on managing the team and he appointed Russell as player-coach, making him the first black man to coach one of the four major North American team sports. It proved to be a prudent move because Boston won two more titles with Russell in the dual role.

CAREER HIGHLIGHTS

- Second all-time in average career-minutes-per-game, averaging 42.3
- Won 11 NBA championships with the Boston Celtics, including 8 in a row from 1959–66
- Went to high school with MLB Hall-of-Famer Frank Robinson
- One of only two players in NBA history, the other being Wilt Chamberlain, to grab at least 50 rebounds in a single game. Russell had 51 rebounds on February 5, 1960, against the Syracuse Nationals
- A 12-time NBA All-Star
- NBA All-Star Game MVP in 1963
- Averaged a career-high 24.7 rebounds per game in 1963–64

"Russell's raw physical ability was amazing," Bill Bradley, the New York Knicks star (and later a U.S. senator), wrote about his rival. "No center has ever moved laterally as well as Russell. When he blocked four opponents' shots on one possession, he seemed to be playing against five men simultaneously, which in fact he was."

That only explained part of the Russell mystique. He always sought an advantage and typically found it.

"It was Russell's competitiveness — like Michael Jordan's or Larry Bird's — that set him apart from the game's other players," Bradley said. "He wanted to win every matchup, every game, every title. He waged psychological warfare, on and off the court. He would ignore an opposing rookie player in a restaurant the night before a game so that the next night the rookie would try too hard to make an indelible impression … and, in the process, throw himself off his game. After Russell blocked a player's shot, he often simply faked a block the next time, and the same player would rush his shot and miss."

He respected his opponents, particularly Wilt Chamberlain, whom he battled so often and so successfully, with the Celtics coming out on top. Rivals? Yes. But they were also friends.

"He was the best I ever played against — not even close," said Russell. "And I told him in the last year he was alive, 'Wilt, I'm the only person on this planet who really knows how good you are.'"

There are many ways to measure Russell's success: A record 11 championships in 13 seasons; top three in rebounding every season he played and second only to Chamberlain for career rebounds per game with 22.5; five times an NBA MVP and five times in the top-10 in assists. They didn't track blocked shots in his era, but he'd have been among the career leaders in that category, too.

How many MVP Finals awards did he win? Well, they didn't give out the award until Russell's last NBA season, and that year Jerry West of the Los Angeles Lakers became one of only two players to ever earn MVP Finals honors on a losing team.

How many might Russell have won? Six, as Michael Jordan did? Eight? Ten? Who knows.

And Russell didn't care. He only cared about winning. Nothing else mattered.

JERRY **WEST**

A young West poses in his Lakers uniform for this photo, taken during the 1960s. West played his entire career with the Lakers.

He has always been successful. Hugely successful. Jerry West has had a career virtually unmatched in professional sports. For 14 years he ranked among the very best players of his or any other era in the NBA. He took up coaching and did well there, too, leading his Los Angeles Lakers to the playoffs for three straight seasons, though the stress of it nearly drove him mad. Then he became an executive, building not one, but two Lakers dynasties and then — just for good measure — as the Memphis Grizzlies' president of basketball operations he helped lift the lowly team to a 50-win season.

How successful is West? He's nicknamed "Logo" because it's his silhouette, frozen in mid-dribble, that the NBA has as its official stamp, appearing on every piece of merchandise it sells. His other nickname is "Mr. Clutch" because he played his best when the stakes were highest.

Consider the seventh game of the 1969 Finals, the sixth time West had led the Lakers to the Western Conference title en route to meeting the powerful Boston Celtics for the NBA championship. Playing with a hamstring injury so severe he needed to be helped onto the court for warm-ups, West scored 42 points and added 12 assists and led a furious fourth-quarter comeback that fell short by a basket. Afterward, Celtics great John Havlicek felt moved to console his valiant opponent, saying simply, "I love you Jerry."

West was voted an All-Star all 14 years of his career. He was a first- or second-team All-NBA 12 consecutive seasons. The league introduced the All-Defensive Team in 1970, and West placed on it for four straight seasons.

When West left the game after the 1973–74 season, he ranked third in NBA career scoring behind Wilt Chamberlain and Oscar Robertson with 25,192 points. Among retired players, only Michael Jordan, Chamberlain and Elgin Baylor have higher scoring averages than West's 27.0 a game. Only Jordan had a higher career-scoring average in the playoffs than West's 29.1 per game, and only Kareem Abdul-Jabbar tallied more career points in the postseason.

But perhaps what's most interesting about West is that for all his success he was known almost as well for his persistent failures. As Frank Deford wrote in a defining profile of West that appeared in *Sports Illustrated* late in West's career, it added to his legacy rather than detracted from it: "What makes West so appealing is that his frailties are not his fault. They are imposed on him by

West jumps and shoots during a 1973 contest against the Washington Bullets. West retired prior to the 1974–75 season.

an arbitrary, even unfair, world … That is the real stuff of identity; he really is you and me. For in our world, although we like to believe that we are veritable saints, deserving of the very best, our dishwasher breaks down, the neighbor's children are better looking, there is water in the cellar and our best friend gets promoted. It is a special comfort to know that Jerry West is just as put upon as we are."

As if to make the point more clearly, Deford's profile ran during the 1971–72 season when West's seemingly endless quest for perfection was met, or at least, as nearly as it possibly could be. The Lakers powered to a 33-game winning streak, a record that still stands, and a 69–13 regular-season mark, the best in NBA history at the time.

To cap it off, the Lakers beat the New York Knicks in five games in the Finals, with West winning his only NBA championship. It could not have been more deserving based on his career achievements, but West being West, he wasn't satisfied given that he endured a rare shooting slump — connecting on just 37.6 percent of his attempts — during the postseason.

"I'd played better every year in the playoffs than I did in the regular season, except the one time we won," he said.

It's West in a nutshell: the All-American Charlie Brown who could never convince Lucy not to move the football. But in his undying efforts, he gained a mountain of respect.

"Jerry, I once wrote that success is a journey, and that the greatest honor a man can have is the respect and friendship of his peers. You have that more than any man I know," Bill Russell said at a tribute for him upon his retirement. "Jerry, you are, in every sense of the word, truly a champion. If I could have one wish granted, it would be that you would always be happy."

- Drafted: 1st overall by the Los Angeles Lakers in 1960
- Los Angeles Lakers: 1960–74
- College: West Virginia University

But would a happy Jerry West be Jerry West? Growing up the son of a coal-mine electrician in rural West Virginia, West's obsessive perfectionism showed itself early when he would spend hours developing his shooting on a basket attached to a neighbor's garage. West's closest brother died in the Korean War, after which the 12-year-old sibling retreated into a private world. "I think I became a basketball player because it is a game a boy can play by himself," he wrote in his autobiography.

Success — and failure — followed him everywhere. Even after twice being named the College Player of the Year at the University of West Virginia, he was forever the poor kid from the country, never believing he really fit in. It's a belief that continually drove him to try to prove himself.

He never missed a beat when he came into the NBA, but perhaps no player has been closer to being at the absolute top of the NBA heap without being named the league's Most Valuable Player, a result of playing in an era dominated by the Celtics and by the likes of Chamberlain. When the NBA began awarding a Finals MVP in 1969, it chose West as the first recipient, though true to form he became recognized for his valor in defeat.

His true reward came as an executive. He became general manager of the Lakers in 1982, after Magic Johnson and Kareem Abdul-Jabbar had won their first title together, but in time for him to expertly mix and match the ingredients around the two stars to help the Lakers to four more championships. In the summer of 1997, he maneuvered to draft a little-known high-school star, Kobe Bryant, and signed Shaquille O'Neal as a free agent, laying the groundwork for three more titles.

In all he spent 40 years with the Lakers, between being drafted and leaving to join the Grizzlies in 2002 and helping to turn around the franchise. With West in the fold in one capacity or another, Los Angeles went to the playoffs 39 times, advancing to the Finals 21 times.

It's not clear if West's gut ever stopped churning long enough to enjoy any of it.

But Mr. Clutch created a lot of fond memories for everyone else.

CAREER HIGHLIGHTS

- Led the NBA in scoring average in 1969–70 with 31.2 PPG
- Had an NBA playoff record 6 consecutive 40-plus point games from April 3–April 13, 1965
- Won an Olympic Gold Medal in 1960 with the U.S. Men's Basketball Team
- Scored a career-high 63 points on January 17, 1962, against the New York Knicks
- Was the NBA All-Star MVP in 1972

West dribbles against a Knicks player during a game at Madison Square Gardens in this undated photo.

The International
GAME

So much had already happened in the world of international basketball by the time the United States gathered a group of college kids to prepare for the 1988 Olympic Games in Seoul, South Korea. The Americans were boys sent to do what had become a man's job, so how could the likes of David Robinson and Mitch Richmond know the basketball world was changing before their very eyes?

The 1992 United States Olympic Dream Team — back row (L-R) Patrick Ewing, Christian Laetner, Magic Johnson, David Robinson and Karl Malone; middle row (L-R) Larry Bird, Michael Jordan, head coach Chuck Daly, Charles Barkley and Chris Mullin; front row (L-R) Scottie Pippen, John Stockton and Clyde Drexler — were the first American professional basketball players to take part in Olympic competition.

Basketball had been an Olympic sport since the Berlin Games in 1936, but never really an Olympic game. It was an *American* game, invented by a Canadian living in the United States, and like jazz and Hollywood movies it radiated out from its humble beginnings. The game found its way around the world, to some extent thanks to the U.S. military, who taught it to local kids as part of outreach programs on its bases. Later, it was coaches like Red Auerbach and Hubie Brown who ventured to spread the basketball "gospel," teaching the rudiments of the game to willing pupils. Stalwarts like Maurizio Gherardini, the first European to become an NBA executive, advanced the cause by personally translating coaching books into Italian, while Dan Peterson, an American who spent most of his coaching career in Italy, helped popularize the game for European audiences as a television commentator.

Mike Bantom (No.7), Jim Forbes, (No.10) and Ed Ratleff (No.15) of the 1972 U.S. men's Olympic team react after a hotly contested final three seconds of play that saw Russia's Alexander Belov score the gold-medal-winning basket off a controversial inbound play.

But the game itself was virtually owned by the Americans, who won every gold medal ever awarded at the Olympics, going undefeated for decades. The Amateur Athletic Union (AAU) squads and college all-star teams would gather for a few weeks before the Olympic tournament, familiarize themselves with the subtleties of the international rule book, and then take on all comers. They never lost and were almost never challenged.

That changed in the gold medal final in Munich in 1972, the U.S. lost 51–50 in one of the most controversial moments in Olympic history, ending the U.S. Olympic win streak at 71. Doug Collins hit a pair of free throws with three seconds left to put the U.S. ahead 50–49. But in a storm of confusion, Russia got three chances to inbound the ball as officials of all stripes intervened, creating a chaotic scene. The third time was the charm, and Russia's Alexander Belov gathered a floor-length pass

to score the winning basket. The United States never accepted the result, and the team unanimously voted to refuse their silver medals (the medals remain in a Swiss vault to this day). But lost amidst the controversy was that, at the very least, the United States had been played even.

With the U.S. recovering to win the gold in Montreal in 1976, the significance of the previous defeat took a while to register: The boycott of the 1980 Moscow games by the U.S. (a diplomatic disagreement with the Soviet Union) and the boycott of the 1984 Los Angeles games by the Soviet Union (a retaliation for the U.S. boycott of Moscow) meant that the U.S. teams had missed measuring themselves against best of the Eastern Bloc. The job finally fell to the 1988 team in Seoul, led by Robinson, and they came up short, losing 82–76 in the semifinals to the Soviet Union, the first time the countries had met since 1972.

"It was a disgrace," Robinson said later. "We shamed our country. I remember the feeling that everyone had, and it wasn't a fun feeling." This time there was no controversy about their bronze medals, just disappointment. "The one thing I remember is going up to get the medal," Robinson said. "Guys didn't even want to go up to the stand. All the years I had watched the Olympics on TV, all those guys were so proud to get their medals. But I was right in the middle of it and we felt like we let everybody down. When your country wins every Olympic Games, and then you're the first team to go out there and lose without a major controversy, it's a distinction you don't want."

American Professionals Play the World

How could Robinson have known that he was standing on the precipice of basketball history? The American loss to the Soviet Union was a crucial moment in time that helped change everything for basketball. And sometimes, when you are wrapped up in the details, it's hard to appreciate the greater significance of such a moment. That the U.S. lost was less telling than that someone else was winning. And seeing the United States lose did a funny thing. Rather than inspire the world basketball community to seek more opportunities to humble U.S. amateurs, the internationals wanted to test themselves against the best the U.S. could offer.

The gap between the country that gave birth to the game and the rest of the world, so vast for so long, was closing. The year before the Seoul Olympics, in the Finals of the 1987 Pan American Games in Indianapolis, the U.S. had been torched by Brazil's Oscar Schmidt to the tune of 46 points, as the Americans lost a game on home soil for the first time. Further proof came in 1990 when a team of U.S. college players could do no better than bronze at the World Championships. By that time, the winds of change were blowing harder. At an International Basketball Federation (FIBA) meeting on April 7, 1989, the governing body stunned the athletic world by ruling that NBA players would be eligible to compete in the Olympics. The United States voted against the motion, concerned that their best would overwhelm what the rest of the world had to offer. The rest of the world said, "bring it on."

The wheels were in motion for a seismic shift in the sport that is still being played out today in the NBA and in international competition. The basketball world was becoming flat. "There were two reasons," for including the best U.S. professionals in the international game, FIBA secretary general Boris Stankovic explained years later. "Our competition was closed to NBA players, but no one else. For years, we had professional players from other countries. The only ones who could not play were NBA players. That seems immoral."

"[And] in 1936, the U.S. was represented by AAU (Amateur Athletic Union) players," Stankovic continued. "They dominated for awhile, but the world caught up. Then the U.S. changed to college players, and they dominated for awhile, but the world caught up. Now NBA players are dominating, but one day — not in my lifetime, but one day — the world will catch up."

The floodgates were open, but this was a very good thing. "The vision of Boris Stankovic started in 1987," NBA commissioner David Stern said. "He said there was simply no way the world would improve in basketball unless the NBA agreed to allow their players to play. We did, and the payback is our sport is so much more global and competition is so much more intense."

Stankovic's comments were made at the 1996 Olympics, four years after the legendary Dream Team (with a roster that included 10 players

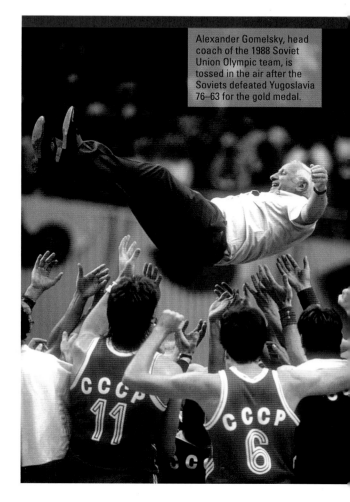

Alexander Gomelsky, head coach of the 1988 Soviet Union Olympic team, is tossed in the air after the Soviets defeated Yugoslavia 76–63 for the gold medal.

later voted to the NBA's 50th Anniversary Team) had rolled through the Barcelona Olympic tournament, winning by an average of 44 points a game and pausing only to pose for pictures with their opponents. The situation wasn't much different in Atlanta in 1996, as Dream Team II swamped the competition, with no opponent coming within 20 points of the U.S. powerhouse.

But the basketball world had begun to shrink. International players were slowly becoming a fixture in the NBA, if only tentatively at first. And as the NBA expanded, some of the best players in the world were out there, waiting to be found, and the NBA went looking.

The First Wave of Internationals

Brazil's Oscar Schmidt was the first international player drafted by an NBA team, taken in the sixth round of the 1984 draft by the New Jersey Nets, but he never tried his luck in the NBA, preferring to make his mark as one of the most prolific scorers in European basketball history. The Phoenix Suns were the first to go out on a limb and bring an international player over without serving an apprenticeship in the U.S. college system, choosing Georgi Glouchkov of Bulgaria in the seventh round of the 1985 draft.

Glouchkov, known as the Balkan Banger, played 49 games for Phoenix during the 1985–86 season. It didn't go particularly well. The Suns had to negotiate his contract with the Bulgarian Athletic Federation, which was paid directly by Phoenix, but that organization neglected to remit Glouchkov's share on a timely basis. Language also became a problem for both the Bulgarian and his teammates, and when Phoenix arranged English classes for Glouchkov, he ended up dating his teacher. And while he showed a spark early in the season, successfully throwing his 6-foot-9, 240-pound frame around on the glass, he withered as the year went on. Some wondered if it was Glouchkov's predilection for unlimited amounts of junk food, or if he had suddenly stopped using steroids, as had been rumored. His play declined, but he was able to put it into perspective. "Yes, I play terribly," he once said through an interpreter, "but I will be neither lynched nor beaten, so there is no reason to be nervous."

Maybe. But the men whose task it was to go out and find talent for NBA teams had cause to be worried. Apart from being the answer to a trivia question, Glouchkov turned into an expensive mistake for the

Georgi Glouchkov, the first internationally-born NBA player, catches a rebound during a 1985 game in Boston. Glouchkov played only 49 games with the Phoenix Suns before returning to Europe.

Vlade Divac shoots over Hakeem Olajuwon in Game 3 of the 1996 Western Conference Quarterfinals. Unlike Glouchkov, Divac became a mainstay in the NBA, playing over 1,000 games.

Suns. They spent more than $500,000 to bring him to the NBA, an experience that briefly soured them on international players.

However, by 1989, there were NBA talent evaluators who believed that a young man from Serbia might be the most gifted player available in the NBA draft that year, better even than University of Louisville star Pervis Ellison, who ended up going first overall to Sacramento. The communication gap and other issues that had made the Glouchkov experiment go south, and the uncertainty surrounding a foreign 21-year-old's ability to adjust to a new land and culture while adjusting to the NBA, caused the young Serb's stock to slip. The Suns, still gun-shy of international players, picked 24th and decided to take Anthony Cook out of the University of Arizona. Two picks later, the Los Angeles Lakers helped themselves to a kid named Vlade Divac. "We think he's very good," said then-Lakers' general manager Jerry West, long one of the shrewdest talent evaluators in basketball. "People look at him as a gamble, but from a talent standpoint, it's not a gamble. He's no project at all. There's no question that there's a risk. The negative right now is his inability to communicate. But he plays very fluidly and easily."

It worked out pretty well. Divac played 20 minutes a game off the bench as a rookie for a Laker team that won 63 games the year after Kareem Abdul-Jabbar retired, and he became a starter on an NBA Finalist team in his second NBA season. Divac is surely one of the most accomplished 26th picks in NBA history and he enjoyed a longer and better career than either Ellison, an oft-injured role player during his 11 NBA seasons, or Cook, who played just four years, none with distinction. Divac was the draft pick that kept on giving, as his combination of size and skill earned him 16 seasons in the NBA, during which his teams made the playoffs 14 times.

He was good enough that the Lakers were able to trade him for Kobe Bryant in 1996 and — and as you might have guessed, based on his performance — his adjustment to North American life was not a problem. "West Germany is capitalist," he said once as a rookie in discussing the politics of the divided Europe he grew up in and left behind. "East Germany is socialist, but socialists can't eat. They always say capitalism is bad, but now they see it's better. Socialists say everyone same. OK, nobody eats. Now everybody is same."

The 1989–90 season saw four other players from the old Eastern Bloc play in the NBA: Drazen Petrovic and Zarko Paspalj, teammates on the former Yugoslavian national team, and Sarunas Marciulionis and Alexander Volkov from the former Soviet Union.

Their impact was notable. Marciulionis was an explosive scorer in between some significant injuries and Petrovic was a rising star named to the All-NBA Third Team in 1993 before his death in a car accident in Germany that summer. Volkov had some bright moments with the Hawks, but struggled with the culture and language barriers and returned to Europe after two seasons. Paspalj didn't last that long either, playing just one season in San Antonio. A talented, high-scoring forward, Paspalj couldn't quite make it over the hurdle imposed by the San Antonio Spurs' coach Larry Brown. After being manhandled by Terry Cummings during one practice, Paspalj was trying to explain the challenge he was facing, his English notwithstanding: "No defense," Paspalj said. "Only offense." To which Brown replied, "No play, only bench."

But even with the injection of five international players in 1989–90, the basketball universe was divided, a decade or more away from becoming the fluid, flowing market of talent it has become today.

Over the Hills and Far Away

Suddenly there was a talent search on for international players. Strangely, even Glouchkov helped, despite his struggles on the court. His mere presence proved, in a roundabout way, that there were roster players to be found in far-flung places; but it took a special breed of talent evaluator, one who could afford to take risks to find those players. It may be a coincidence, but one of the most influential figures in the broadening of the NBA's horizons was Donnie Nelson, now the president of basketball operations for the Dallas Mavericks. He was then working as an assistant coach with the Golden State Warriors with his dad, Don Nelson, the head coach. "During those years, there was virtually no emphasis internationally, and there were a number of reasons for it. The thing that I heard most frequently was, 'Well, Georgi Glouchkov was the best player from over there, and he couldn't even make the NBA, so those guys just aren't good enough,'" Nelson said. "I heard that little battle cry for a long period of time." But Nelson didn't listen and, perhaps with the security of someone working for his father — who is one of the most prolific coaches in NBA history — he pursued his own path.

As a student at Wheaton College in Illinois in the early 1980s, Nelson had been on basketball tours of Europe, including one of the Soviet Union. Later while playing with Athletes in Action in South America he had been blown away by the skill of some of the players he'd encountered. Having been around NBA players his entire working life, not to mention his father, Donnie Nelson had a pretty good idea of what it took to succeed in the NBA, and he was seeing first-hand that the gifts required for this didn't stop at borders. The problem was convincing people in the NBA to see things his way. "If you're a general manager, the last thing you want to hear when your rear end is on the line while making a draft pick is 'high risk,'" Nelson said.

Fortunately, his father was willing to take a risk. Based on Donnie's scouting in Eastern Europe, Golden State selected Sarunas Marciulionis, the Lithuanian star, in the sixth round of the 1987 draft. When he came to play in the NBA for the 1989–90 season, Golden State immediately profited as Marciulionis scored 19 points in his NBA debut.

While Nelson was ahead of the curve by the summer of 1989 — having noted what happened to the talented group of American college players at the 1988 Olympics — other progressive teams were overseas in earnest, trying to expand their talent base. The San Antonio Spurs are another franchise that has benefitted greatly from international stars, be it drafting an unknown Argentinean named Manu Ginobili 57th overall in 1999 and then standing back in wonder as he became one of the most dangerous scorers in the NBA; or plucking French point guard Tony Parker with the No. 28 pick in 2001, starting him as a rookie and reaping the benefits as he steered San Antonio to two titles. Those gains could be attributed to the Spurs' early embrace of the international game.

"Nellie [Donnie] and I were like kids in a candy store with all these players," recalled Gregg Popovich, the long-time coach of the San Antonio Spurs, of the early recruiting trips to Europe. "It was, 'You're going to get him, I'm going to get him. You're going to get him, I'm going to get him.'"

The irony being, of course, that there were so many players to get, this just a few years after the first international players had struggled, and well before they began coming to the NBA in waves. The struggles of Glouchkov and later Volkov and Paspalj proved the exception, not the rule. But who could have predicted the international tidal wave? Like any paradigm-shifting event, it's not attributable to any one thing. The decline in U.S. basketball supremacy helped; the fall of the Berlin Wall likely helped. The increasingly capitalist shift in China probably helped, as it's unlikely Yao Ming would have been selected first overall in 2002 without that country becoming more international in its outlook. The expansion of the NBA from 23 teams in 1987–88 to 30 by 1995–96 helped, as it required the league to find roughly 80 new NBA players.

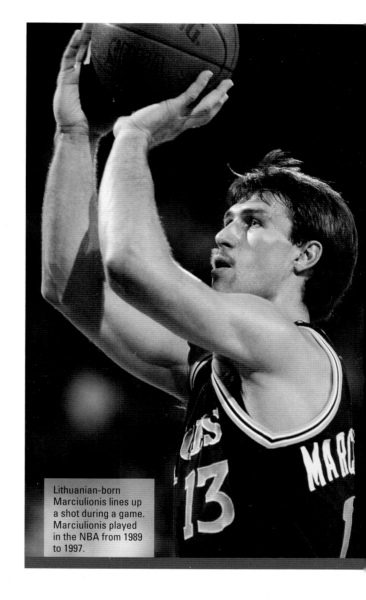

Lithuanian-born Marciulionis lines up a shot during a game. Marciulionis played in the NBA from 1989 to 1997.

Toni Kukoc attempts a layup during a game against Washington in 1996. Kukoc retired in 2006, playing a total of 846 games over the course of his NBA career.

A watershed moment for international talent was the 1996 draft. Peja Stojakovic and Zydrunas Ilgauskas were among the five internationally trained players taken in the first round, selected 14th and 20th, respectively. Before this draft, between 1990 and 1995, the international trend was more a trickle, as only 8 of the 324 players picked came from foreign teams, and none were taken in the first round, though Toni Kukoc, picked 29th overall (the second pick of the second round in the then 27-team league) by the Chicago Bulls in 1990, became a superb role player for the Bulls. He made an immediate impact after coming over from Europe for the 1993–94 season (the start of an impressive 13-year NBA career), and helped the Bulls to three titles: 1996, 1997 and 1998.

When the Dallas Mavericks — in another move engineered by Donnie Nelson — managed to acquire a little-known German named Dirk Nowitzki in 1998 by trading the No. 6 pick (Robert Traylor) to Milwaukee (who had taken the 20-year-old Nowitzki ninth), it marked a sea change. Nowitzki's success meant every NBA team felt they couldn't afford to miss on the so-called "next Dirk" — a European-trained big man who had the shooting skills of a two guard in the package of a center. After struggling as a rookie, Nowitzki became one of the most prolific and consistent scorers in the league, racking up All-Star nominations routinely before earning the league's MVP award in 2007. The success of Spain's Pau Gasol, taken No. 3 by Atlanta in 2001 but then traded immediately to the Memphis Grizzlies, intensified the search.

Every trend has a point of diminishing returns, and inevitably there were mistakes as NBA teams took bigger risks on less proven players. In 2002 Denver took Nikoloz Tskitishvili with the fifth pick and never got a return on a talented seven-footer who had many of the skills associated with European-trained big men, but little feel for the game, as reflected by his 30.4 career shooting percentage. And for all the success Joe Dumars has had in the NBA, as both a player and then general manager with the Detroit Pistons, he'll always be living down his decision to take Serbia's Darko Milicic with the No. 2 pick in the extraordinarily deep 2003 draft, ahead of perennial All-Stars Carmelo Anthony, Chris Bosh and Dwyane Wade among others. Milicic has never delivered on his potential, though each draft has its share of U.S.-born players with the same problem.

That there were, nevertheless, so many exciting prospects overseas wasn't just attributable to NBA teams doing a better job finding players internationally (by the late 1990s a club without a director of international scouting was deemed as simply not trying hard enough). There were also more players to find, which in turn could be credited to the NBA itself.

The Boston Celtics play Real Madrid during the 1988 McDonald's Open at the Palacio de Deportes in Madrid. The Celtics defeated Real Madrid 111–96.

The NBA and Global Growth

Well before international players began showing up in the NBA, the league was taking its show on the road, spreading basketball gospel and finding believers. As early as 1979, the NBA had made a goodwill visit to China with the Washington Bullets — winning two games, one against the Chinese national team and the other against the Bayi Rockets.

Though the NBA's players were almost exclusively American in the early 1980s, the league — under the watch of commissioner David Stern — saw at that time an opportunity to bring the game to an international audience. With the likes of Magic Johnson and Larry Bird at their peak, Stern literally got on the phone and personally negotiated broadcast deals in various international markets. In 1985 the NBA hosted the Chinese national team for a tour through several NBA training camps. Then, in 1987, the Milwaukee Bucks hosted the Soviet Union's national team and European powerhouse Tracer Milan of Italy for the inaugural McDonald's Open. A year later, the four-team round-robin format was established, featuring one NBA club against three top European teams, moving to various European centers each year. The format was put aside after 1997, NBA clubs having gone undefeated in the process.

Nonetheless, the NBA's international presence is a constant, as exhibition appearances in Europe, Mexico, Japan and China eventually gave way to the establishment of EA SPORTS' NBA Europe Live, where today, multiple NBA teams hold training camps and start their exhibition season overseas. Similarly, the league now holds exhibition games in China annually during the preseason. The emergence of the Michael Jordan era in the 1990s only accelerated the international appetite for the NBA — and it didn't hurt that Nike was striving to make Jordan a global brand right alongside it. The NBA did its part too, and now has satellite offices in China, Japan, Mexico, Brazil, France, Italy, Spain and England with plans to open offices in Africa, India and Russia.

Foreign Impact

The give-and-take relationship the NBA has fostered with foreign countries, associations and players is a trend that shows no sign of slowing. In the 2001–02 season all eight teams to make the second round of the playoffs had a foreign-born player on their roster and 5 of the 10 spots on the First and Second All-Rookie Teams were given to foreign-born players. On All-Star Weekend in 2003, five of the 20 players in the Rookie-Sophomore Game had come to the NBA straight from Europe, and nine international players were taken in the first round of the draft.

Then there was the triple crown of 2006–07, when the No. 1 player selected in the 2006 draft was Italy's Andrea Bargnani (the first time a European was taken first overall); the regular season's Most Valuable Player award went to Germany's Dirk Nowitzki and the Finals MVP went to Tony Parker of France. Incidentally, Parker led the San Antonio Spurs to a sweep of LeBron James and the Cleveland Cavaliers, a team that also featured Lithuania's Zydrunas Ilgauskas, Brazil's Anderson Varejao and Sasha Pavlovic of Montenegro in their rotation. Overall, the two Finals teams included nine internationally-born players on their rosters.

Turkey's Hedo Turkoglu (Orlando) tries to shoot by Spain's Pau Gasol (L.A.) during the 2009 NBA Finals. The Turkish and Spanish stars were just two of eight internationally born players in the Finals.

The 2009 NBA Finals — 20 years after the first wave of foreign-trained talent arrived on the NBA's shores — further emphasized the basketball world is borderless. However, the eight international players on the two conference rosters were just an indication of something much bigger: The 2009 NBA Finals between the Magic and the Lakers were televised in 215 countries and territories and in 42 languages; of the 1,800 media members credentialed for the games in Orlando and Los Angeles, more than 250 of them were international media from 32 countries; a total of 55 international television, radio and Internet outlets covered the Finals, with 14 of them providing live commentary of the action; on the league's Web site, more than 30 million daily page views were registered by fans outside the United States.

Turkish star Hedo Turkoglu, playing for the Magic, got a good-luck phone call from Turkey's Prime Minister, Recep Tayyip Erdogan, just before the start of the Finals. And Marcin Gortat, the Magic's Polish-born backup center, was suddenly a star. "If I wanted to run for president of Poland right now, I think I might win," said Gortat, the third Polish player ever to play in the NBA and the first to appear in the Finals. "The response from back home has been incredible. People there are staying up late and watching basketball games instead of soccer. It's amazing."

Just as amazing, or perhaps surprising, was how quickly the rest of the basketball world caught up with and, arguably, surpassed the United States after the inclusion of NBA players in international competition. At the 2000 Olympics in Sydney, only a missed three-pointer at the buzzer by Lithuanian guard Sarunas Jasikevicius allowed a talented U.S. team, led by the likes of Kevin Garnett and Vince Carter, to survive the semifinals and win gold. Then at the 2002 World Championships in Indianapolis, a team of NBA stars could do no better than a sixth-place finish, as Argentina won gold. At the 2004 Olympics, the U.S. was reduced to bronze again, and at the 2006 World Championships in Japan, it was bronze once more for the Stars and Stripes. The tables were now turned: Having taught the rest of the world, the United States basketball program was forced to relearn its own approach.

Jerry Colangelo, the Phoenix Suns executive who brought over Georgi Glouchkov from Bulgaria in 1986, was named chairman of U.S.A. Basketball in 2005. He instilled a true national team concept where a roster of hopefuls gathered each summer to familiarize themselves with each other and the international game. Positions had to be earned on merit. Teams were constructed with specific roles in mind.

How much had things changed? The U.S. team that headed over to China for the 2008 Olympics was dubbed "The Redeem Team." The United States and the NBA had something to prove. Mike Krzyzewski, the legendary Duke University coach entrusted with coaxing a team concept from a group of stars accustomed to having teams built around them was able to draw on the recent history of international stumbles to focus the American team for the Olympics. After the gold medal final against Spain in 2008, Krzyzewski talked of the importance of playing together

The US Men's Basketball team, including LeBron James, Carmelo Anthony, Chris Paul, Chris Bosh and Dwight Howard, celebrate their gold medal victory over Spain at the 2008 Beijing Olympics.

as a team, "If we didn't have three years together, we wouldn't have won this game. The three years gave us character to beat a great team that had character ... It was one of the great games in international basketball history."

What's Next?

And so, international basketball has become just basketball — no need for the adjective. But it's a story very much still being written. No one would have predicted two decades before, when David Robinson and his teammates despondently accepted their bronze medals, that a United States' team full of NBA stars would play the plucky underdog in international competition. And no one could have predicted that the loss by Team USA at the 1988 Seoul Olympics would have been the catalyst for the globalization of the sport over the past 25 years.

Losing in Seoul in 1988 opened the door for the Dream Team in 1992 in Barcelona. Watching there was a young Pau Gasol, the Spanish star who teamed with Kobe Bryant to win the 2009 NBA championship for the Lakers, just a year after he had faced Bryant and Team USA in the epic U.S.-Spain gold medal final in Beijing.

What will be the impact of the Olympic tournament on basketball in China, the world's most populous nation? "The opportunity for

basketball and the NBA in China is simply extraordinary," said NBA Commissioner David Stern while announcing the league's investment, along with the likes of The Walt Disney Company (owners of U.S. cable giant ESPN) in NBA China — a wholly owned subsidiary to operate all of the NBA's business in China, including building a network of NBA-caliber arenas and perhaps an NBA-sanctioned league in partnership with the Chinese Basketball Association. And what of Africa, where most agree the NBA has only begun to scratch the surface? The Indian subcontinent is another area targeted for growth.

"As a player you want to focus on what you've got on the table here, but at the same time you want to stop and think about what's going on around these Finals," said Gasol during the 2009 NBA Finals. "A lot of kids from around the world are watching us play, dreaming about maybe one day being here."

Best of the REST

Patrick Ewing jumps to defend a Scottie Pippen finger roll in Game 5 of the 1993 Eastern Conference Finals. Pippen poured in 28 points while Ewing posted 33 points, a personal best in the series. The Knicks lost the game 97–94, and Chicago went on to win the series in Game 6.

G	FG%	FT%	ORB	DRB	TRB	AST	STL	BLK	PTS
876	.467	.810			2.3	7.4			18.8

NATE ARCHIBALD

In the universe of basketball the creation myth centers around New York City and the playgrounds out of which the slick, authoritative and skilled point guards that gave the sport its urban roots seemed to flow like a river.

Some of them thrived in the NBA. For some it didn't matter. Being a star in New York was enough.

"But to know the New York point guard is to know that the NBA has not, does not and will not define him," basketball writer Scoop Jackson wrote for ESPN in July 2008. "Because unlike any other place on this planet, having a million people in New York know who you are and what you do is more rewarding than having a million people around the country watch you on TNT or collecting a check with a million dollars on it."

Nate "Tiny" Archibald was a New York City point guard who grew up rough and earned his reputation on the hot blacktop courts. But unlike so many before, and since, starring in New York was just a start for him. His legend was formed in the Big Apple crucible, but his game was bound for a much bigger stage.

Archibald, born September 2, 1948, in New York, had a nightmare of a childhood. He was the eldest of seven children raised in the Patterson Housing Projects in the South Bronx, one of the most dangerous neighborhoods in the country. He became the effective head of the household at age 14 when his father — from whom he got his nickname — left his mother and family. Without a father and with worlds of responsibility beyond his age, living in chaos,

Archibald could have, and probably should have, spiraled downward at an early age. It did not turn out that way, however.

"It's interesting how guys who are into drugs are always looking to get other guys involved, as if they want company when they go under," Archibald would later say about his upbringing. "Me? I was always into basketball."

His career did not go altogether smoothly. He was cut from the DeWitt Clinton High School team in his sophomore year, and he considered dropping out of school after that. A local coach named Floyd Lane, however, took him up as a cause, getting him back onto the team for his junior year. By his senior season, he was a member of the All-City team.

Still, that was not a ticket to the usual basketball star system. His grades were still poor, not allowing him to go to a Division 1 school. Instead, he went to Arizona Western Community College, using that as a springboard to three years at the University of Texas at El Paso. Despite a solid career at UTEP, he was not picked until the second round of the 1970 draft, chosen by the Cincinnati Royals.

- Drafted: 19th overall by the Cincinnati Royals in 1970
- Cincinnati Royals: 1970–72
- Kansas City–Omaha Kings: 1972–76
- New York Nets: 1976–77
- Boston Celtics: 1978–83
- Milwaukee Bucks: 1983–84
- Jersey: #7; alternates: #10, #1
- College: University of Texas

Archibald would be a better professional than collegiate player. His history of playground basketball had made his ability to get into the paint unparalleled. Once he got there, he could find a teammate, get himself a layup or hit a pull-up jumper with equal precision.

By his third season (1972–73), by which point the Royals had moved to Kansas City–Omaha and renamed themselves the Kings, Archibald was already one of the league's elite players. The point guard averaged 34.0 points and 11.4 assists per game that season, becoming the first player in league history to win both individual titles in the same season. (Oscar Robertson had the highest averages for both points and assists in 1967–68, but the titles were determined by totals at that time.)

However, Archibald's teams never achieved much success. In his first eight seasons — with three different franchises — his team made the playoffs just once.

After his disastrous first season with the Boston Celtics (1978–79), Archibald, battling several injuries, was considered to be nearing the end of his career. He returned to the South Bronx that off-season.

"Here I was, coming off the most frustrating year of my career, and it was the kids who were counseling me," Archibald said. "They kept saying, 'Don't worry, Tiny. Don't get down. You can do it. The Celtics need you.' I'll never forget them for that."

Indeed, those kids were right. With a bevy of other weapons, the Celtics turned Archibald into a pass-first, shoot-second point guard. He responded by averaging 8.4 assists per game in 1979–80, his best average since his career high in 1972–73.

The next year, Archibald averaged 15.6 points and 6.3 assists per game in 17 playoff games and the Celtics won the title.

That gave him something that many of the great New York City point guards that followed him — Mark Jackson, Rod Strickland, Kenny Anderson and Stephon Marbury, to name a few — never attained: a championship ring to go his with status as a playground legend.

His 1991 induction into the Hall of Fame was nice, too.

CAREER HIGHLIGHTS

- Averaged 34.0 points and 11.4 assists per game, both career highs, for the Kansas City–Omaha Kings in 1972–73

- One of only 9 NBA players to average at least 34 points per game in a season

- Was a six-time NBA All-Star

- NBA All-Star MVP in 1981

- Was named to the All-NBA First Team three times

Archibald goes up for a shot against the San Antonio Spurs in 1980. The 1980–81 season marked a high point for Archibald, after struggling for several seasons.

DAVE COWENS

The NBA was well-established by the time Dave Cowens made his way onto the scene in 1970 and it has continued to grow and thrive since his retirement in 1983, but before he arrived and since he left, the league has never seen a player quite like him.

Ferocious, fearless, competitive; and fun, funny and quirky, too.

In 1991 Cowens was inducted into the Naismith Basketball Hall of Fame. And his credentials explain why.

In the prime of his career — from his rookie season as a wild-eyed redhead out of Florida State University in 1970–71 until the 1977–78 season — he was never worse than the seventh-best rebounder in the NBA. And most of the time he was comfortably in the top three. His career average of 13.9 rebounds per game remain the eighth-best in NBA history.

In 1972–73, he averaged 20.5 points, 16.5 rebounds and 4.1 assists and was named the NBA's Most Valuable Player. The Celtics posted a 68–14 record, one of the best regular-season marks in NBA history. A season later, he led the Celtics to an NBA championship, scoring 28 points and grabbing 14 rebounds in Game 7 of the NBA Finals against the Milwaukee Bucks, led by center Kareem Abdul-Jabbar. Two seasons later, the Celtics won another title, and once again Cowens was in the middle of things.

But the accomplishments

- Drafted: 4th overall by the Boston Celtics in 1970
- Boston Celtics: 1970–80
- Milwaukee Bucks: 1982–83
- Jersey: #18; alternate: #36
- College: Florida State

barely tell half the story. Cowens, born October 25, 1958, in Newport, Kentucky, always did things his own way — and thank goodness for that.

"You try things, meet a lot of people, go down that road," he said. "I haven't followed the same path as a lot of other people. I didn't stay on the NBA course for my entire career. I got off of it, went out and saw what the big, real world was about.

"And I liked it."

Among NBA players he's likely on a short list who took self-improvement courses during the season. One year it was a course in auto mechanics, coming to practice with grease underneath his fingernails. He studied sign language during another. He took a night off during the playoffs one year to drive a cab. Citing burnout, he took a 30-game sabbatical at the start of the 1976–77 season. He spent nine years and raised $100,000 to cover legal fees to prevent a company from developing a prime piece of pasture land in rural Massachusetts. He worked as the full-time volunteer chairman of the New England Sports Museum for a time. After he retired from the NBA at age 31, he immediately took a job as the athletic director of a women's college. And after a few years there, he came back for half a season at age 34 to play for the Milwaukee Bucks, coached by his Celtic friend Don Nelson, "just to prove he could."

He established a legacy as one of the most determined players in NBA history. At 6-foot-8, he knew he didn't have the physical tools to compete with Wilt Chamberlain or Abdul-Jabbar. But he was crafty, so the Celtics created a role for him as "point-center" where he would draw opposing big men away from the basket and direct the offense from there. And on defense he would battle and scratch and claw, and fight, if necessary.

"It was simple — for 48 minutes I played as hard as I could," Cowens says.

But even in that context he did it with style. Once, playing against the Houston Rockets, he took offense when Mike Newlin drew a charge on him by flopping. On the next trip up the floor, Cowens took aim at Newlin, sprinted at him, elbows raised, and knocked him over, turning to the referee and shouting, "Now *that* was a foul!"

Cowens was widely criticized for the foul, and in response he wrote a long letter to the editor of the *Boston Globe* explaining his reasoning, and why flopping was a scourge that had to be eradicated from all right-thinking minds.

"Fraudulent, deceiving and flagrant acts of pretending to be fouled when little or no contact is made is just as outrageously unsportsmanlike as knocking a player to the floor," he wrote. "Pretending makes players think they can achieve their goal without putting in the work or effort that it takes to develop any skill or talent ... It distracts anyone who attends the game to study fundamental basketball skills and traits of the game."

This was not a problem for anyone who watched Cowens throw his body around the floor and into the stands in pursuit of loose balls and, in his own way, the truth.

CAREER HIGHLIGHTS

- Is eighth all-time in NBA history with a 13.6 rebounds-per-game career average

- Nicknames included "Redhead," "The Cow" and "Big Red"

- In 1977, Cowens briefly worked as a taxi cab driver to help "clear his head"

- Seven-time NBA All-Star

- He was head coach for the Charlotte Hornets from 1996–99 and the Golden State Warriors from 1999–2001

- In 1972–73 posted PPG career highs of 20.5 points and 16.2 rebounds

DAVE **DeBUSSCHERE**

Nicknamed "The Big D," DeBusschere helped the Knicks win two championships. Here, he grabs a rebound from the L.A. Lakers' Happy Hairston during a 1970 game.

The most fitting tribute to Dave DeBusschere, the hard-as-rock, team-first forward on the great New York Knicks teams of the 1970s, came in the first line of his obituary that appeared in the Associated Press: "It's hard to believe Dave DeBusschere's heart gave out on him," it read. "That was always the strongest part of his game."

The former Knick star died of a heart attack on a Manhattan sidewalk in 2003, a moment both sudden and saddening. But his passing created an opportunity to revisit the man and what he stood for, which was, above all, his team.

His eulogy was delivered by Bill Bradley, the former New Jersey senator and presidential candidate with the smooth outside shot who roomed with DeBusschere on the road for six years, looking up to him as a big brother as they made their way through the rough-and-tumble NBA.

In a packed church Bradley talked about loyalty and teamwork and what made the Knicks a special group in the annals of professional sports as they provided each other what Bradley called, "the depth of a sense of belonging."

The Knicks were already a very good team when DeBusschere joined them by way of a trade from Detroit late in the 1968–69 season, but he was, as Hall of Fame teammate Walt Frazier said, "the final piece of the puzzle."

DeBusschere provided an ample dose of toughness, defense, rebounding and the ability to hit shots with seemingly unlimited range. And he delivered in the big moments. In the Knicks' 1970 legendary Game 7 win over the Los Angeles Lakers — remembered mostly for the emotional return of limping, injured center Willis Reed and an incredible performance by Frazier — DeBusschere made a significant contribution, tallying 18 points and 17 rebounds while blanketing Laker star Elgin Baylor. In the pivotal Game 4 of the 1973 championship series win over the Lakers, Debusschere totaled 33 points and 14 rebounds. It was one of the greatest games of his career.

The son of a Detroit saloonkeeper, he was a blue-collar guy, most comfortable after a game with a cold beer in hand, swapping stories and dissecting the wins or losses, inviting everyone to join in. But DeBusschere's everyman image doesn't capture

his athletic gifts. A two-sport star at the University of Detroit, he was a gifted pitcher who played four seasons of professional baseball with the Chicago White Sox organization. He had a 3–4 record with a 3.09 ERA as a Major-League call-up in 1963, and compiled a career 25–9 Triple-A mark before making basketball his full-time job. He was named to the NBA's All-Rookie Team in 1962–63, and his leadership skills were such that the Pistons appointed him player-coach early in the 1964–65 season, making DeBusschere the youngest coach in NBA history at age 24.

The Pistons struggled, however, and relieved DeBusschere of his coaching duties after three seasons. Without that added responsibility, his game soared. "I realize now there were things I wasn't mature enough to handle," DeBusschere said later. "As soon as I was back on my own again, I had my best season. I was scoring better, rebounding better, defending better and doing everything else better." He became a three-time All-Star with Detroit, but the losing took a toll on him, and he welcomed the trade to the Knicks in December 1968.

- Drafted: by the Detroit Pistons in 1962 (territorial selection)
- Detroit Pistons: 1962–68
- New York Knicks: 1968–74
- College: University of Detroit Mercy

The Knicks were already good, but DeBusschere's brand of toughness, smarts, skill and hustle provided a missing element to the New York club. Lining up at power forward, he allowed Reed to shift to center and specialized in taking opposing stars out of their games. "He took away my first, second, third and fourth offensive moves," said fellow Hall of Famer Connie Hawkins.

Tellingly, DeBusschere was a fixture on the NBA's All-Defensive Team from the moment it was established in 1969 until he retired in 1974. He was inducted into the Hall of Fame in 1983, the year the NBA introduced the Defensive Player of the Year award, a title DeBusschere owned informally several times in his career. Over 12 seasons, he averaged 16 points and 12 rebounds a game, but it was the points he took away that made him an All-Star and a member of the NBA's Top-50 Team in 1996.

For all his gifts and talents, perhaps his most significant contribution came as a teammate, helping to make those around him better. DeBusschere did the things on the floor that didn't always show up as numbers in a box score, and he did things as a person that made his team better before they took the court: accepting blame, distributing credit, supporting those who mattered most to him.

As his teammate Bill Bradley remembered in delivering DeBusschere's eulogy: "He seemed to say, 'What's the point of achieving anything in basketball if you can't share it?'"

CAREER HIGHLIGHTS

- Averaged a double-double, with points and rebounds, in 10 consecutive seasons

- Was named to the NBA All-Defensive First Team six times

- Played professional baseball with the Chicago White Sox in 1962–63

- An eight-time NBA All-Star

- Was an assistant coach and worked in the front office for the New York Knicks in the 1980s

G	FG%	FT%	ORB	DRB	TRB	AST	STL	BLK	PTS
1086	.472	.788	2.4	3.7	6.1	5.6	2.0	0.7	20.4

CLYDE **DREXLER**

When you play the same position during the same time as Michael Jordan, you are bound to be overshadowed. As such, Clyde Drexler's accomplishments were often dimished by the man who sold a billion shoes.

Drexler served as the backup to Jordan on the 1992 Dream Team. He finished as the runner-up to Jordan in MVP voting for the 1991–92 season. His Portland Trail Blazers lost to Jordan's Bulls in the 1992 NBA Finals. It was a pattern that started early on, when Jordan's North Carolina Tar Heels beat Drexler's Houston Cougars en route to a national championship in 1982.

Sure, Drexler was eclipsed by Jordan, but so was everyone else. Really, Drexler might have been Jordan's closest competitor during the reign of the Bulls' star.

"We basically played the same game," Drexler said. "The main difference in our games … is that he shot the ball more. You look at every other aspect of the game, and you'll see that the numbers are startlingly close. But FGA [field goal attempts] he almost shot twice as much as I did … and scored almost twice as many points. But that was amazing because it's hard to get up 30-plus shots every game. I was getting between 16 and 18 shots, he was getting 30 or 35. That's the difference in our games."

Drexler overstates it a bit, but Jordan shot the ball more than his counterpart — almost 7,000 more times over the course of their careers. Drexler actually averaged more assists per game than Jordan, while Jordan averaged 6.2 rebounds per game compared to Drexler's 6.1.

And Drexler entered the public consciousness before Jordan, too. Born June 22, 1962, in New Orleans, Drexler played for the most famous college team of its time: the Phi Slama Jama Houston Cougars.

The Cougars made three straight Final Fours from 1982 to 1984, with Drexler a member of the first two of those teams. Playing with the likes of Hakeem Olajuwon, Larry Micheaux and Michael Young, Drexler previewed the type of play that Jordan would typify while dominating NBA: A slashing, full-court game predicated on athleticism and dunking.

"Phi Slama Jama revolutionized the way basketball was going to be played in the future," Drexler said. "We had guys who were 7 feet tall, a 6-10 power forward, we had two 6-8 swingmen, and a 6-3 point guard. That's an NBA line-up, in college, and all were very talented. And the way we played, with our pressing defense and our up-tempo style, was fun to watch. So people realized that while these guys

- Drafted: 14th overall by the Portland Trail Blazers in 1983
- Portland Trail Blazers: 1983–95
- Houston Rockets: 1995–98
- College: University of Houston

do have a fair amount of athletic ability, they play extremely hard. And when people play hard, it's infectious."

He said that with the benefit of hindsight. But Drexler perhaps best articulated Houston's mission statement during his college career: "Sure, 15-footers are fine, but I like to dunk."

Although Houston never won a championship, Drexler's exceptional play earned him national recognition, and eventually the 14th-overall selection by Portland in the 1983 draft.

After playing sparingly in his first season, Drexler averaged at least 17.2 points per game in each of his final 15 seasons. He led Portland to two NBA Finals (1990, 1992), both losses, and at his peak Drexler could fill the box score like few players in his era or any other, finishing seasons in the NBA's top-10 in an array of categories, from points, assists and steals to free throw attempts and offensive rebounds.

He did some of his best work in the post-season — he averaged at least 21 points, 7 rebounds and 7 assists per game in three straight playoffs between

1989 and 1992. His best year was that 1991–92 season, but, as with the Cougars, he could never bring a championship to Portland.

So, with the Trail Blazers' fortunes fading, Drexler was dealt to the defending champion Houston Rockets in the middle of the 1994–95 season and reunited with Olajuwon. Despite finishing just sixth in the Western Conference, the Rockets would improbably win the title, including a sweep of the Shaquille O'Neal-powered Orlando Magic. A 32-year-old Drexler averaged 21.5 points, 9.5 rebounds and 6.8 assists per game in the Rockets' four game sweep, providing more than able support for his old college teammate.

After Houston clinched that series, Rockets' coach Rudy Tomjanovich famously exclaimed, "Don't underestimate the heart of a champion."

Finally, like Jordan, Drexler could be mentioned in that breath.

CAREER HIGHLIGHTS

- Averaged a career high 27.2 points per game in 1988–89

- With John Havlicek and Oscar Robertson is one of only three players to have recorded at least 20,000 points, 6,000 rebounds and 6,000 assists in a career.

- Was a 10-time NBA All-Star

- Won a gold medal with the U.S. Men's Olympic Basketball Team in 1992

- Shares the NBA record for most steals in a half with 8

Drexler goes for a layup in a 1995 contest against the New Jersey Nets. Nicknamed "The Glide," Drexler was known for his high-flying drives to the basket.

G	FG%	FT%	ORB	DRB	TRB	AST	STL	BLK	PTS
1183	.504	.740	2.3	7.5	9.8	1.9	1.0	2.4	21.0

PATRICK **EWING**

Ewing shoots a hook shot against Houston's Hakeem Olajuwon during a 1994 game. Olajuwon and the Rockets would foil Ewing and the Knicks' bid for the 1994 championship.

Patrick Ewing arrived in the United States a shy and lonely 11-year-old, a stranger in a strange land. Ewing settled in Cambridge, Massachusetts from Kingston, Jamaica, and arrived just in time to see snow fall for the first time.

Big for his age, Ewing left behind his love of cricket and soccer and took up basketball in a local park soon after his arrival. He became a highly sought-after high-school player and enrolled at prestigious Georgetown University, where he led the Hoyas to the NCAA Tournament's championship game three times in four years. The New York Knicks made the 7-foot center the first player taken in the 1985 NBA draft and he won the Rookie of the Year award in 1986.

Ewing lifted a drifting New York Knicks franchise back to glory, helped them become annual championship contenders and led them to 13 straight playoff appearances, 11 times advancing beyond the first round.

By the time he retired in 2001–02, he had won a gold medal at the 1992 Olympics, been chosen to the NBA's 50th Anniversary Team and led the Knicks to Game 7 of the NBA Finals in 1994.

But some might say his exemplary career somehow fell short. Ewing left the Knicks in 2000 in a transaction that was as much a divorce as a basketball trade. The fans at Madison Square Garden, where Ewing had become the franchise leader in points, rebounds, blocked shots, steals and field goals made, were happy to see him go, frustrated that his best years weren't good enough to bring New York a championship. Towards the end of his time with the Knicks, he was booed and mock-cheered by the fans, such as the time he got into foul trouble early in his 1,000th career game, normally an occasion for looking back through a warm and fuzzy lens.

"Nothing surprises me anymore," said a stoic Ewing. He ended up finishing his 17-year NBA career with unsatisfying seasons in Seattle and Orlando.

But a strange thing happened to Ewing in retirement, almost as amazing as his immigrant-to-stardom tale.

Bit by bit, fans in New York looked at what they had had with Ewing and what was left after he was gone. The Knicks rapidly descended into the NBA's cellar and the fans realized they had sold the big man short.

"I think people appreciate Patrick now," Allan Houston, his teammate from 1996–2000, said when Ewing returned to Madison Square Garden for his jersey retirement ceremony on February 28, 2003. "It's funny. When we had him, people were saying one thing. Now they're saying another thing. Sometimes you don't appreciate things until they're gone. I think that's definitely the case with Patrick and the fans and New York."

What they had was one of the best shooting big men in NBA history, and a rugged, shot-blocking presence who played with an almost unprecedented level of effort and consistency, exchanging buckets of sweat for one 20-point and 10-rebound season after another.

When Ewing was at his peak, playing for Pat Riley, the Knicks were the best defensive team in the NBA and one of the best of all time, winning an average of 56 games a season from 1991–92 to 1994–95.

- Drafted: 1st overall by the New York Knicks in 1985
- New York Knicks: 1985–2000
- Seattle Supersonics: 2000–01
- Orlando Magic: 2001–02
- Jersey: #33; alternate: #6
- College: Georgetown University

How good were the Knicks and Ewing? After losing to the Chicago Bulls in seven games in the second round of the playoffs in 1992, the Knicks worked hard all season to secure home-court advantage in the playoffs the following year. They finished first overall in the Eastern Conference with a 60–22 record, led by Ewing who averaged 24.7 points, 12.1 rebounds and two blocks per game. After splitting the first four games of the Eastern Conference Finals, the Knicks fell short in Game 5 at home. Charles Smith, the Knicks' power forward, had what would have been the go-ahead basket blocked four times. After stealing the win on the road, the Bulls closed the series at home.

Ewing's best chance at a championship came in 1994–95 when Jordan retired to play baseball. Ewing led the Knicks to the NBA Finals against the Houston Rockets. Again the Knicks fell short by the smallest of margins, losing Game 6 and Game 7 to the Rockets after leading the series 3–2, with Ewing struggling against Hakeem Olajuwon, who was playing at the top of his game. The next season with Chicago's Michael Jordan still out, the Knicks advanced to the Conference Finals against the Indiana Pacers but lost in seven games. Ewing missed a three-foot layup at the buzzer that would have sent the final game into overtime.

There was lot of frustration and a lot of heartbreak for Ewing, but time has treated him well. He led good teams far into the playoffs, and in failing to overcome the best of the Jordan era and the best Olajuwon had to offer, he and the Knicks are still regarded in fine company, along with the likes of Charles Barkley, Karl Malone and John Stockton among others.

For Ewing, the ultimate recognition came in 2008 when he was inducted into the Hall of Fame in Springfield Massachusetts, a short journey from his childhood home in Cambridge, a vast distance for a shy Jamaican kid who accomplished more than he could have ever imagined.

CAREER HIGHLIGHTS

- 11-time NBA All-Star
- 16th all-time in NBA scoring history with 24,815 points
- Is a two-time Olympic gold medalist, winning in 1984 and 1992 with the U.S. Men's Basketball Team
- Averaged at least 20 points and 10 rebounds for 9 straight seasons from 1989–90 to 1997–98
- Had a career-high 327 blocks in 1989–90, which is the 14th highest single-season block total in NBA history
- Averaged a career-high 28.6 points per game in 1989–90 and was selected to his only All-NBA First Team that same year
- Is seventh all-time in NBA history with 2,894 career blocks

G	FG%	FT%	ORB	DRB	TRB	AST	STL	BLK	PTS
1122	.452	.801			5.0	4.0			19.2

HAL **GREER**

They don't give awards for attendance in the NBA, but if they did Hal Greer would be at the front of the class, a picture of consistency alongside heroes. Playing in the shadow of legends and going head-to-head against the greats of his era, Greer spent his entire 15-year career (1958–73) with the same franchise — the Syracuse Nationals which, in turn, became the Philadelphia 76ers — compiling steady and sometimes spectacular statistics for some of the best teams in NBA history.

His early years were spent playing alongside Dolph Schayes when the team was in Syracuse, and then as a running mate with Wilt Chamberlain during the golden years after the team moved to Philadelphia. Despite his 21,586 points and 1,122 games — both marks still well within the NBA's Top-50 All-Time — Greer's legacy is as a sidekick. He was one of the best Robins to a teammate's Batman that a franchise could ever hope to have.

Graduating out of Marshall University in West Virginia, he never expected to have a long NBA career, even after being named an All-American in 1958. He says he didn't even unpack his bags in training camp, figuring he'd have a short stay.

That modest outlook carried him all the way to the Hall of Fame.

"Hal Greer always came to play," Schayes said upon Greer's induction into the Hall of Fame in 1982. "He came to practice the same way, to every

- Drafted: 13th overall by the Syracuse Nationals in 1958
- Syracuse Nationals: 1958–63
- Philadelphia 76ers: 1963–73
- College: Marshall University at El Paso

team function the same way. Every bus and plane and train, he was on time. Hal Greer punched the clock. Hal Greer brought the lunch pail."

A strong, slim guard with spectacular speed that he used to set up his trademark pull-up jumper, it could be said that Greer had his best years playing alongside Chamberlain, but then again Chamberlain had perhaps his best season playing alongside Greer.

By the 1967–68 season, Chamberlain had been in the NBA for eight years but had never won a title. He had become known not only for his scoring and rebounding exploits, but also for his inability to lead teams past Bill Russell and the Boston Celtics.

To Greer's chagrin, he was the scapegoat for one of those stumbles. He was the inbounder in the final seconds of Game 7 in the 1965 Eastern Conference Finals in which the 76ers seemed poised to upset the Celtics in Boston Garden. Bill Russell had turned the ball over on his inbound pass, and with Philadelphia trailing by a point, Greer was charged with getting the ball in for a potential game-tying basket. To Greer's regret Celtics' great John Havlicek read the play and intercepted the pass intended for Chet Walker, leading to Johnny Most's famous "Havlicek stole the ball" radio call.

"And people have never let me forget it," said Greer. "But I'd like to forget about it."

He made Philadelphia fans forget just two seasons later when the 76ers put together one of the most dominant seasons in NBA history, rolling to a 68–13 regular-season record in 1966–67, the best in league history at the time. They blew by Oscar Robertson and the Cincinnati Royals in the first round and the hated Celtics in the Eastern Conference Finals on their way to an NBA championship.

Greer was brilliant all year. His 22.8 points a game made him the second-leading scorer to Chamberlain in the regular season and his 27.7 points a game in the playoffs led Philadelphia and accounted for a fair number of Chamberlain's nine assists a game in the post-season. "It was a beautiful, beautiful season," Greer said later. "We had everything. We knew we were going to win most of our games — it was just a matter of by how much."

Not long after came perhaps his greatest moment in the sun when he was named the Most Valuable Player of the

1968 NBA All-Star Game — one of 10 he played in — as he scored what was then a record 19 of his 21 points in a single quarter. As a guard who played in the same era as Oscar Robertson and Jerry West, moments in the spotlight were hard to come by for Greer, but his seven selections to the All-NBA Second Team indicate the respect he earned.

But some of Greer's greatest moments came well away from the spotlight. Growing up a black man in Huntington, West Virginia, he didn't expect to go to a Division 1 school, but late in his senior year of high school in 1955 he was offered a scholarship at Marshall University in his hometown, the first black athlete to ever enroll there.

He wasn't by nature a trailblazer, but he stuck it out and become a beloved figure at the school.

"He was such a likable person," a teammate said. "All the athletes liked him and the other students liked him. He just was a role model. There was no way you could have any hard feelings toward him."

He graduated from Marshall a star, and went on to become a pro's pro in the NBA — not the name on the marquee, but the guy everyone in the know appreciated.

CAREER HIGHLIGHTS

- Averaged at least 20 points per game seven seasons in a row in the 1960s

- A 10-time NBA All-Star

- Named MVP of the 1968 NBA All-Star Game

- Has scored 21,586 points in his career which puts him 26th on the all-time NBA scoring list

- Named to the All-NBA Second Team seven times

Greer goes up for a shot against the New York Knicks. One of Greer's strengths was his jump shot, which he liked to take from inside the top of the key.

G	FG%	FT%	ORB	DRB	TRB	AST	STL	BLK	PTS
1303	.452	.670			12.5	1.8			21.0

ELVIN **HAYES**

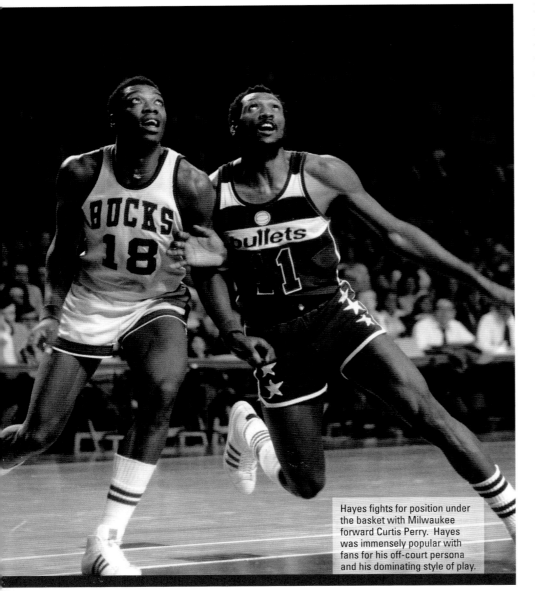

Hayes fights for position under the basket with Milwaukee forward Curtis Perry. Hayes was immensely popular with fans for his off-court persona and his dominating style of play.

Fair or not, Elgin Hayes was saddled with the reputation of being a selfish star for most of his remarkable career. He was a statistically overwhelming power forward, who could dominate games with the force of his talent, posting amazing numbers. But he was also perceived as someone who could undermine teams with the force of his personality.

Hayes was gifted, on par with the very best players of his or any other era, and he was as reliable as an alarm clock. In 16 seasons, he missed just nine games and in no single season did he play fewer than 80. Additionally, in the first seven years of his career, he never averaged less than 42 minutes a game. His 50,000 career minutes ranks third all-time.

Perhaps the best illustration of Hayes' talent comes not from his prolific NBA career, but from his college days.

On January 20, 1968, Hayes, a senior at the University of Houston, led the No. 2 and undefeated Cougars against the No. 1-ranked UCLA Bruins, led by Kareem Abdul-Jabbar (known then as Lew Alcindor). The Bruins were on a 47-game winning streak; the upstart Cougars were 16–0. The game was played at the Houston Astrodome in front of a national television audience and a crowd of 52,693, the largest ever to watch a college basketball game at the time.

In a stunning upset, Hayes' Cougars defeated the Bruins 71–69. The Houston center outplayed the UCLA star, finishing with 39 points, 15 rebounds and 4 assists, and won the game with a pair of free throws in the final minute. John Wooden, legendary UCLA coach, called Hayes' game "one of the great individual performances in a game I ever saw."

Hayes didn't skip a beat in the NBA, averaging 28.4 points and 17.1 rebounds as a rookie in 1968–69 with the expansion San Diego Rockets. He also began a streak of playing in 12 straight All-Star games. At 6-foot-9 and 240 pounds, Hayes was chiseled and athletic, putting the "power" in the power forward position, yet his trademark offensive move was the high-arching fall-away jumper.

The problem in explaining Hayes is that despite his big numbers and ranking fourth all-time in career rebounding (16,279) and seventh all-time in career scoring (27,313), his teams, for the most part, didn't do very well. He didn't play on a team with a winning record in his first four NBA seasons, and didn't play on a team that advanced past the first round of the playoffs until his seventh season.

Alex Hannum, one of Hayes' coaches with the San Diego Rockets, once described Hayes as "the most despicable person I've ever met in sports." Rocket teammate Mike Newlin said, "Elvin Hayes was quintessentially the most selfish hog in the history of basketball."

When Hayes was traded to the Baltimore Bullets in 1972, Baltimore coach Gene Shue joked that Hayes' psychiatrist was part of the package.

- Drafted: 1st overall by the San Diego Rockets in 1968
- San Diego Rockets: 1968–71
- Houston Rockets: 1971–72 and 1981–84
- Baltimore Bullets: 1972–73
- Capital Bullets: 1973–74
- Washington Bullets: 1974–81
- Jersey: #11; alternate: #44
- College: University of Houston

Said John Lally, a trainer with the Washington Bullets, "For some players and coaches, being around Elvin every day is like a Chinese water torture. It's just a drop at a time, nothing big, but in the end, he's driven you crazy."

Hayes attributed his reputation to his determination to stand up for himself and speak the truth, regardless if it wasn't what others wanted to hear, a by-product of growing up poor in segregated rural Louisiana. He said it was a lesson he learned from his father, who died when Hayes was in eighth grade, just as he took up basketball.

But Hayes' ability couldn't be denied. With the Bullets, Hayes was on a talented veteran team, and he proved he could be part of a winner, as he helped the Bullets to two NBA Finals appearances and the NBA title in 1977–78.

Hayes acknowledges that playing well with others was something that he had to learn as his career went along. "When I left basketball, I was much more humble than when I first came," says Hayes, who has enjoyed a successful business career in retirement.

As he finished his career back in Houston, the truculent star was a mentor to a new generation.

"I was never the easiest guy to play for when I was coaching," said then Rockets' coach Bill Fitch. "But I have absolutely not one bad thing to say about Elvin Hayes. He played his behind off for us, and he showed those kids what it meant to be a professional."

CAREER HIGHLIGHTS

- Grabbed 16,279 rebounds in his career, fourth all-time in NBA history
- Played at least 80 regular season games in every year of his 16-year career
- Played exactly 50,000 minutes in his regular season career, which places him third all-time behind Kareem Abdul-Jabbar and Karl Malone
- 12-time NBA All-Star
- Led the NBA in PPG with 28.4 in his 1968–69 rookie season

G	FG%	FT%	ORB	DRB	TRB	AST	STL	BLK	PTS
489	.575	.599	3.6	9.1	12.7	1.5	0.9	2.1	17.5

DWIGHT HOWARD

The National Basketball Association, for the most part, is full of genetic marvels. Sure, the uber-talented can sometimes make the league without an extraordinary frame, but it is rare. Most of these guys are built differently.

So, it's particularly telling when NBA players are amazed by a peer's physicality, the way they are with the Orlando Magic's Dwight Howard.

"That kid is a freak of nature, man," Kevin Garnett, himself 6-foot-11 and a chiseled 250 pounds, said. "I don't know what they put in the milk these days for these young kids, but that kid is a freak of nature. I was nowhere near that physically talented. I wasn't that gifted, as far as body and physical presence."

"He is so developed. He doesn't look like a 19- or 20-year-old," Tim Duncan, also an inch under seven feet, said of Howard after his rookie season. "He has so much promise and I am just glad that I will be out of the league when he is peaking."

With apologies to the other facets of Howard's game, his sheer size is the thing that jumps off the page. He measures 6-foot-11 and 265 pounds, pretty typical for an NBA center. But his near-perfect physique and the athleticism that accompanies it is just plain unfair.

The only obstacle to a career for the ages, some feel, is his status as a friendly, joking giant. The Atlanta native, born December 8, 1985, is famous for his multi-watt smile, not to mention his exaggerated impersonation of his tense head coach, Stan Van Gundy. In the 2009 NBA Finals, as the Los Angeles Lakers took

out the Orlando Magic in five games, some pointed to Howard's laid-back demeanor, in stark contrast to Kobe Bryant's drive, as a reason for the result.

"The point was made that Dwight has only got us out of the first round one time in four years," Van Gundy said during those playoffs. "I wanted to ask the guy, 'How many times did Kevin Garnett get his team out of the first round in his early years?' It took eight years. Eight years of not getting out of the first round. But what, because Kevin Garnett yells and scowls and screams, he cares and Dwight doesn't? It doesn't add up."

And really, Howard made the Magic hardly wait at all, but his talent has always made those around him impatient with anticipation. Going to Southwest Atlanta Christian Academy, where his father worked as athletic director, Howard progressed so rapidly he registered per-game averages of 25 points and 18 rebounds as a senior, leading his school to a state championship.

His spectacular season allowed him to enter the draft as a prep player. Orlando had the choice to take Howard or Connecticut center Emeka Okafor, who was considered a sure thing because of his college pedigree. Of course, Orlando went the riskier route. And while Okafor outperformed the youngster early, winning the 2005 Rookie of the Year award, Howard quickly passed him, becoming an All-Star by his third season.

- Drafted: 1st overall by the Orlando Magic in 2004
- Orlando Magic: 2004–
- High School: Southwest Atlanta Christian Academy in Atlanta, Georgia

At that point, the comparisons to Shaquille O'Neal were in full swing. O'Neal started his career in Orlando, dominating as a big man with a deadly combination of power and athleticism. However, he bolted Orlando at the first chance, even after he led the Magic to the NBA Finals in 1995.

"You can easily make the parallel," Magic general manager Otis Smith said. "What Dwight is going to do for the team and the city hasn't been done since Shaq left."

Howard, though, would not repeat Magic history. In 2007, he signed a contract extension with Orlando. The following season, he averaged 14.2 rebounds per game, becoming the youngest player to ever win the rebounding crown. And by 2008, he was the starting center for the United States' gold-medal-winning team at the Beijing Olympics.

And the year that followed was his best. In addition to his spectacular offensive numbers, he averaged 2.9 blocks per game to win the Defensive Player of the Year. He punctuated the season with a 40-point effort in the decisive game of the Eastern Conference Finals. Howard repeated as Defensive Player of the Year in 2009–10.

His post game is becoming more polished, his athleticism is still peaking. For the NBA's most exciting young center, the best is still to come.

CAREER HIGHLIGHTS

- Has grabbed at least 1,000 rebounds in five consecutive seasons

- He is the youngest player in NBA history to lead the league in rebounding and blocks in the same season (2008–09)

- Has averaged a double-double, with points and rebounds, in all six seasons of his NBA career

- Was the NBA Slam Dunk Champion in 2008

- Has recorded at least 20 rebounds in a game 40 times in his career

- Four-time NBA All-Star

- Has won NBA Defensive Player of the Year twice (2009 and 2010)

- Is the only player in NBA history to lead the league in rebounds and blocks in the same season twice

Howard goes up for a shot against Sacramento's Jon Brockman on January 12, 2010. Orlando won the game 109–88, with Howard posting a double-double (30 points, 16 rebounds).

3

GUARD

ALLEN IVERSON

Iverson dishes to Kenny Thomas during a game against the Toronto Raptors in 2004. The Raptors went on to defeat the 76ers 93–80, despite Iverson's 36 points.

For more than a few moments, Allen Iverson was on top of the basketball world. But one moment stands out more than any other because it was so typically Iverson: Uncommon talent plus uncommon bravado.

In the first game of the 2001 NBA Finals against the Los Angeles Lakers — a series in which his Philadelphia 76ers were given no chance — Iverson had somehow coaxed the game into overtime. The Lakers had not lost in the playoffs up until that point. Iverson made play after play, capped by losing defender Tyronn Lue with his patented crossover dribble and draining a jumpshot from the baseline. After that came the moment that everybody remembers: With Lue on the floor, Iverson stepped over him with two defiant strides.

The Lakers won the series as they were supposed to, but that play was the exclamation point on Iverson's dream season: Philadelphia had won the Eastern Conference and Iverson was named the league's 2001 Most Valuable Player, averaging a league-best 31.4 points per game and 2.8 steals per contest.

"I believe in my heart I'm the best player in the world," Iverson said the following season. "I'm just a scorer. I try to put the ball in the basket for my team. I'm just confident in my ability to play ball."

That swagger defined Iverson who, in turn, defined the NBA's post-Jordan crop of superstars. While it endeared him to millions of mostly younger fans, it also turned off many basketball purists. For each of his four scoring titles, he also had several run-ins with the authorities, be it coaches, the police or NBA commissioner David Stern. Making the easy play — hitting an open teammate or falling in line with the rules — was not the Iverson way.

But given his upbringing, not to mention his stature, his me-against-the-world stance made plenty of sense. Iverson's mother, who would become famous for supporting her son during his career, had Allen when she was just 15. Iverson's father was never in the picture. While his mother was going from job to job — and sometimes unemployed — Iverson played basketball for money in the projects of Hampton, Virginia.

"There were times when Allen never knew where his next meal was going to be," Mike Bailey, Iverson's coach at Bethel High School in Hampton, said. "Here's a kid who couldn't take a bath because he had no running water because it had been turned off."

Despite his economic hardships and despite being relatively undersized — even in the NBA his being listed at an even six feet was generous — Iverson flourished athletically in his early life. He was the quarterback of a state champion football team in high school and dominated on the basketball court until legal troubles caught up with him. He was given a 15-year jail sentence, with 10 years suspended, for his role in a brawl that took place at a bowling alley. However, he was granted a pardon after serving four months in prison, and his guilty verdict was eventually overturned.

Although his troubles always defined him in part, so did the skills that launched his amazing career. As a favour to his mother, legendary coach John Thompson took Iverson on to play at Georgetown University. He

- Drafted: 1st overall by the Philadelphia 76ers in 1996
- Philadelphia 76ers: 1996–2006 and 2009–10
- Denver Nuggets: 2006–2008
- Detroit Pistons: 2008–2009
- Memphis Grizzlies: 2009
- Jersey: #3; alternate: #1
- College: Georgetown University

starred there for two years and, as a result, the 76ers chose him first overall in the 1996 draft; a class that included Ray Allen, Kobe Bryant and Steve Nash.

And for the better part of the next decade, Iverson was the 76ers, for better and for worse. He was the Rookie of the Year, a ten-time All-Star, a three-time steals leader and a seven-time All-NBA selection. After 13 seasons he has the fifth-highest scoring average in league history. However, his tiffs with his coaches, most notably Larry Brown, and the league are legendary. Brown bristled as Iverson would miss countless practices due to his battered body, leading to Iverson's famous rant against the importance of practice. This player-coach relationship eventually worked, with Iverson ultimately speaking reverently of Brown, and vice versa. Iverson's commitment to practice may have wavered, but his competitive fervor when the lights came on was impossible to ignore.

"I love Allen," Brown said. "Everybody documents our issues, but think of the body of work when he played for me. Pretty incredible."

Iverson also clashed with Stern, especially over the NBA dress code instituted in 2005 that banned clothes such as baggy t-shirts, throwback jerseys and boots, which were associated with hip-hop culture. And Iverson typified that.

"Just because you put a guy in a tuxedo, it doesn't mean he's a good guy. It sends a bad message to kids," Iverson said. "It's just not right. It's something I'll fight for."

In the end, fight was what Iverson was all about. Critics knocked Iverson, claiming he was a selfish player incapable of making those around him better. However, in that remarkable 2000–01 season, he took a team that included the unremarkable Theo Ratliff as its second-leading scorer to the NBA Finals. Despite failed stints in Denver and Detroit, his 2000–01 season, as much as anything, is a testament to Iverson's immense talent and tenacity.

CAREER HIGHLIGHTS

- Listed at 6 feet tall, he is the shortest player in NBA history to be named MVP
- Has led the NBA in scoring average in a season four times
- Two-time NBA All-Star Game MVP
- Nicknames include "The Answer" and "AI"
- Scored a career high 60 points on February 12, 2005 against the Orlando Magic
- He averaged at least 26 points per game 10 seasons in a row (1998–99 to 2007–08)

G	FG%	FT%	ORB	DRB	TRB	AST	STL	BLK	PTS
871	.456	.803			4.9	2.5			17.7

SAM JONES

If your team is the greatest dynasty in the history of North American professional sports, it goes without saying you have star power.

And the 1960s-era Boston Celtics, winners of 11 NBA titles in 13 years, had their stars. Bill Russell, the anchor for all 11 of those wins, was obviously the biggest, but there was also Bob Cousy, Bill Sharman and John Havlicek, too. But even with all that talent, perhaps the untold story behind the Celtics' domination was the quality of their so-called secondary players.

Sam Jones won 10 NBA titles playing alongside his more famous teammates, the most of any NBA player not named Russell. But when he was inducted into the NBA Hall of Fame in 1984, the smooth, 6-foot-4 shooting guard seemed almost put out by his moment of professional glory, the culmination of 12 years spent being a vital cog in one of the NBA's most amazing machines.

"I know I was just a role player," Jones said. "Just as I know the whole Celtic team, and not me, should be in the Hall of Fame. There are 26 other Celtics who are not here who made it possible for me to be here."

Of course his star-powered teammates knew better. It's a team sport, and on the greatest team the NBA has ever seen, there was no such thing as a weak link.

"Sam probably never got quite the attention he deserved," Bob Cousy said. "That's one of the difficulties of playing with six or seven Hall of Famers. Somebody's going to get overlooked. The way I looked at it, Sam and Bill Sharman are probably most

responsible for me getting into the Hall of Fame, because whenever I'd throw them the ball, they'd put it in the damn hole."

Jones did it with a signature shot, knocking his rock-solid jumper in off the glass from nearly any angle or distance.

He made his mark in other ways, too, including a willingness to taunt and tease his close friend Wilt Chamberlain. Jones' specialty was — on occasions when the big center had been switched out to cover him — to keep his dribble alive, daring Chamberlain to creep further and further out on the floor. And then at the last possible second, when it seemed inevitable the 7-foot-1 Chamberlain would block Jones' shot, the crafty guard would let it go just that much higher and watch it sail past his rival's fingertips.

"Too late!" he would yell at Chamberlain as another jumper settled off the glass and through the net.

Growing up in segregated South Carolina, Jones didn't get a lot of exposure in high school and attended North Carolina Central University, a traditional black college in Division II. Celtics' general manager Red Auerbach learned of Jones' ability from a former player and selected him with the team's first-round pick in 1958 despite never seeing him play. After four years as a backup, Jones claimed the starting role from Sharman in 1961–62 and carved himself a place in NBA history for his ability to hit big shots at big moments.

In Game 7 of the 1961–62 Eastern Finals against Chamberlain and the Philadelphia Warriors, Jones hit a shot

- Drafted: 8th overall by the San Diego Rockets in 1957
- Boston Celtics: 1957–69
- College: North Carolina Central University

with two seconds left to give Boston a 109–107 win. In the 1962–63 Eastern Finals, he scored 47 in a Game 7 win over Cincinnati. In 1964–65, he averaged 28.6 points in the playoffs, including a 37-point effort in Game 4 of the Finals against the Lakers.

But his best moment might have been in his final year in a Celtics uniform. For the 1968–69 season, Jones, at 35, was the oldest player in the league, and the Celtics were seen as a team on the decline. But matched up against Chamberlain, now playing for the Los Angeles Lakers, Jones hit an off-balance fadeaway at the buzzer to give Boston a key Game 4 win.

"If we lost [that] game, we'd go to Los Angeles down 3 games to 1," Jones said. "We called a timeout, and Russell, then the coach, called a play for me. Later, he told me he almost didn't call it because it was my last season, and he said that people always remember the one you missed. But I made it, and I knew it was good from the time it left my hand."

Some role player. When Jones retired, he had numerous Celtics records: total points in a season (2,070 in 1964–65); total points in a regular-season game (51 at Detroit on October 29, 1965); total points in a playoff game (51 at New York on March 28, 1967) and career playoff points (2,909 in 154 games). He trailed only Cousy in career points in the regular season (16,955). He was named to both the NBA's 25th and 50th Anniversary Teams.

Most important? He was a guy his teammates could count on in the clutch.

CAREER HIGHLIGHTS

- Averaged a career high 25.9 PPG in 1964–65

- Nicknamed "The Shooter"

- A five-time NBA All-Star

- Is a 10-time NBA Champion, second-most to Bill Russell who is an 11-time NBA Champion

The affable Jones at Boston Garden in 1967–68. Jones averaged 20.5 points in the playoffs, helping Boston claim the championship over the L.A. Lakers.

G	FG%	FT%	ORB	DRB	TRB	AST	STL	BLK	PTS
1187	.403	.782	1.4	5.2	6.6	9.2	2.0	0.3	13.6

GUARD

JASON **KIDD**

The veteran Kidd works against the rookie Brandon Jennings of the Milwaukee Bucks in 2010 in a 108–107 Dallas victory. Kidd led all players with 12 assists, and he added 11 points for the double-double.

As spectacular a player as Jason Kidd is, the better word for him is unique.

In the history of the sport, there have been virtually no point guards, especially at Kidd's 6-foot-4 size, who could control any given game on so many fronts. He's established himself as one of the game's best passers, rebounders and defenders for his position. Scoring is secondary for him, but few players are more dangerous in transition, and he has never feared taking the big shot.

At more than 200 pounds, he plays with the speed and toughness of an NFL free safety. He isn't the greatest leaper or best shooter — for most of his career he has struggled to shoot better than 40 percent from the floor.

But Kidd has excelled by perfecting some skills that aren't easily measured.

"He's one of my favorite players," former Celtic star and current Boston general manager, Danny Ainge, said. "You look at Jason's fundamentals, they're not great. You look at his shooting, it's not great. The guy just finds ways to win, defensively and offensively."

How does anybody with Kidd's relatively ordinary physical gifts become an elite player, to the tune of a Rookie of the Year award, five All-NBA First Team berths, four All-Defensive First Team selections and five-time Assists champion? By playing out of his depth as a child and following that up with boatloads of hard work. As a result Kidd is just one of two players — John Stockton being the other — to pass for more than

10,000 assists. He's sixth all-time in steals, too, and could conceivably finish second all-time on that list by the time he's done.

Growing up in Oakland — where he would play against fellow future-star point guard Gary Payton, among others — Kidd did not bother playing within his age group.

"When I was a little kid I used to play with guys twice my age, so, I was the last one picked," Kidd said. "So if I was picked I knew that I had to get the ball to the scorer if I wanted to stay on the court. So that was pretty much my job."

When Kidd started focusing on his age level, though, almost-immediate success followed. He led his high school, St. Joseph Notre Dame, to back-to-back California championships. He was the state's High School Player of the Year twice, and in 1992 he was named the Naismith High

School Player of the Year. Both *USA Today* and *PARADE* followed suit, calling him the best prep player in the country.

He went outside the box with his college choice, choosing to play at the University of California at Berkeley over such basketball heavyweight universities as Kansas and Kentucky. Kidd helped the school turn around its performance — following a 10–18 season the year before — with two straight trips to the NCAA Tournament.

Kidd declared for the NBA draft in 1994 and was selected second overall by Dallas. While Kidd fit in seamlessly with the professional game, team success did not follow. The Mavericks, despite a core of Kidd, Jim Jackson and Jamal Mashburn, were one of the worst franchises in sports and Kidd was shipped out to Phoenix after three seasons.

He excelled as a Sun, but despite five straight seasons in the playoffs, Phoenix dealt him to New Jersey in 2001 for a package that included fellow point guard Stephon Marbury.

As a Net, though, Kidd established himself as an NBA great. In 2001–02 Kidd led the Nets to a 26-win improvement in the regular season from 2000–01, and propelled New Jersey to its first of two straight trips to the NBA Finals. Although the Nets would lose both series — in 2002 to the Los Angeles Lakers, in 2003 to the San Antonio Spurs — Kidd's impact could not be doubted.

"If you look at our team my first year, the areas we were weak were rebounding and defense, and our team chemistry was not what you'd like to have," Nets' president Rod Thorn said. "We didn't play together. And those are the three strengths of Jason Kidd's game. He's as good a rebounding guard as you're going to find. Defensively, he's right there with anybody, and because he thinks 'pass first,' our team chemistry automatically got better."

Indeed, with the Nets, he brought all of that. He is one of just three players with at least 100 triple-doubles, evidence of his versatility. He routinely chased down defensive rebounds, got them on the run and sprinted past the defense, faster with the ball than most are without

it, constantly looking to set up easy baskets. Before he was dealt back to Dallas in 2008, Kidd had established franchise records for the Nets for three-pointers made, assists, steals and, of course, triple-doubles.

And he has been a significant piece of the United States national team, winning gold at the Olympics in 2000 and 2008, and having never lost a game against an international opponent while wearing his country's colors.

"He plays with passion, he plays with love, he's a winner," former coach and broadcaster Doug Collins said. "He's going to win games for you. He transforms a whole team."

G	FG%	FT%	ORB	DRB	TRB	AST	STL	BLK	PTS
658	.441	.820			4.2	5.4			24.2

44

GUARD

PETE MARAVICH

Pistol Pete dribbles near the net during a game in this undated photo. Despite his individual success, Maravich never played on a championship-winning team.

Pete Maravich was a classic case of a player being far ahead of his time. He was a do-it-all shooting guard in an era when point guards almost exclusively dominated the ball. He was a showboat of a player who dribbled between his legs and tossed no-look passes long before those things were in style. He was a proficient long-range shooter who only got to play with the three-point arc late in his career.

His peers did not always like him. But trailblazers are rarely universally adored.

"I'm just trying to push the game to its limits. We have so much to discover in basketball. Ten years from now, a lot of guys will be doing what I do," Maravich said during his career. "Every team will have a seven-foot guy on their roster. Basketball has to grow and change if we expect people to keep coming and paying good money." Over time, Maravich was proved right.

Born June 22, 1947, in Aliquippa, Pennsylvania, Maravich was a fixture in his local gym, and the flash he became famous for was the product of hours of practice to master the fundamentals of the game. He used drills taught to him by his father, Press, a former professional player and long-time college coach. Although Pete had long planned to attend the University of West Virginia, he eventually chose to play at Louisiana State. The reason was simple: The school recruited his father as head coach.

"I don't want to be hanged or shot, or die a natural death," Jim Corbett, the athletic director who brought the Maravichs to Baton Rouge, said. "I want to be trampled to death by the crowd trying to get in to see an LSU basketball game."

It was apparent what the presence of the younger Maravich — dubbed "Pistol Pete" for his funky shot that started from the side of his body — would mean for a team's box office. Maravich gave students and basketball fans alike a reason to flock to see the Tigers play.

Despite not being allowed to play for the varsity team in his freshman season — it was NCAA policy at the time — Maravich rewrote the collegiate basketball record books: He averaged a startling 44.2 points per game in his three varsity seasons. He managed to shoot 52 percent from the floor in his senior season, despite shooting more than 37 times per game. He became the all-time scoring leader in NCAA history in only three years.

However, Maravich's personal success never translated to tremendous team success, either in college or professionally. Drafted by the Atlanta Hawks with the third pick of the 1970 draft, he spent his first four years with the franchise. The Hawks made the playoffs in his first three years, but were easy post-season fodder.

While he put up huge numbers — averaging 26.1 points and a career-high 6.9 assists per game in his third season (1972–73) — he could not bring the team together. Veterans resented his million-dollar-plus contract, and his flashy style went against the conventional play at the time.

Maravich never felt it necessary to defend his game. "They don't pay you a million dollars for two-hand chest passes," he said.

Atlanta traded Maravich to the expansion New Orleans Jazz before the 1974–75 season, repatriating a local hero. He peaked as a professional with the Jazz, but sticking him with a burgeoning expansion team ensured he would never enjoy much team success as a professional.

Still, he put up some of the most spectacular stat lines the league has ever seen. In 1976–77 he averaged a league-best 31.1 points, logging almost 42 minutes per game. He also averaged 5.1 rebounds and 5.4 assists. In one game against the New York Knicks that year, Maravich scored 68 points, despite the presence of ace defender Walt Frazier.

That was the peak for Maravich. He injured his knee the following year and never quite regained his previous form. He was waived midway through the 1979–80 season — the Jazz had left New Orleans for Utah the season before — and was picked up by the Boston Celtics, coming off the bench during Larry Bird's rookie season. With his skills eroding, Maravich retired prior to the 1980–81 season, and his timing was off again, as he missed the Celtics championship that season.

As a result he was inducted into the Hall of Fame in 1987 having never tasted

- Drafted: 3rd overall by the Atlanta Hawks in 1970
- Atlanta Hawks: 1970–74
- New Orleans Jazz: 1974–79
- Utah Jazz: 1979–80
- Boston Celtics: 1979–80
- Jersey: #44; alternate: #7
- College: Louisiana State University

postseason glory. He died tragically a year later from a previously undiscovered congenital heart defect while playing pickup basketball.

His individual success meant that in 1996 Pete Maravich was named as one of the NBA's top 50 players of all time. And when the group of players got together to celebrate the NBA's 50th Anniversary, he was the only player named to the list who was not there.

The style and flair of generations of players who came after him remain proof he has not been forgotten.

G	FG%	FT%	ORB	DRB	TRB	AST	STL	BLK	PTS
1015	.489	.903	0.5	2.4	3.0	8.3	0.8	0.1	14.6

STEVE **NASH**

In an age where celebrites hone carefully-crafted public images that often have only a partial connection to their private personas, there is no mystery to Steve Nash.

If you want to know the man, just watch him on the floor.

"If you really understand the game, it's really easy to understand what he's like as a person," said Rowan Barrett, one of Nash's oldest friends and a teammate on the Canadian Olympic team. "I mean, he's constantly trying to give the ball away! He's running around, dribbling, cutting, slashing, tiring himself out just so he can go, 'here's the ball.' He makes it easy for you."

Scoring in bunches is a more proven route to basketball stardom, but Nash, like his seeing-eye passes, is all about taking the path less traveled. Born in South Africa and raised in Canada, Nash became the first Canadian in NBA history to win recognition as the NBA's Most Valuable Player, which he claimed after the 2004–05 season when he led the Phoenix Suns — just 29–53 the season before he arrived as a free agent from Dallas — to a league-best 62–20 mark.

The Nash-led Suns used a high-tempo, quick-shooting style to win in a league characterized for most of the previous decade by lane-clogging, off-the-ball wrestling matches.

The Suns became the darlings of the NBA and just to prove it wasn't a fluke,

- Drafted 15th overall by the Phoenix Suns in 1996
- Phoenix: 1996–98 and 2004–
- Dallas: 1998–2004
- College: University of Santa Clara

they kept it up the in 2005–06 with Nash again being named MVP, becoming just the ninth player to earn back-to-back awards and the first point guard to be recognized as such. For good measure he finished a close second to Dirk Nowitzki in the 2006–07 MVP race. Had he won he would have joined Bill Russell and Larry Bird as the only players to win three straight MVP awards.

Nash has led seven teams to 50-plus win seasons and twice sparked teams to 60-win seasons, but has yet to win an NBA title, twice being thwarted in the Western Conference Finals. But his approach has won him the respect of champions.

"I think, on the world stage, he's one of our great athletes in all sports ... I'm a big fan," said Celtics great Bill Russell. "The two MVPs he got, he deserved. Part of the reason that he's so good and so effective is that the guys like playing with him. He creates an atmosphere where they win games."

Nash's game is a throwback in ways his career averages of 14.6 points and 8.3 assists might not indicate. His league-leading 11.48 assists in 2004–05 were the most since John Stockton was in his prime a decade before, and the first of four seasons (through the 2009–10 season) that Nash has led the NBA in helpers.

And when he chooses to shoot, he rarely misses.

Only four players have completed a season making at least 90 percent of their free throw attempts, 50 percent of their shots from the field and 40 percent of their shots from three-point territory — Larry Bird, Reggie Miller and Mark Price, each having done it once. Nash has managed the 90–50–40 season four times.

"That's the part that separates him," Toronto Raptors guard Jarrett Jack said about trying to match up with Nash. "I don't know too many people, if they had their own team and were out here by themselves, could [shoot] like that."

The heights are even more remarkable given where he began. He was a soccer and hockey player growing up in Victoria, British Columbia, before taking up basketball in earnest in Grade 8. His only scholarship offer came from the lightly regarded University of Santa Clara, but he ran with the opportunity, lifting the Broncos to three NCAA tournament appearances in four seasons and becoming the 15th pick in the guard-rich 1996 draft. Success in the NBA was hardly

CAREER HIGHLIGHTS

- Was in the top-three in assists seven straight years, beginning in 2003–04

- Is the second-most accurate free-throw shooter in NBA history at 90.3 percent

- Ranks fifth in the NBA in career three-point shooting percentage at 43.1 percent

- Has played on the NBA's highest-scoring team nine times

- Led Canada to a 5–2 record at the 2000 Sydney Olympics

Steve Nash flies under the hoop and dishes the ball to a teammate in Game 4 of the 2010 Western Conference Quarterfinals.

immediate. Through his first four seasons (split between his draft club, Phoenix, and Dallas) he was playing part-time minutes and averaging seven points and four rebounds a game.

But with the emergence of Dallas teammate Dirk Nowitzki, and given the trust of then-Mavericks head coach Don Nelson, Nash flourished, unveiling his trademark water bug style to great effect.

As his notice grew — Nash made the All-Star Game seven of the next nine years beginning in 2002 — much was made of his seeing-eye passes to teammates for lay-ups and open jumpers.

It all seemed natural to Nash. "I'm unselfish. I like being part of a team and I like being a teammate, and it's not preconceived or contrived," he said. "For a lot of people who never played at this level, that's what they remember about this sport — being a teammate, playing together and sharing those things."

G	FG%	FT%	ORB	DRB	TRB	AST	STL	BLK	PTS
920	.473	.876	1.2	7.2	8.5	2.7	0.9	1.0	22.9

DIRK NOWITZKI

If Kevin Garnett paved the way for high-schoolers to flood the NBA, Dirk Nowitzki was the pioneer for international players.

When Nowitzki was selected ninth overall by the Milwaukee Bucks in 1998, no player from a European team had ever been drafted in the lottery. Because of Nowitzki's success, it has become commonplace: Pau Gasol and Vladimir Radmanovic (2001), Nikoloz Tskitishvili (2002), Darko Milicic and Mickael Pietrus (2003), Andris Biedrins (2004), Fran Vazquez and Yaroslav Korolev (2005) — all were given shots in the lottery because Nowitzki flourished.

The problem is, for every Gasol, there have been many more like Tskitishvilis, all picked in the name of not missing out on the next Nowitzki.

"He has definitely helped European basketball," former player and current television analyst Kenny Smith said in 2004. "But all these [general managers] go to Europe now and think they have to find that guy under a rock who can play like Dirk. It makes it look like they're doing their jobs. There is only one Dirk. If you start taking all these kids and expecting them to be the next Dirk Nowitzki, that is going to hurt the European kids, and it is going to hurt American basketball."

Only such a prodigious talent could inspire such a hunt. When the Toronto Raptors took 7-foot Italian

forward Andrea Bargnani with the first overall pick in the 2006 draft — the first European taken No. 1 — the Nowitzki comparisons were the justification. Fresh off leading the Dallas Mavericks to the NBA Finals, there was never a better time to invoke the German's name.

Nowitzki always figured to be a star, even if it took a while for North American general managers to figure that out. He was born on June 19, 1978, in Wurzburg, Germany. His mother was a professional basketball player, while his father was a top-flight handball player. That he was both tall and athletic wasn't a surprise.

However, what made Nowitzki so special, at least from an NBA perspective, was that he defied expectations for a player his size. Instead of being trained as a bruiser with post moves, his mentor, former German international player Holger Geschwindner, trained Nowitzki as a prolific jump shooter and ball handler. By 19, he was named his country's best player and bound for a bigger stage.

"The boy is a genius," Hall of Famer Charles Barkley said after playing against a teenaged Nowitzki in an exhibition game. "If he wants to enter the NBA, he can call me."

But still, NBA general managers were blind to his talent until the Nike Hoop Summit in San Antonio, when he scored 33 points and 14 rebounds, dominating future NBA players Rashard Lewis and Al Harrington.

"Anybody who had not heard about him before that definitely knew who he was after that," Seattle general manager Rick Sund would later say. "It was quite a show."

Dallas coach and general manager Don Nelson loved him, orchestrating a trade to get him one pick before Boston surely would have. He also dealt for Phoenix point guard Steve Nash that summer, and Nowitzki, the shy German, and Nash, the thoughtful Canadian, formed a friendship that along with Michael Finley made the Mavericks an elite team.

"We were both joining a new club, living in a new city, we were both single and outsiders: this creates a bond," Nash said. "Our friendship was something solid in a very volatile world."

"He would have also become a good friend if we had met at the supermarket," Nowitzki added.

Those Maverick teams were always held back by poor

- Drafted: 9th overall by the Milwaukee Bucks in 1998
- Dallas Mavericks: 1998–2010
- High School: Rontgen Gymnasium in Wurzburg, Germany

defense. Nash left for Phoenix in 2004, and won two straight MVP awards. Nowitzki, however, enjoyed greater success. In an epic series in 2006, Nowitzki led Dallas past Nash and the Suns in the Western Conference Finals. Nowitzki's 50-point performance in Game 5 was the turning point.

While Nowitzki's play would fall off in the NBA Finals against Miami, he rebounded the next season, becoming the first European to win the MVP award — though Dallas was upset in the playoffs by Golden State.

"It is an incredible feeling," Nowitzki said. "Who would have thought back then when I left Germany aged 19 or 20 that I would be sitting here one day and call myself the MVP of the best league in the world?"

The milestones have kept coming. Through 2010 he'd led the Mavericks to ten straight 50-win seasons and counting. He's the first European to score 20,000 career points. He's on a fast-track to the Hall of Fame.

And if the NBA didn't know what they were getting when Nowitzki was drafted as an unknown teenager, perhaps the most telling tribute to the ground-breaking German is the league's general managers have been trying to find the "next Dirk" ever since.

CAREER HIGHLIGHTS

- Won the NBA Three Point Shootout in 2006

- Is a four-time All-NBA First Team selection

- Has averaged at least 21 points per game for 10 consecutive seasons

- Has career free throw percentage of 87.6 percent, good for 14th all-time

- A nine-time NBA All-Star

Nowitzki battles for a rebound with Oklahoma City's Nick Collison on December 16, 2009. Nowitzki is often considered the best international player in the NBA.

CHRIS PAUL

It might not go down as a mistake on the level of the Portland Trail Blazers choosing Sam Bowie over Michael Jordan in the 1984 draft, but it was a franchise-altering blunder. In the early part of the 2000s, the Atlanta Hawks collected high draft picks by the bushel. As a result, the Hawks procured more than their share of young, talented players, but the only thing missing was a point guard.

In 2005, the Hawks were presented with the perfect chance to rectify that. They had the second pick in a draft that had two surefire stars at the position. Given a choice of selecting either Illinois' Deron Williams or Wake Forest's Chris Paul, they chose neither, taking North Carolina swingman Marvin Williams.

While Deron Williams would turn into an elite point guard in his own right, Paul is the player who has made that decision look comical. Just five years into his career, Paul has become the best point guard in the league. He has invoked comparisons with some of the all-time greats at the position — everyone from Isiah Thomas to John Stockton — and is among the new crop of NBA stars such as Dwight Howard and LeBron James, who are expected to shape the NBA for a decade or more.

In just his third season in 2007–08, he finished second in the league's MVP voting. He placed fifth the following season while earning All-NBA honors for the second straight season with the best yet to come from the still-improving star.

In that sense, the NBA is lucky to have him in New Orleans, a troubled franchise in the league, especially after Hurricane Katrina. Paul, with his GQ looks and camera-attracting smile, has been the perfect player to keep a troubled city engaged with its team.

Born on May 6, 1985, in Winston-Salem, North Carolina, Paul always seemed destined for greatness. Kept in line by his parents, who sent him and his brother to work at their grandfather's gas station, Paul's on-court skills were always tempered by his humility. Even as he averaged 30.8 points, 9.5 assists, 5.9 rebounds and 6.0 steals per game as a high school senior, he kept close to his family. After Paul's grandfather, Nathaniel Jones, was murdered during a robbery in his driveway, Paul scored 61 points in one game. It was a point for every year his grandfather — his best friend — lived.

Paul played his college ball locally at Wake Forest and led the school, often seen as an also-ran in its own state compared to North Carolina and Duke, to two consecutive NCAA tournaments. He raised the school's profile after it had struggled since Tim Duncan graduated in 1997.

While Paul served notice that he would be an elite player after that fateful draft — he was named the 2006 Rookie of the Year — it was not until he first made the playoffs, in his third season, that the world knew he would be capital-S Special.

In 12 games in the 2007–08 playoffs, Paul averaged 24.1 points and 11.3 assists per game, all while registering more steals than turnovers and shooting better than 50 percent from the field. The Hornets defeated Dallas in the first round, a series that saw Paul destroy Jason Kidd in their one-on-one matchup, but fell to San Antonio in seven games in the next round.

"Sitting there watching Chris really develop into the best point guard in this league, it's amazing to watch how he's really risen his game to another level," Hornets' coach Byron Scott said after Paul's 32-point, 17-assist performance in Game 2 of the series against Dallas. "But that's what great players do. He's definitely one of the best in this league right now."

A spot on the United States' "Redeem Team" at the 2008

- Drafted: 4th overall by the New Orleans Hornets in 2005
- New Orleans Hornets: 2005–
- College: Wake Forest University

Beijing Olympics validated that. Although Kidd started in front of Paul, it was Paul who played the majority of minutes in front of both Kidd and Williams.

"Chris Paul is a magician with the ball," Utah's Carlos Boozer said. "At practices with Team USA, D-Will, J-Kidd, Kobe — nobody could stop him."

Just four years into his career, Paul has been unable to lift the Hornets to the NBA stratosphere. Whether or not he will be able to do that will depend on the players he's surrounded with as the cash-strapped Hornets try to stay competitive and manage their budget. But one safe bet is that he will continue to make the Atlanta Hawks — and every other NBA franchise — wish they had him on the floor in their uniform.

CAREER HIGHLIGHTS

- He has an NBA record of recording at least one steal in 108 consecutive games

- Is also known for being an excellent 10-pin bowler

- Won an Olympic Gold Medal with the U.S. Men's Basketball Team in Beijing in 2008

- Averaged a career-high 11.6 assists per game in 2007–08. Only six players in NBA history have had a better single-season average

- A three-time NBA All-Star

Paul drives past Paul Millsap of the Utah Jazz in a game on January 4, 2010. Paul has led the league in steals three times and assists twice in his first five seasons.

G	FG%	FT%	ORB	DRB	TRB	AST	STL	BLK	PTS
1335	.466	.729	1.0	2.9	3.9	6.7	1.8	0.2	16.3

GARY **PAYTON**

The saying used to be that the only person who could ever hold Michael Jordan under 30 points a game was Dean Smith, his coach at the University of North Carolina and a man who favored a measured, equal opportunity offense.

It turns out there was one other: Gary Payton, the fiery point guard who carved out a Hall-of-Fame-worthy career with his willingness to get into the face of opponents and a defensive approach born on the rough streets of East Oakland, where he played for a club team coached by his father, who proudly drove around the neighborhood with a license plate that said "Mr. Mean."

In 1996 Payton's Seattle Sonics broke through after years of promise and found themselves in the NBA Finals where, if little else, they were able to prove to the world that the dynastic Chicago Bulls were more than a one-man team.

The Bulls, coming off their NBA record 72–10 regular season, were up 3–0 on a young Seattle club, but Payton, a wiry 6-foot-4, 180 pound point guard, known for his quick hands, quick feet and quick mouth (though not necessarily in that order) had been switched over to cover Jordan for most of the Game 3 and seemed to have had some success against the most feared scorer in NBA history.

"I can lock up anybody," Payton said when asked about guarding Jordan, who — predictably — picked up the gauntlet.

"I invite anybody to guard me," a miffed Jordan said when asked about Payton's challenge. "I'm not discriminating. Anybody

wants to guard me, guard me."

Huffed Jordan: "I can only stop myself."

Unbowed, Payton said: "That's fine with us. If he's the only one that can stop himself, we'll give him a good chance to stop himself."

And in a potentially series-clinching Game 4, Jordan either stopped himself, or Payton and his teammates helped him. Payton held Jordan to nine points in the second half, and only one shot over a crucial nine-minute stretch of the fourth quarter when the game was decided. In Game 5 it was more of the same, as Jordan was held to just 26 points (his Finals average in three previous visits was 36.2 points per game). And while the Bulls stopped the Sonics' comeback in its tracks in Game 6, the Bulls' star scored just 22 points on 5-of-19 shooting while committing five turnovers.

The Bulls won and Jordan was the Finals MVP, but his 27.3 points-per-game series average was by far the lowest of his career.

To Payton, it was just another couple of weeks' work for the multi-skilled guard who earned the nickname "The Glove" for his ability to cover his opponents like a mitt does a baseball, a habit he brought into the NBA as the No. 2 pick in the 1990 draft.

Another habit Payton brought to the NBA was his ability to talk and play at the same time. "My way is to talk to my opponent so he makes it a personal thing," Payton said. "He starts playing me one-on-one, and forgets about his team. Meanwhile, I'm still playing team ball and eating him up."

Bound for the Hall of Fame, Payton's path there will be paved with defense. The same year he helped the Sonics to the Finals, Payton was recognized as the NBA's Defensive Player of the Year, the only time a point guard has ever received the award. He was an NBA All-Star nine times and nine times was named to either the All-NBA First, Second or Third Team. But his defensive bona fides never wavered, earning First-Team All-NBA defensive recognition

- Drafted: 2nd overall by the Seattle SuperSonics in 1990
- Seattle SuperSonics: 1990–2003
- Milwaukee Bucks: 2003
- Los Angeles Lakers: 2003–04
- Boston Celtics: 2004–05
- Miami Heat: 2005–07
- Jersey: #20; alternate: #2
- College: Oregon State University

Payton drives to the basket against the San Antonio Spurs during a 1994 game. 1994 marked the first of Payton's nine First-Team All-NBA defensive team nominations.

nine straight seasons, beginning in 1994, with Jordan the only other player to earn as many First-Team selections.

Not that his offensive game was suspect. He retired with 21,813 points, good for 23rd all-time, while his 8,966 assists stand him seventh in NBA history. And his last great moment in the NBA came in his 15th season when he was a veteran role player for the Miami Heat: He stepped up and hit a game-winning shot in Game 3 of the NBA Finals, saving the Heat from falling 3–0 to the Dallas Mavericks and paving the way for a Miami comeback that earned Payton his only championship ring.

He's the only player in NBA history to have at least 20,000 points, 8,000 assists and

2,000 steals; but for all the numbers, it was his attitude that stood out. "Gary's not a stat guy," said his long-time Sonics' coach George Karl. "He's a winner. He makes teams play the right way and with the right toughness."

CAREER HIGHLIGHTS

- Nine-time NBA All-Star
- Won the NBA Defensive Player of the Year award in 1996
- Nine-time NBA All-Defensive First Team selection
- Is a two-time Olympic gold medalist, winning in 1996 and 2000 with the U.S. Men's Basketball team
- Is seventh all-time in NBA history in assists with 8,966
- Is third all-time in NBA history in steals with 2,445
- Averaged at least 20 points per game in a single season seven times in his career

G	FG%	FT%	ORB	DRB	TRB	AST	STL	BLK	PTS
1178	.473	.704	1.8	4.6	6.4	5.2	2.0	0.8	16.1

SCOTTIE **PIPPEN**

Scottie Pippen didn't care about statistics, but numbers do help capture the subtle aspects of his otherwise extraordinary talent.

Pippen, the Robin to Michael Jordan's Batman for six Chicago Bulls' championships in the 1990s, is one of just four players in National Basketball Association history to lead his team in points, rebounds, assists, steals and blocks in the same season. He did it in 1994–95, one of the two years he played with the Bulls as the featured attraction when Jordan retired to try his hand at baseball. The other three players? Legends all: Dave Cowens, Kevin Garnett and LeBron James.

The irony is that when Jordan was on the floor, Pippen's best work defied quantification. He could be the most important player on his team just on the basis of his exceptional defense, which earned him eight berths on the league's All-Defensive First Team. He directed the offense from the forward spot and gave Jordan the freedom to be Jordan.

"When we went into battle, I knew I had someone to watch my back," Jordan said. "I love him like a brother. He pushed me to be the best basketball player every day in practice. And I pushed him to be the best Scottie Pippen he could be."

Pippen ended up being exceptional, named one of the league's greatest 50 players of all time in 1996

- Drafted: 5th overall by the Seattle SuperSonics in 1987
- Chicago Bulls: 1987–98 and 2003–04
- Houston Rockets: 1998–99
- Portland Trail Blazers: 1999–2003
- College: University of Central Arkansas

when he was only 32. It was an unlikely rise for the native of Hamburg, Arkansas. A walk-on to the basketball team at the University of Central Arkansas, he could only afford to stay in school because of the stipend he was paid for being the team manager and his summer job as a welder. Pippen's height was a big reason for the lack of attention around him. He entered college at just 6-foot-1, but rocketed up to 6-foot-8 by the end of his four years. A bit player as a freshman, he eventually averaged a double-double in points and rebounds by his senior year, shooting an astounding 59 percent from the floor.

All of that led to his fifth-overall selection in the 1987 draft. But it was not Chicago who took him. Seattle did, but dealt him quickly for the eighth pick, center Olden Polynice. In that sense, the Bulls can thank the Pacific Northwest for their six championships. Portland, of course, passed on Jordan in the 1984 draft.

While Pippen would not immediately take his spot alongside Jordan — he backed up nondescript Brad Sellers for most of his rookie year — by the time the playoffs rolled around that year the two started together. Three years later, the duo led the Bulls to their first championship.

If, however, Jordan's almost-two-year departure from the league was Pippen's chance to validate his own superstar standing, the results were decidedly mixed. On the one hand, Pippen enjoyed his most spectacular statistical seasons. In 1993–94 he ended up on the All-NBA First Team for the first time and finished third in MVP voting as the Bulls barely missed a step, winning 55 games with Pippen averaging a career-high 22 points, 8.7 rebounds, 5.6 assists and 2.9 steals.

However, he also experienced the lowlight of his career that season. Down 2–0 in the second round against New York and tied at the end of Game 3, head coach Phil Jackson drew up a play for Toni Kukoc instead of Pippen, who ultimately refused to get off the bench to serve as the inbound passer. Kukoc hit the shot, but it showed Pippen did not thrive as the lone star on a team.

"He is such a great teammate and maybe the pressure was getting to him and he just could not take it anymore," teammate Steve Kerr theorized.

But as Jordan returned, there would be little doubt of Pippen's importance. Together, they pulled off another three-peat, with Pippen averaging at least 19 points, 6 rebounds and 5 assists per game in each season.

And while neither of his stints in Houston or Portland resulted in a seventh championship, his impact on the game is undeniable.

"He directed a lot of what happened, and was one of the reasons why we were so successful over those six championships," Jackson said. "He had the big, bass voice so he could boom out and help guys on where to go. He was really a spokesperson on the floor. He could stunt, he could trap, he could play guards, he could play centers. He was a great presence to have out there."

He appeared in the playoffs every season of his 17-year career, and in 2010 he was inducted into the Hall of Fame, one year after his good pal Michael Jordan.

CAREER HIGHLIGHTS

- One of only four players to record at least 200 blocks and 100 steals in a single season

- Holds the NBA record for career steals by a forward with 2,307

- Led the Chicago Bulls in points, rebounds, assists, blocks and steals in 1994–95

- Is an eight-time NBA All-Defensive First Team selection

- Is a seven-time NBA All-Star

- Named the NBA All-Star Game MVP in 1994

Pippen attempts a shot against New York's Anthony Bonner during Game 1 of the 1994 Eastern Conference Semifinals. Pippen scored 24 points, but the Bulls fell to the Knicks, ultimately losing the series in seven games.

G	FG%	FT%	ORB	DRB	TRB	AST	STL	BLK	PTS
987	.518	.736	3.1	7.5	10.6	2.5	1.4	3.0	21.1

DAVID ROBINSON

In the instant gratification world of the NBA, it is amazing that the San Antonio Spurs and David Robinson had such a long, happy marriage. At the beginning of his career, Robinson tested the Spurs' patience, and as his career progressed, the Spurs tested Robinson's.

But they saw through their differences and built a relationship that can only be envied.

The Spurs took Robinson, a 7-foot-1 center with unnatural athleticism, first overall in the 1987 draft out of the United States Naval Academy. But Robinson made the Spurs wait for two years while he completed his mandatory tour of duty with the Navy, making it very difficult for management to start building a team around the prized pick.

It was an unusual arrangement because the Spurs were willing to wait and Robinson never gave a serious thought to trying to get out of his service commitment. But that was part of the package the Spurs were getting: An athlete who saw the big picture. As such winning never completely consumed Robinson as it did some of his peers, and that was one of the best things anybody could say about him. As teammate Steve Kerr pointed out, Robinson placed being a decent person above being a champion, extolling strength of character over everything else. "Winning a championship doesn't make you a better person," Kerr recalled Robinson saying. "It doesn't validate you."

It was a likely mantra for the league's gentle giant, given his upbringing. His father was also in the Navy, meaning Robinson grew up moving around often and with strict parents. Also, Robinson's early life was not defined by athletics. Due to a late growth spurt, Robinson did not play basketball competitively until his senior year in high school in which he shot up to 6-foot-7. Despite a tremendous season, he drew fleeting interest from major colleges. It did not matter much to Robinson, who was bound for the Naval Academy and a degree in mathematics.

With the Navy Midshipmen he excelled, becoming the nation's best college player. He continued to grow, but still defied expectations of a jock. He was an elite chess player and, despite his height, ended up with the highest gymnastic scores in his class.

And once he joined the NBA, he did not act as expected, either. Due to his two-year tour with the Navy, Robinson could have elected to not sign with the Spurs, who were struggling both on and off of the court. The Lakers made it known they would sign Robinson if he elected for free agency, but he showed his commitment to the team that had taken a chance on him.

"The term 'franchise player' is overused," Red McCombs, a former owner of the Spurs, told *Sports Illustrated* after Robinson was named one of two Sportsmen of the Year by the magazine in 2003. "But I'm not sure there would be a franchise here without David."

Entering the league at age 24, he proved worth the wait, averaging 24.3 points, 12 rebounds and 3.9 blocked shots a game. San Antonio improved by a then-record 35 wins in his rookie year (1989–90). In 1992, he was named the league's outstanding defensive player. In the final game of the 1993–94 season,

CAREER HIGHLIGHTS

- Scored 71 points on April 24, 1994, against the Los Angeles Clippers. Only five players have ever scored 70 or more points in a game

- One of only four players to have recorded a quadruple-double, which happened on February 17, 1994, against the Detroit Pistons. Robinson had 34 points, 10 rebounds, 10 assists and 10 blocks

- Averaged 4.5 blocks per game in 1991–92, which is the seventh highest NBA single-season block average

- Averaged at least 23 points, 10 rebounds and 3 blocks per game in his first seven seasons

- Drafted: 1st overall by the San Antonio Spurs in 1987
- San Antonio Spurs: 1989–2003
- College: United States Naval Academy

Robinson attempts a basket against former teammate Dennis Rodman during a 1995 game in Chicago. Robinson scored 30 points, but the Bulls defeated the Spurs 106–87.

Robinson scored 71 points to win the scoring title that year, averaging a career-high 29.8 points a game. In 1995, he was named the league's Most Valuable Player.

For a big man, Robinson moved exceptionally well. He could block shots, run the floor, hit jumpers, and yes, he had some post moves, too.

"No center in the history of the game," Spurs coach Gregg Popovich said, "did the athletic things that David did in his prime." In his third season, Robinson became the third player in NBA history to finish in the top-10 in five categories and the first to finish in the top five in rebounding, blocks and steals in a single season. In 1993–94, he had 34 points, 10 rebounds, 10 assists and 10 blocked shots in a win over Detroit, recording the fourth quadruple-double in league history.

Time after time, though, Robinson's teams failed in the playoffs, most notably during the 1994–95 season when he was bested by fellow center Hakeem Olajuwon and the Houston Rockets in the Western Conference Finals.

Indeed, Robinson would not taste a championship until 1999. It came about after injuries sidelined the otherwise durable Robinson for all but six games in 1996–97 and the Spurs fell to 20–62. As a result, however, San Antonio gained the first overall pick in the 1997 draft, which it used to select Tim Duncan, Robinson's successor as the Spurs' franchise player.

Together, the pair won championships in 1999 and 2003. Quite quickly, Robinson knew that emphasizing Duncan in the offense was the best thing for the team.

"When I came in, David was the Man and I was just trying to learn the game, develop under his wing," Duncan said. "And when it was time for me to do more, David understood it without a word being spoken."

For a man known for his proclivity to give — the winners of the league's Community Assist Award are given the David Robinson Plaque — a final act of selfless consideration on the court was a fitting way to go out.

G	FG%	FT%	ORB	DRB	TRB	AST	STL	BLK	PTS
650	.476				12.9	1.8			18.7

WILLIS **REED**

Reed boxes out Dave Cowens of the Boston Celtics during a 1973 game. Reed and the Knicks won the championship in 1970 and again in 1973.

Some greats are remembered for a career of achievement. Willis Reed is remembered for a moment of courage.

Reed, the bruising New York Knicks' center spanning the 60s and 70s, famously jogged onto the court just minutes before Game 7 of the 1970 NBA Finals started, despite a torn muscle in his thigh. His presence ignited the crowd and inspired his team.

"[Reed] literally had to have a shot, a horse shot, three or four of them in his thigh to come back out and play," said his then Knick teammate Phil Jackson.

As a burly center, Reed was already known for his toughness. That game, however, made him a legend.

"I'll play if I have to crawl," Reed told team doctors before the game.

It's a moment so iconic that it's become the measure for brave turns in sports ever since. So, when Boston Celtics' star Paul Pierce improbably returned from a knee injury in Game 1 of the 2008 NBA Finals after writhing in pain just moments earlier, nobody needed to search for a reference point: This was Pierce's Willis Reed moment — as much a statement about the toughness of Paul Pierce as it was about the inspiration of Reed.

More than any of the 50 greatest players of all time, Reed's career was likely defined by one game, one moment. But take away that game and Reed still would have been an unquestioned Hall of Famer.

Reed was born on June 25, 1942, in

Hico, Louisiana, a place so small that Reed once joked, "They don't even have a population." He attended Grambling State University, a historically black university more famous for its football program than its basketball team. Still, the small stage did not prevent Reed from making a name for himself.

His numbers simply could not be ignored. He averaged 18.7 points and 15.2 rebounds per game in his university career, products of his 6-foot-10, 240-pound frame and his tenacity in the paint. In the 1963–64 season, his senior year, he averaged an outrageous 26.6 points and 21.3 rebounds per game. Grambling played in the NAIA, a less-competitive organization than the NCAA, but Willis' numbers were eye-popping whatever the competition.

It was enough to catch the attention of the Knicks, the team with which he would spend his entire career. New York took him with the 10th pick in the 1964 draft, just as the team was in the midst of a bad spell. As Reed ascended, so did the Knicks.

Reed averaged a points-rebounds double-double in each of his first seven seasons in the league. He averaged a career-best 14.7 rebounds in his rookie season, winning Rookie of the Year honors. By his third season, the Knicks were in the playoffs, with Reed averaging 20.9 points and 14.6 rebounds per game.

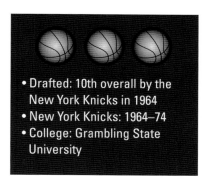

- Drafted: 10th overall by the New York Knicks in 1964
- New York Knicks: 1964–74
- College: Grambling State University

But the 1969–70 season, Reed's sixth in the league, cemented his status as an all-time great. In 1968–69, New York acquired Dave DeBusschere, allowing Reed to slide back to his natural center position from power forward. While they could not get past the Eastern Division Finals that season, the unit gelled perfectly the next year.

The team cruised to a 60–22 record, with Reed averaging 21.7 points and 13.9 rebounds per game. With coach Red Holzman at the helm, the Knicks finally made it through the Eastern Division playoffs and beat the Los Angeles Lakers in seven games to win the Finals. Reed accomplished a rare feat that season: He was named the most valuable player of the All-Star Game, regular season and playoffs.

And, oh yes, there was that game. Reed fell in Game 5, injuring his thigh and missed Game 6 because of it, and the Lakers won. With Game 7 back at Madison Square Garden, the crowd was palpably nervous.

"He's better on one leg than anybody else we have," DeBusschere said.

Indicating a flair for the dramatic, Reed let his teammates go on the court without him for warm-ups. He came on the court with just minutes to spare. He scored four points, New York's first two baskets of the game, and did not score again. But his defense was key in negating Wilt Chamberlain, and the Knicks won easily.

"He can barely walk and we asked him to run," teammate Cazzie Russell said.

And because he was determined to try, he will always be the reference point for gritty, improbable, comeback performances.

G	FG%	FT%	ORB	DRB	TRB	AST	STL	BLK	PTS
711	.426	.883			3.9	3.0			17.8

BILL SHARMAN

The NBA is full of athletes who have compiled amazing statistics, been part of great teams and authored great moments on the floor.

That will never change.

But it's safe to say no one has had a career quite like Bill Sharman's, and no one ever will.

Sharman was drafted out of the University of Southern California by the Washington Capitols in 1950. The Boston Celtics acquired the gifted shooting guard after the Washington franchise folded in the middle of the 1950–51 season. Sharman quickly became a fixture in the Boston backcourt alongside Bob Cousy and he starred on the Celtics' first four championship teams; teams that set the foundation for the dynasty that won 11 titles in 13 years between 1957 and 1969.

In 1952–53 he shot .436 from the floor to lead all guards in a season when the league's field-goal percentage was .370. Further proof of his ability to make shots came at the free throw line, where Sharman converted 88.3 percent for his career — an NBA record upon his retirement — and led the league for seven seasons.

But Sharman's star really took off when the NBA introduced the 24-second shot clock in 1954–55 and perimeter shooting became increasingly important. Having earned a spot on the All-Star Team in 1953 and Second-Team All-NBA honors, Sharman established himself as the best shooting guard in the game in the mid-1950s, earning four straight All-NBA First-Team honors beginning in 1955.

He led the Celtics in scoring with 21.1 points per game in 1956–57 en route to Boston's first NBA title.

He played with a fire that set a tone for Boston and made him a favorite at the Boston Garden, earning him the nickname "Battling Bill" from Celtics' announcer Johnny Most.

Los Angeles Lakers' star Jerry West was once asked to name his "all-thug" team — a list of NBA tough guys — and Sharman was the first one on it.

"It was my rookie year ... I hit seven straight jumpers over Bill," West said. "On the last one, he took a swing at me ... Bill was tough. I'll tell you this: you did not drive by him. He got into more fights than Mike Tyson. You respected him as a player."

But his basketball feats only tell part of the story. He served in the navy in World War II and was a minor-league call-up to the Brooklyn Dodgers in 1951. In fact, he was seated in the dugout when Bobby Thomson hit "the shot heard 'round the world" that won the National League pennant for the New York Giants in 1951.

When he retired from the Celtics in 1961, making way for the emerging Sam Jones, Sharman took a coaching job in the American Basketball League, a short-lived rival to the NBA started by Abe Saperstein, founder of the Harlem Globetrotters. Sharman led the Cleveland Pipers to the title in 1962, but more significantly it was Sharman whom Saperstein consulted when he introduced the three-point line for the new league. The former Celtics marksman convinced Saperstein that the proper distance should be about the dimensions still in place today — 22 feet in the corners to 23.75 feet behind the top of the key — and not the 25 feet Saperstein had proposed.

Sharman's coaching career peaked in 1971–72 when he led the Los Angeles Lakers to a then-NBA record 69–13 season. The season included a 33-game winning streak, the longest of any of the four major North American professional sports. He is also known for inventing the game-day shootaround, now standard in the NBA, where teams come to

- Drafted: In the 2nd round by the Washington Capitols in 1950
- Washington Capitols: 1950–51
- Boston Celtics: 1951–61
- Jersey: #21; alternates: #10
- College: University of Southern California

the arena early on the day of a game for a light workout. Later as an executive, he helped the Lakers win more titles, becoming the only person in NBA history to record championships (15 in all) as a player, coach, general manager and team president.

In 1976 he was inducted into the Hall of Fame as a player, and in 2004 he was honored as a coach, one of only three people to be honored twice, along with John Wooden and Lenny Wilkens.

But he's perhaps the only man in NBA history to be recognized in the Smithsonian, The Library of Congress and the National Civil Rights Museum. As a rookie in Washington, he drove Earl Lloyd, the first African American to ever play in the NBA, to and from practice. It was a gesture Lloyd never forgot, and he recognized it in his essay "Handprints" that was included in the collections of those most revered American institutions.

"In my life, there were many good people who restored my faith in human nature. Bill Sharman is one I will never forget," Lloyd wrote. "In my early days with the Capitols, we would practice at American University and Bill would drive me there and home every night. Do you understand? If he hadn't, no one would have criticized him … No one succeeds alone."

CAREER HIGHLIGHTS

- Led the NBA in free throw percentage seven times including a then-NBA record 93.2% in 1957–58

- He played in the Brooklyn Dodgers minor league system for five years in the early 1950s while playing professional basketball in the winters for the Boston Celtics

- One of only three people to be inducted into the Basketball Hall of Fame as both a player and a coach, John Wooden and Lenny Wilkens being the other two

- Was an eight-time NBA All-Star and the NBA All-Star Game MVP in 1955

Bill Sharman dribbles the ball in his Celtics uniform in this undated photo.

G	FG%	FT%	ORB	DRB	TRB	AST	STL	BLK	PTS
1504	.515	.826	0.6	2.1	2.7	10.5	2.2	0.2	13.1

JOHN **STOCKTON**

John Stockton was in his 11th season in the NBA when he broke Magic Johnson's record for career assists, and it says everything about the way Stockton played the game that Johnson was pleased for him.

"Nobody distributes the ball and reads his team like John Stockton," Johnson said when the longtime guard of the Utah Jazz made his 9,922nd helper. "No one knows how to get everyone involved like John."

But it was the second half of Johnson's compliment that really captured Stockton's star quality: "But what sets him apart is his toughness. He gets knocked down and gets right up."

Stockton didn't look particularly tough. In fact he looked more like a professional golfer than an NBA star. But at 6-foot-1 and 180 pounds on a good day, he was a bundle of wiry muscle with unlimited nerve.

To perfect the pick-and-roll, sometimes you are going to have to set picks on bigger players. And in the NBA, those bigger players are a lot bigger.

"It's unfortunate we couldn't keep statistics on screens," Stockton's longtime Utah Jazz coach Jerry Sloan said. "That's one of the most important things he does for a team and that tells you a little bit about who he is and what he's about — to try to make somebody else better. He wasn't screening midgets. The rules probably changed because of the way he set screens on big guys."

Yes, he held, grabbed and clutched opponents to free his teammates from coverage (often Karl Malone) but Stockton was frequently over-matched by sixty or more pounds. And not everyone liked having the little point guard screen them, as he would lean in (often with his elbows high) and block their path allowing the man they were covering to score. But no matter who he screened Stockton never backed up, and that's as much a reason for his greatness as his huge hands and uncanny vision.

Stockton played university ball at Gonzaga in his hometown of Spokane, Washington. Almost 15 years after Stockton left school, Gonzaga developed a reputation as an underdog in the NCAA tournament. In Stockton's tenure they were a national non-factor. But his senior-year averages of 20.9 points and 7.2 assists per game put him into the national spotlight, paving the way for his selection, 16th overall, in 1984 draft — the same year fellow Hall of Famers Hakeem Olajuwon, Michael Jordan and Charles Barkley were selected.

A year later, the Jazz took Karl Malone with the 13th overall selection. With that pick, the Jazz set a foundation that remained in Salt Lake City for 18 seasons. Stockton would never be a member of the Jazz again without Malone as a teammate; the same can be said for Malone, who played the final year of his career, the one after Stockton retired, with the Los Angeles Lakers.

"He's a great, great friend of mine," said Stockton. "And I'm thankful we're part of each other's family."

Stockton and Malone became inseparable on the court, and one was rarely mentioned in the media without the other. Fittingly, the two won co-MVP honors at the 1993 All-Star Game in Utah.

CAREER HIGHLIGHTS

- Shares the single-game playoff assists record (24) with Magic Johnson
- Played in every game in 17 of his 19 seasons
- Averaged 3.2 steals per game in 1988–89, which is the sixth highest average for steals in an NBA season
- Averaged an NBA record 14.5 assists per game in 1989–90
- He is one of only three players to record at least 1,000 assists in a season, which he achieved seven times
- 10-time NBA All-Star

Stockton goes for a layup against Chicago's Scottie Pippen during Game 4 of the 1998 Finals. Despite making the Finals twice, Stockton and the Jazz never won a championship.

However, in a sense, they also became the poster boys for not being able to win the championship. Both players were surefire first-ballot Hall of Famers, but the pairing could never propel Utah to an NBA title, losing in both the 1997 and 1998 Finals to Michael Jordan's Chicago Bulls.

But it was Stockton who managed to get Utah to its first finals in 1997. In a 25-point outing in Game 6 against Houston in the Western Conference Finals, Stockton hit a three-pointer over Barkley at the buzzer for the win. He was mobbed as he unleashed a rare on-court smile.

Some of Stockton's records look close to unreachable. His 15,806 assists are a little less than 5,000 ahead of second-place Jason Kidd, who, while still active, is nearing the end of his career. Stockton is one of just three players to record at least 1,000 assists in a year. Kevin Porter and Isiah Thomas each managed the feat once; Stockton did it seven times. His 3,265 steals, meanwhile, are 751 more than runner-up Michael Jordan.

Perhaps as impressive as those feats is that in 19 seasons Stockton missed just 22 games in total, 18 of which came in the same season.

In a league with a lot of swagger, Stockton's no-frills style gave him a career of unmatched substance.

"I hope and I pray people realize a couple of things," Malone said after Stockton's retirement. "There absolutely, positively, will never ever be another John Stockton — ever."

- Drafted: 16th overall by the Utah Jazz in 1984
- Utah Jazz: 1984–2003
- College: Gonzaga University

ISIAH THOMAS

As scars go, it's a good one — a thick, moon-shaped arc above his left eye. And as with nearly everything involving Isiah Thomas, there's a story behind the story.

The former Detroit Pistons great got it thanks to the generous elbow of Karl Malone. That Thomas got hit while driving into Malone, a 6-foot-9, 260-pound slab of muscle was typical — you don't become great in the NBA at Thomas' size (6-foot-1, 180 pounds) by playing scared.

Blood stained the hardwood and Thomas was hustled off to a nearby hospital for treatment, including 40 stitches to close the gaping wound. Malone was ejected, suspended and fined. Thomas, of course, returned to play the fourth quarter.

Thomas rose to fame on a Pistons team known around the league as the "Bad Boys" whose take-no-prisoners approach to basketball earned them consecutive NBA championships in 1989 and 1990, with their flashy, baby-faced point guard setting the tone for the team of bruisers.

"As tough as they come," Pistons' coach Chuck Daly said of Thomas.

Wherever Thomas went, he circled the wagons, determined his loyalties and took on all comers, making his share of enemies along the way. The incident in Utah was typical.

Malone always claimed the elbow was inadvertent, but the back story said otherwise. The last time the two teams played, Thomas had made a point of taking on Jazz great John Stockton, miffed that he had been chosen to the 1992 Olympic team — the Dream Team

— instead of him. Determined to settle a perceived slight, Thomas enjoyed a 40-point night at Stockton's expense.

The back story doesn't end there. With Thomas it rarely does.

Why was Thomas left off the Dream Team? The snub, the story goes, stems from his personal rivalry with Michael Jordan that developed after the 1985 All-Star Game, when (it's alleged) Thomas helped orchestrate a freeze-out of Jordan on the basis of him being an upstart rookie. Thomas always denied the accusation, but by the time the Barcelona Olympics rolled around, Jordan was the biggest star in the sport and watchers were quick to conclude that it was his influence that kept Thomas off the team. "Isiah should have been on that team," Daly said later. "Why wasn't he? That's a book; we don't have time to talk about that."

Olympic medal or not, Thomas' basketball legacy will always be secure. He was the kid from the wrong side of town who made good. The youngest of Mary Thomas' nine children, he grew up a basketball prodigy in one of the toughest neighborhoods in Chicago, the lure of the game stronger than the lure of the streets. "The environment was one where you didn't really have much to base your opportunities on, and that creates a desire to explore them," said Demetrius Brown, a childhood friend and basketball rival. "Sports gave you a chance to travel around and see that there were courts with nets on the rims, gyms with air-conditioning. It gave us a chance to see that there were opportunities."

Thomas joined the Pistons as the second player taken in the 1981 draft, fresh out of Indiana University where he had helped Bobby Knight win the NCAA championship in his sophomore season. Originally, he wasn't that thrilled about joining a 21–61 team. "My job is to get the ball to somebody who can score," he said. "In Detroit, who would I pass to?"

He found his way. In his NBA debut Thomas counted 31 points, 11 assists and three rebounds in a 118–113 victory over Milwaukee before 9,182 at the Pontiac Silverdome. Thomas had the Pistons in the playoffs by the 1983–84 season and among the NBA's very best teams by his sixth season. Along the way he accumulated his share of individual honors: he was named an All-Star 12 straights seasons; he was an All-NBA selection from 1983 to 1987; and in 1984–85, set an NBA record by averaging 13.5 assists a game, still the second highest per-game average in NBA history.

But perhaps Thomas' most important accomplishment was his realization that he needed help to win the ultimate prize.

"I was scoring all sorts of points, I was getting all sorts of assists. People said I was a great basketball player," said Thomas. "[But] Looking good was no longer satisfying to me."

The Pistons' championship teams reflected his approach. They were tough and played together. Offensively, no player averaged more than 18.4 points over those two seasons, yet six players averaged at least 13.5 points a game. The Pistons were the best defensive team in the game and they followed their leader.

"It's funny, because I really don't know what people around the country think of us," says Thomas. "And the reason is that five years ago we sat down, 12 guys, and said, 'Let's get out of this with a championship.' Ever since, we've more or less been in a cave."

He emerged battered and bloody, but a champion.

CAREER HIGHLIGHTS

- In 2000, he was elected into the Basketball Hall of Fame in his first year of eligibility
- Passed for a career-high 25 assists February 13, 1985 against the Dallas Mavericks
- Was the executive vice-president and part owner of the expansion Toronto Raptors franchise from 1994–98
- Was the head coach for the Indiana Pacers from 2000–03 and the New York Knicks from 2006–08
- Sixth all-time in career assists with 9,061
- Was a 12-time NBA All-Star
- Was a two-time NBA All-Star Game MVP

- Drafted: 2nd overall by the Detroit Pistons in 1981
- Detroit Pistons: 1981–94
- College: Indiana University

Thomas attempts a basket against the Boston Celtics during a 1992 game.

G	FG%	FT%	ORB	DRB	TRB	AST	STL	BLK	PTS
471	.482	.770	1.3	3.6	4.9	6.6	1.8	1.0	25.4

DWYANE **WADE**

The NBA and the number three have an affinity for one another. Over time, good things in the league have tended to come in groups of three. The San Antonio Spurs of the 2000s were built on a nucleus of Tim Duncan, Manu Ginobili and Tony Parker. The Chicago Bulls, who won three straight titles from 1996–98, were defined by Michael Jordan, Scottie Pippen and Dennis Rodman. The Showtime-era Lakers were all about Magic Johnson, Kareem Abdul-Jabbar and James Worthy.

In that fine tradition came the 2003 draft, one with unparalleled hype surrounding it because of the presence of three players: high school star LeBron James, European star Darko Milicic and college star Carmelo Anthony. But of all the stars taken in that deep draft, it is appropriate that the guy who wears No. 3 — Dwyane Wade — was the first to lead his team to a championship. Quite naturally, he did that in his third season in the league.

"You can have LeBron James. You can have Kobe Bryant," Washington Post columnist Michael Wilbon wrote after Wade's 42-point, 13-rebound performance on an injured knee in Game 3 of that Finals series against the Dallas Mavericks. "You can have any pick on the playground ... anybody. Just let me have Dwyane Wade."

Getting selected fifth overall in a thoroughly deep draft is certainly no slap in the face — he went behind the so-called big three in 2003, along with Chris Bosh, an NBA All-Star who was chosen fourth — but revisionist history would have him, along with James, in the conversation for that first pick. But that

meshes well with the personal history of Wade, a Chicago kid who grew up idolizing Michael Jordan and who, like his hero, was not a basketball prodigy.

Wade was largely a non-factor for his first two years at Harold L. Richards High School, thanks to being relatively height-challenged. A four-inch spurt before his junior year changed that, but he was still not populating the world of all-star games for high school stars. Due to academic problems, only three schools scouted the 6-foot-4 combo guard, and they were hardly basketball powers. He chose Marquette over Illinois State and DePaul because North Carolina, Duke, UCLA and other big-name schools ignored him.

It was fitting, then, that his triple-double in the 2003 NCAA tournament — only the third in tournament history — came over Kentucky, one of those schools that overlooked him. It was that game that put him in the national spotlight and in the thick of the draft conversation.

And that is where his underdog story ended. Wade so impressed in his rookie season that Heat general manager Pat Riley refused to part with him when three-time champion Shaquille O'Neal became available on the trade market. Instead, Riley gave the Lakers a package of three players, Lamar Odom, Brian Grant and Caron Butler. In return, O'Neal gave Wade and the Heat their first title. More accurately, Wade gave O'Neal his fourth.

Wade was the first player who made O'Neal accept the role of secondary threat. In Orlando, O'Neal never gave way to Anfernee Hardaway. Despite three championships with Kobe Bryant and the Lakers, there was a perpetual battle for alpha dog status. In Miami, O'Neal realized who was "the Man,"

CAREER HIGHLIGHTS

- Named *Sports Illustrated* Sportsman of the Year in 2006
- Won an Olympic Gold Medal with the U.S. Men's Basketball team in Beijing in 2008
- Led the NBA with 30.2 points per game in 2008–09
- Achieved a Miami Heat record by scoring 20 points or more in 21 consecutive games from January 30 to March 14, 2009
- Is the shortest player in NBA history to record at least 100 blocks in a single season, which he achieved in 2008–09 with 106 blocks

leading to one of the all-time great Shaqisms: "The difference between those three is in *The Godfather* trilogy," O'Neal mused. "[Hardaway] is Alfredo, who's never ready for me to hand it over to him. [Bryant] is Sonny, who will do whatever it takes to be the Man. And [Wade] is Michael, who, if you watch the trilogy, the Godfather hands it over to Michael. So I have no problem handing it to Dwyane."

In 2004–05, Wade averaged 24.2 points, 6.8 assists and 5.2 rebounds to explode to stardom, earning Second-Team All-NBA honors and Second-Team All-Defense recognition. He's averaged at least 24 points and 6.7 assists each season since and earned a spot on the All-NBA First Team in 2008-09 by leading the NBA in scoring with 30.2 points a game and averaging 7.5 assists.

But it was in the 2006 Finals that Wade showed himself a player for the ages, able to dominate the highest stage. After being slowed by a knee injury and the flu in two losses to the Mavericks, Wade averaged 39.3 points over the last four games of that series, all Miami wins. In a relentless display of aggressiveness, Wade got to the free-throw line 83 times over those last four games. The Mavericks could not stop the player known as "Flash" for his graceful quickness.

"Tonight he really had it on his mind that he was going to be aggressive getting to the basket, especially in that fourth quarter," Dallas' Jason Terry said after Game 3. "He really, really took over."

ESPN analyst John Hollinger would later call it the greatest performance of any Finals' MVP in history. With a spectacular season in 2008–09 that lifted a talent-barren Heat team to the playoffs, and a gold medal in the 2008 Olympics, Wade showed that he still is in the same class as James.

And certainly, Anthony, Bosh, Milicic et al look up at No. 3.

- Drafted: 5th overall by the Miami Heat in 2003
- Miami Heat: 2003–
- College: Marquette University

Wade drives against Jared Jeffries of the Knicks in a game on December 25, 2009. Wade contributed 30 points to the Heat's 91–87 victory over New York.

G	FG%	FT%	ORB	DRB	TRB	AST	STL	BLK	PTS
1074	.461	.811	2.7	3.9	6.7	2.5	1.3	0.6	24.8

DOMINIQUE **WILKINS**

Dominique Wilkins was one of the most electric players in the history of basketball, with his fame coming primarily from his other-worldly leaping ability.

Twice Wilkins won the NBA's slam dunk contest and he finished second two other times. But his best work came in games where he could unfurl his powerful frame using his estimated 42-inch vertical jump to ferociously attack the rim and anything that was in the way.

But the 6-foot-7 small forward scored more than 26,000 points in his 15-year NBA career by the time he retired in 1999, a total exceeded by only eight others — and his points were not all dunks.

Wilkins' legend preceded him. He was nicknamed the Human Highlight Film before he ever arrived in the NBA as the No. 3 pick in the 1982 draft by the Utah Jazz (who traded his rights to the Atlanta Hawks), a raw bundle of energy out of Georgia. No story seemed too outlandish. "Somebody put a basketball on the top of the backboard, balanced it up there. He went up, got it and dunked it. That's what I heard," his teammate Johnny Davis once said. "Now what I've seen is him up there so high, I believe he did it. Nothing he does amazes me. The man is a phenomenal athlete."

It took him a while to became a polished professional player, but each year he listened to the critics who suggested he shot too much and badly, or had suspect defense, or was more interested in personal accolades than team success. Over time, he proved them all wrong.

In his second NBA season, he averaged 21.4 points a game but took only 11 three-point shots and missed them all. A decade later he averaged 29.1 points a game and shot 38 percent from deep, converting 120 of 316 attempts. For the first four seasons of his career, he had more turnovers than assists, but he reversed that ratio for the next eight seasons.

His teams made the playoffs seven of his first eight seasons, but in an era when the Boston Celtics ruled the Eastern Conference and the Chicago Bulls and Detroit Pistons were ascendant, the Hawks never advanced beyond the second round.

Because Wilkins was the focal point of the franchise, whatever problems arose were laid at his feet. Those who worked with him knew the truth: Whatever success the Hawks had was because of him, not in spite of him.

"It's easy to forget about it now, but there was a widespread media impression in those years that we never

- Drafted: 3rd overall by the Utah Jazz in 1982
- Atlanta Hawks: 1982–94
- Los Angeles Clippers: 1994
- Boston Celtics: 1994–95
- San Antonio Spurs: 1996–97
- Orlando Magic: 1998–99
- Jersey: #21; alternate: #12
- College: University of Georgia

CAREER HIGHLIGHTS

- Averaged at least 25 points per game in 10 straight seasons from 1984–85 to 1993–94

- Two-time NBA Slam Dunk Contest champion

- Nine-time NBA All-Star

- Is 10th all-time in NBA scoring history with 26,668 points

- Led the NBA in scoring in 1985–86, averaging 30.3 points per game

- Has been the Atlanta Hawks' Vice President of Basketball since 2004

Wilkins shoots a basket against Philadelphia in a match on November 17, 1993. Wilkins was the Hawks' all-time leading scorer when he was traded midway through the season.

could win because of Dominique," recalled Stan Kasten, the Hawks' general manager who swung the trade with the Utah Jazz to acquire Wilkins before his rookie season. "I always thought, and I said so at the time, that all those people were always wrong. Whatever we accomplished during the decade we won, we did because of him."

"He's probably the most underrated player of our generation," said fellow Hall of Famer Charles Barkley, who remains one of Wilkins' biggest fans. "He carried the Hawks. When you went to Atlanta, you had to bring it ... because of him."

He relished the opportunity to matchup against the best the NBA had to offer. In 1986, with the building abuzz about Chicago's Michael Jordan as the brightest new NBA

star, Wilkins set the record straight about who was the best player that night in Atlanta at least, dropping a career-high 57 points on the Bulls to Jordan's 41.

Wilkins' signature moment came in the 1988 playoffs against Larry Bird and the Celtics when the pair put on one of the best duels in league history. Bird and the Celtics came out on top, scoring 20 of his 34 points in the fourth quarter, but Wilkins' gutsy 47-point effort in defeat cemented his status as one of the league's greats in a way his nine All-Star Team berths and seven All-NBA nominations never quite did.

Wilkins was left off the 1992 Dream Team, and even more controversially, wasn't named to the NBA's 50th Anniversary Top-50 Team in 1996. But his body of work made him an obvious choice to be inducted into the Hall of Fame in 2006. Wilkins had long had had the respect of his peers. Now he had the recognition his legacy deserved.

"I don't think people ever really appreciated what I've done, especially during that era, one of the greatest eras in history, almost all of the greatest players in one era," he said. "To not play with another superstar and to carry a team to the playoffs eight out of 12 years is a pretty amazing feat. I don't think people really appreciated that, until now. It wasn't by accident."

JAMES **WORTHY**

History has doomed James Worthy's role on championship teams to second billing. He might have been the best player on the 1982 national champion North Carolina Tar Heels, but Michael Jordan's game-winning jumper is the enduring memory of that team. He was instrumental in bringing three championships to the Los Angeles Lakers in the 1980s, but Magic Johnson and Kareem Abdul-Jabbar headlined those teams.

But his value was never forgotten by his teammates or his coaches. Before Scottie Pippen defined the small forward position in the 1990s, Worthy blueprinted it.

"I don't think there has been or will be a better small forward than James, and I don't think people appreciated that," Worthy's longtime Lakers' coach Pat Riley said upon the forward's retirement. "He was always such a quiet guy. But when he was in his prime, I can guarantee you, there wasn't anybody who could touch him."

Perhaps Worthy will never earn the one-name endearment as Magic and Kareem have, but "Big Game James" earned Hall of Fame status for his career work, not to mention a spot on the league's top-50 list in 1996.

Born on February 27, 1961 in Gastonia, North Carolina, Worthy was a Carolina guy through and through. He played for Ashbrook High School in his hometown under Larry Rhodes, a coaching disciple of longtime Tar Heels' boss Dean Smith. So it came as no surprise when Worthy committed to attend North Carolina.

On his way to a remarkable freshman season at UNC in 1979–80, Worthy broke his ankle after just 14 games, placing his career in doubt.

"I wasn't sure I would be able to come back with the same type of intensity I'd always had," Worthy said. "I wasn't traveling with the team, I wasn't going to all the practices, and I wasn't a part of the day-to-day routine. It really made me wake up and expose myself to all kinds of people — not confine myself to just basketball."

But the injury proved to have no long-term effect when he returned to the floor. Just two seasons later, Worthy headlined a team that included Jordan and Sam Perkins. Averaging 15.6 points, 6.3 rebounds on 57 percent shooting, Worthy was named Co-Player of the Year, along with Virgina's Ralph Sampson. And it was Worthy — not Jordan — who was named the Final Four's Most Outstanding Player. In the championship game against Patrick Ewing and Georgetown, Worthy scored 28 points and secured the late-game steal that closed out the contest.

Worthy declared his intention to enter the NBA draft after his junior season and the Lakers finagled the first pick. He served as an apprentice to Jamaal Wilkes at first, but did not waste much time in taking his starting his spot.

And by the middle of the decade, when the Lakers and Boston Celtics routinely met in the NBA Finals, he was in the middle of things. However, that did not necessarily come naturally at first.

"The young guys, with the exception of Kareem, really didn't understand that rivalry that the Celtics and the Lakers had back when the Celtics were dominating the league in the 60s and early 70s," Worthy said. "It wasn't until Larry and Magic faced off again that the whole history was conjured up and put on our shoulders, and it was an overwhelming experience for me."

But it rarely looked as such for Worthy. He gained a reputation as one of the greatest clutch players, averaging 21.1 points per game in his playoff career, compared to 17.6 in the regular season. He was particularly brilliant in the 1988 playoffs, averaging 21.1 points, 5.8 rebounds and 4.4 assists per

- Drafted: 1st overall by the Los Angeles Lakers in 1982
- Los Angeles Lakers: 1982–94
- College: University of North Carolina

game. In Game 7 of the Finals against the Detroit Pistons, Worthy scored 36 points, 16 rebounds and 10 assists, his first-ever triple-double. He earned Finals MVP honors in the Lakers' championship win.

But even if that championship marked his career peak, it did not represent his favorite memory. That belonged to his first title, in 1985, when the Lakers finally vanquished the Celtics.

"It's not just because it was my first NBA championship, but that we did it in the [Boston] Garden," Worthy said. "That was the one I cherish the most. There was a lot of attention to the fact that they'd pretty much dominated us, even though that was back in the 60s."

Worthy revered history. And despite being overshadowed, he has his place in it, too.

CAREER HIGHLIGHTS

- Was named MVP of the NBA Finals in 1988

- Seven-time NBA All-Star

- Worthy played the part of a Klingon in an episode of *Star Trek: The Next Generation*

- Averaged at least 20 points per game in a season four times in his career

- Was on the All-Rookie First Team in 1982–83

Worthy looks to make a pass during a 1988 game against the Seattle SuperSonics. His trademark move was a one-handed dunk.

The New MATH

The thing with basketball is, as glorious as it is to watch, you can't always trust what you see. We know great players when we see them, and we know what good teams look like. But do we really understand what makes them great? Can we measure it and account for it?

We know Michael Jordan is spectacularly talented; we can see that, and certainly the numbers prove it. But how many of the things he made look so easy — or that he did even though they looked so hard — were possible because the defense didn't want to leave the slick-shooting Steve Kerr alone at the three-point line? Or because Dennis Rodman was sealing his man off, preventing that player from coming over to help cover Jordan? Or how many times were those degree-of-difficulty maneuvers bad plays that simply ended up good ones? An extra pass might have ruined the highlight reel, but it might have made for an easier shot. In that sense basketball is very much like how we all know life is most of the time: A series of random events we try to make sense of as we go along, one thing interacting with another in ways we don't always understand.

Baseball doesn't have that problem, or at least not in the same way. For example, time stops when the pitcher looks in for the sign and, for an instant, the pitcher and hitter are the only two people who matter. Sure, there are other players on the field, but they don't have an impact on what happens when the pitcher lets the ball go, and the batter decides to take it or let it rip. What does happen has been captured in a rich statistical mine that can be dug into again and again to help further the understanding of baseball and how it's played.

Kobe Bryant goes up for a shot on April 5, 2009 against the Clippers in an 88–85 Laker victory. In the 2008–09 season Kobe converted on 45.7% of his chances in clutch play (see page 176).

Steve Kerr helps the Bulls eliminate the Knicks from the 1996 Eastern Conference Semifinals. In 1995–96 Kerr hit 51.5% of his 237 regular season 3-point attempts and posted playoff per-game highs in points (6.8) and minutes played (19.8).

Basketball doesn't have any moments like that. So many different things have an impact on whether a play is made successfully or not that it can't really be measured; or at least easily measured. And what's happening at every single moment of a game is a collection of individuals are trying to balance their own interests with the interests of the group. This compromise for the betterment of the group comes in different forms — the ball movement and selflessness epitomized by the early Celtics dynasty is one example, where a group of elite talents — all those Hall of Famers! — sacrificed a little individual offensive glory so that as a whole the team could achieve great things. It was a formula that also worked well for the 2007–08 NBA champion Celtics, as three future Hall of Famers — Kevin Garnett, Paul Pierce and Ray Allen — set personal goals aside for the good of the team. Other times, it's a group of complementary players who accept their roles as the supporting cast for an unquestioned star: the Jordan-era Bulls or the Houston Rockets with Hakeem Olajuwon in charge; or more recently, the Los Angeles Lakers with Kobe Bryant at his peak.

For a long time, watching basketball was like that. You watched, you tried to figure out what may have caused one thing or another to happen, but you couldn't know for sure. Was Russell better than Chamberlain? In their day, the practice of gathering statistics was more rudimentary than it is now, and there was little video to back up first impressions. After all, Chamberlain's 100-point game in 1962 wasn't even televised. As a result, we're left to debate if the Celtics thrived because of Russell's team-first approach and wonder if maybe Chamberlain's teams fell short because he was too busy winning the box score instead of the game. Or maybe Russell's 11 championships had more to do with the caliber of his Celtic teammates, while the fact that Chamberlain had to settle for two titles perhaps was simply because he didn't have as much help. Was Magic better than Bird? Was Dr. J better than Jordan? Is LeBron better than everyone? And what about Kobe? For basketball fans, these riddles are like trying to explain the secrets of the universe: fun to argue about, but essentially unknowable.

But as the NBA enters its eighth decade, a new approach to unraveling the mysteries of the game has emerged, embracing fans and NBA insiders alike. With every game televised, with computers at everyone's fingertips, data can be collected, stored, analyzed, reviewed and compared as never before. The result is an ever-growing way to understand the game; one that can prove and disprove long understood truths while unearthing new ones along the way.

Dork Elvis

Daryl Morey was always a stats hound. While he was growing up in Akron, Ohio, he worked in a movie theater and remembers getting all excited when Steve Kerr was there one day. Not because Kerr, then a back-up point guard with the Cleveland Cavaliers, was lighting up the house with a little low-wattage celebrity — even if some of Morey's fellow staffers mistook him for Mark Price, the Cavaliers starting point guard

— but because Morey knew that Kerr shot an unfathomable 57.3 percent from the three-point line in his senior year at the University of Arizona in 1987–88, which remains the best mark in NCAA Division 1 history for a player with more than 100 attempts. And Morey knew that converting triples at that rate made Kerr quite possibly the most efficient scorer in NCAA Division 1 history. Morey's mind works like that: drawn not to the glamorous or glittery, but to facts and measures and efficiency. It's part of the reason that, as the general manager of the Houston Rockets, he's emerged as an odd sort of celebrity among a specific breed of NBA fans who are enamored by his dedication to using advanced statistical analysis to help chart the course of his club. It's why ESPN columnist, and friend, Bill Simmons dubbed him Dork Elvis.

General manager of the Houston Rockets, Daryl Morey, in 2010.

Playing high school basketball, Morey admits that he used to keep track not only of his own scoring totals, but of the number of points his man scored on him as a way to measure if he was having a positive impact on his team or not. Flash forward a few decades and Morey's instinct for efficiency and a wider view of what goes into winning basketball has made him a pioneer of sorts in the NBA.

Morey was made the general manager of the Rockets in 2007 at age 35, an appointment that was notable not only because he was the youngest member of the NBA lodge, but also because among the 30 men charged with shaping the multimillion-dollar rosters in the NBA, Morey was the only one not to have previously played in the NBA, coached in the NBA or scouted for the NBA. Suddenly, a guy whose basketball claim to fame was winning an intramural championship at Northwestern University was going to be in charge of figuring out the best way to build a roster of NBA talent. "With the high level of competition in this league, you can never have too much information," Rockets' owner Leslie Alexander said at the time. "If we combine the best information with our basketball people, we should be able to make the most informed and best decisions in the NBA."

Morey was short on hands-on experience, but he had something that his new peers didn't have: A math degree from Northwestern and an MBA from MIT for starters, and a deep understanding of quantitative analysis — the practice of using advanced statistical measures to evaluate player and team performance, which Morey then uses to inform decisions about who the Rockets put on the court and how they will play. Early in his career Morey was so taken with the statistical guru Bill James' pioneering work in baseball that he began to work at STATS Inc., a Chicago-based firm that provides sports statistics and analysis primarily to teams, leagues and media outlets, and the company which Bill James himself had joined about a decade earlier. Morey's primary contribution there was to show that James' approach to baseball could be applied to other sports, basketball in particular. That alone didn't launch him into his role as general manager with the Rockets. His entrance into the NBA came while using his MBA in his capacity as a consultant for an ownership group that was buying the Boston Celtics. Once on the inside in a business role, he began to add value by using quantitative analysis to help inform basketball decisions.

In 2006 the Rockets hired him as an assistant general manager and tabbed him as a successor to Carroll Dawson. The result? Morey was able to argue why the Rockets should trade Stromile Swift (a high-flying, former No. 2 pick) and the rights to Rudy Gay (an absurdly athletic if otherwise unproven forward taken No. 8 in the 2006 draft) to Memphis for Shane Battier, a relatively unathletic small forward who couldn't create his own shot and was usually the fifth or sixth leading scorer on his team.

Even a 12-year-old sitting in the farthest reaches of an NBA arena can make a pretty good case why LeBron James helps a team win in the NBA, but Battier's gifts were less obvious. Yet Morey felt he was able to quantify them. "It wasn't a revelation that Shane Battier made a big impact," said Morey. "[Coaches] didn't need anything fancy to tell them he was good … They knew he ran the plays, they knew he moved the ball, they knew he took the charge. They knew all those things were good, but they didn't have any particular catch-all numbers to describe what he did."

But by analyzing all manner of statistics — some available to the average fan and some not — Morey was able to show why Battier made teams better. This was, after all, a player who won three state championships in high school, a national championship at Duke and helped the Memphis Grizzlies to three straight winning seasons — the only three in franchise history — before being traded to Houston. With Battier added to the Rockets' lineup, the team went on to win an average of 53 games the next three seasons; the Grizzlies, without Battier, averaged 23.

What impact does Battier have? One measure is something referred to by the analytics crowd as adjusted plus-minus, where the performance of the team is measured according to an individual player's playing time, but adjusted to reflect the quality of the opponents and his teammates. This is a significant improvement over a simple plus-minus approach, because it's inevitable that whoever backs up LeBron James or Dwyane Wade is going to suffer in comparison, since the Cavaliers or Heat can't be expected to be as good without their top guns on the floor. But by taking into consideration factors like the quality of the other players on the floor, analysts like Morey are able to get a sense for who actually impacts a game and in what way.

No, Battier doesn't reject shots into the fourth row or send bodies sprawling as he rattles the rim with dunks. But he talks on defense, calling out opponents' plays almost as soon as they are signaled in from the bench, and expertly directs the Rockets' coverage. He runs through the Rockets' plays flawlessly and makes timely passes to keep the offense flowing. He's a tireless individual defender and a better-than-average three-point shooter, focusing on taking open corner jumpers — the most efficient shot in basketball, don't you know. What does all that look like when reduced to a math equation? Add it all up (well, if it were only that simple), and in a good year, Battier makes his team better by about 10 points per game, a spectacular result for a role player and on par with the very biggest stars in the NBA. The fact that Battier earns just above the league's average salary makes him a relative bargain in the NBA where teams have a salary cap to govern overall spending. And for Morey, and those convinced that quantitative analysis is an essential new approach to furthering the understanding of basketball, being able to measure Battier's success was a big step into a new frontier.

The New School

But perhaps the most exciting aspect of the way quantitative analysis is shaping the way people appreciate basketball is that the gap in knowledge is shrinking between basketball brass and insiders, and enthusiastic fans.

Morey was able to use his background in analytics to make the jump from business to basketball. Similarly, there was a wave of fans with an enthusiasm and aptitude for studying basketball in a new and different way that was ahead of what was going on inside the league. In his columns for ESPN.com John Hollinger has perhaps played a bigger role than anyone else in popularizing a more quantitative approach to basketball. He knows first-hand that the efforts he was making as a deeply curious fan were ahead of the curve compared to what was happening inside the NBA; that people charged with assembling rosters weren't yet as conversant as many fans in concepts like pace of play, offensive and defensive efficiency, and ways to measure scoring not reflected in traditional shooting stats.

A self-confessed math geek who grew up in New Jersey creating point differential models for his high-school team, Hollinger began making his findings public with a Web site called Alleyoop.com in 1996. In 2002 he published a book, *Pro Basketball Forecast*. It didn't make him rich, but among certain cross-sections of fans and NBA insiders, it made him, in a small way, famous. "I first realized I had made an impact when I was sitting in my kitchen having lunch and I got this phone call and the person calling goes 'This is…' and it was an NBA head coach," says Hollinger. "And I was like 'oh my God.' It was just very surprising; I guess this book has made some kind of impact, not on my wallet but on the league. He just wanted to know more, he was really interested in what else his team could potentially do further."

It's fitting that the adoption of quantitative analysis in basketball was inspired by fans and outsiders. That's

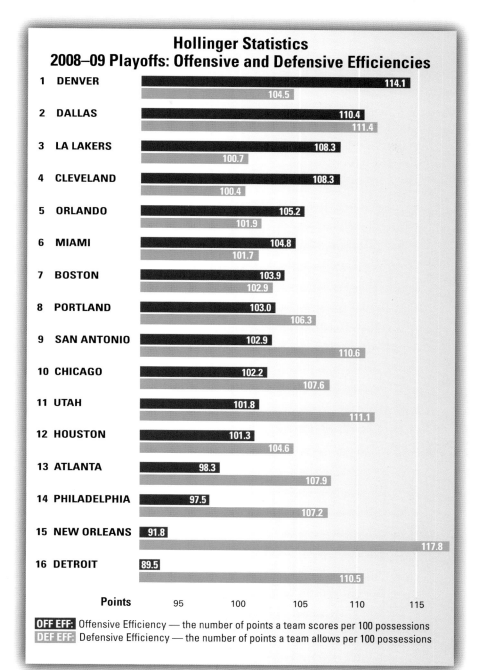

Hollinger Statistics
2008–09 Playoffs: Offensive and Defensive Efficiencies

	Team	OFF EFF	DEF EFF
1	DENVER	114.1	104.5
2	DALLAS	110.4	111.4
3	LA LAKERS	108.3	100.7
4	CLEVELAND	108.3	100.4
5	ORLANDO	105.2	101.9
6	MIAMI	104.8	101.7
7	BOSTON	103.9	102.9
8	PORTLAND	103.0	106.3
9	SAN ANTONIO	102.9	110.6
10	CHICAGO	102.2	107.6
11	UTAH	101.8	111.1
12	HOUSTON	101.3	104.6
13	ATLANTA	98.3	107.9
14	PHILADELPHIA	97.5	107.2
15	NEW ORLEANS	91.8	117.8
16	DETROIT	89.5	110.5

Points   95   100   105   110   115

OFF EFF: Offensive Efficiency — the number of points a team scores per 100 possessions
DEF EFF: Defensive Efficiency — the number of points a team allows per 100 possessions

just what happened in baseball. And while Bill James, the person who popularized analytics in baseball, never wrote about basketball, he's had a significant impact on the way fans and NBA franchises alike look at their teams.

Bill James was a security guard and aspiring writer working the night shift at a Stokely-Van Camp pork and beans factory when he began self-publishing *The Bill James Baseball Abstract* in 1977. It was a new way of looking at the most hidebound of sports. One of James' breakthroughs was showing that a key to understanding baseball — largely ignored by conventional statistics — was that preserving outs was an undervalued trait. Because batting averages and home runs were the dominant offensive descriptors, the ability to get on base wasn't properly reflected in the way players and teams were evaluated. James proved that players who took more than their share of walks and avoided strikeouts, for example, could have a contribution to scoring runs that had been previously underappreciated.

How did James influence basketball? Most of the forward thinkers about the game grew up in the 1980s, drawn in by the exploits of Larry Bird, Magic Johnson and a young Michael Jordan. But many of those thinkers were also baseball fans and fans of Bill James' approach. It was natural for them to begin thinking about basketball in the same way. "At an early age I was very interested in sports and very interested in figuring out what contributed to wins," says Daryl Morey. "And so, like many folks at that time, I gravitated to Bill James and his abstracts. I was a basketball player, and that was my first love, but there really wasn't much information available. I gravitated to reading the stuff that Bill was doing in baseball, grew up studying his work and playing basketball.

Says John Hollinger: "I was a big Bill James junkie growing up. When I started reading his books I was like 'oh yeah, this is what I wanted to do in basketball,' but it took a while to figure out how I could do it, and then when the Internet came along, a light bulb came on: here's how I can do this."

Similarly, another early quantitative basketball pioneer was Dean Oliver, who, like Hollinger, made the jump from Internet hobbyist to the printed page. Like Morey, he also cracked the NBA hierarchy, first as a paid consultant to the Seattle SuperSonics and then as the Denver Nuggets director of quantitative analysis. His book, *Basketball On Paper*, is considered the breakthrough work in the field — basketball's version of Bill James' baseball abstracts.

Oliver was one of the early champions of the idea that the key to understanding winning basketball was measuring for efficiency. It didn't matter how many total points a team scored, but how many points per possession they scored. To Oliver and his counterparts, possession efficiency is basketball's version of on-base percentage, the statistical measure that James showed was previously underappreciated in baseball. "Teams that score a lot of points don't necessarily win games, and teams that prevent opponents from scoring a lot of points don't necessarily win, either," he said. "But if you convert a greater percentage of possessions into points than your opponent does, you win games." Similarly, tracking a team's per-possession efficiency whenever a given player is on the court provides a better idea of a player's contributions rather than simply looking at points per game, rebounds and assists.

An engineering graduate from Caltech and holder of a PhD in environmental science, Oliver was so committed to his views that he quit his job as an engineering consultant to create a new career for himself in basketball. In the spring of 2004, he got in his car and began driving across the country, using his book as a résumé. Interest varied, but he finally landed a job when Wally Walker, general manager of the then-Seattle

SuperSonics, paid him a $30,000 consulting fee. Two seasons later the Denver Nuggets hired him.

What it is exactly that quantitative experts like Oliver and Morey and others do for the NBA teams that have invested to varying degrees in the practice isn't easily known. The information they generate is closely guarded and proprietary. After all, why would the Houston Rockets invest "multiple millions of dollars," according to Morey, on finding ways to beat their opponents and then give the information away? But perhaps what's most exciting is that in just a few short years, data that was unavailable to NBA team presidents a decade ago is now easily accessible to fans today. It's unlikely many fans are going to follow the path taken by Morey and Oliver into the front office of NBA teams, or by Hollinger and become one of the NBA's most influential media figures. But the rise to the professional ranks of these basketball fanatics suggests the understanding of the sport is more egalitarian than ever before.

The True Clutch Player

Nearly any idea previously debated by fans and NBA insiders alike, based on impressions and anecdotes, can today be hashed out and argued with data unavailable to almost everyone a decade ago. One example? The idea of a clutch player — someone who is at his best late in games when the outcome hangs in the balance — is a concept of NBA lore. Jerry West was dubbed Mr. Clutch for his heroics late in games, and late in playoff games in particular. Jordan's reputation was built in large measure on the foundation of his ability to seemingly lift his game to new heights in the dying moments. Today, Kobe Bryant is considered the game's best closer: a cold-blooded operative immune to pressure. But how to know for sure?

Until very recently, even the game's

55.6%

LeBron James drives the hoop for a clutch-time jam against Craig Smith of the Los Angeles Clippers in a 102–101 Cavalier victory in 2010. In 2008–09 James converted 55.6% of his clutch chances (see page 176).

insiders could only rely on anecdotal evidence to determine who were actually able to play their best when the stakes were highest. A single game-winning shot played over-and-over again on highlight reels could do more for a player's reputation than all the misses or turnovers or defensive lapses that never saw the light of a post-game clips package.

But today, if two NBA fans get into a debate about who is best in the clutch, they can head over to a site like 82games.com, founded in 2002 by Roland Beech (now working for the Dallas Mavericks). Thanks to the group of volunteers at 82games.com that watch and catalogue every NBA game, and the inquisitive minds that allow for wide-ranging topics of online discussion, the two arguing fans, if determined to dig deeply enough, will have assuredly more practical evidence to back up their opinions than Red Auerbach and Jerry West did combined during their careers, and quite often these fans will have as much information as many NBA insiders in the league have right at this moment.

Rather than simply debate who may or may not be the best clutch player in the NBA, Beech and his colleagues set out to prove it. Their first step was to define "clutch time" as "the fourth quarter or overtime, with less than five minutes left to play and neither team ahead or behind by more than five points." Then they ran the numbers.

Was Kobe Bryant the best clutch player in the NBA? Not quite. Yes, in the sense that he averaged a league-best 56.7 points per 48 minutes of clutch time play in 2008–09. But what about LeBron James, who averaged a nearly as impressive 55.9 points per 48 minutes? And what of the fact that James shot 55.6 percent from the floor in those key moments, compared to Bryant, who converted just 45.7 percent of his chances? James also averaged 12.6 assists in the clutch compared to Bryant's 5.7 assists. Sure, Bryant has the reputation as the best clutch player in the league, but is it deserved? Beech makes the case that it's not, based on James' greater efficiency. It's a case Mr. Clutch himself, Jerry

West, could never have made even as he was winning championships as a general manager with the Lakers because he didn't have the data.

Want to dig deeper? Beech did an investigation of game winning shots — exactly the kind of moments that live on in highlight-reel glory — by first defining game-winning shots as those taken with "24 seconds or less left in the game, team with the ball is either tied or down by 1 to 2 points." Using data from more than five seasons of play (2003–04 through most of 2007–08) some amazing trends emerge. The first is that making shots at the very end of games where the clock is an enemy, defenses are locked in and scrutiny is the highest is a remarkably difficult task. The entire league converted just 29.8 percent of those chances, compared to the average shooting percentages for the same period, which ranged between 43.9 percent and 45.9 percent. But who rose to the challenge? James made the most shots of any player in the sample, with 17; Bryant made 14, placing him fourth. James converted 34 percent of his chances; Bryant just 25 percent of his.

The best bet to make a shot with the game on the line? How about Denver Nuggets' star Carmelo Anthony, who was good on 13-of-27 chances for 48.1 percent, by far the best accuracy of players with at least 10 game winners on their résumé. But perhaps the most important lesson learned by diving deeper into the numbers is that what sticks in people's minds are the dramatic, walk-off shots that decide games — which don't happen very often and aren't converted with any significant regularity. "The truth seems to be that, while we want to believe in the infallible hero who comes through every time," writes Beech, "in the NBA even the brightest of the bunch are lucky to come through one out of three times."

For fans willing to poke around, the fun doesn't end there. Hollinger's best known contribution to a more advanced statistical approach is his Player Efficiency Rating, or PER — a catch-all number that allows fans to look at a player's achievements across a number of statistical platforms on a per minute basis. By including factors like their team's pace of play and their court time, and comparing production to the league as a whole, fans are better able to compare the contributions of a player with gaudy scoring averages but woeful shooting percentages and sloppy ball-handling. Each season Hollinger sets the NBA average PER at 15 — players with PERs higher than 15 are, by that definition, above average performers; those with PERs approaching or just over 20 are playing at an all-star level or close to it, and those with a PER over 25 are legitimate candidates for most valuable player honors, or at least worthy of mention. "It provides an academic rigor," says Hollinger of the approach he and other quantitative analysts have taken. "You have to make sure you're comparing apples to apples. We're so trained to look at per game numbers [but] when you factor in pace of play and look at what happens on a per-possession basis, you get a better picture."

As an added bonus, PER allows fans a better measure than ever before to compare the stars of today with the stars of previous eras, or at least as far back as 1973–74 when the NBA began tracking individual turnovers (the last stat to be tracked by the NBA that is needed for Hollinger's PER evaluation). During James' 2008–09 MVP season, Hollinger shed new light on his performance by using PER to illustrate that James was playing not

48.1%

Carmelo Anthony pulls up for jumper over LeBron James on February 18, 2010; Anthony's Nuggets won 118–116 on his buzzer beater. Over the six years previous the 2010 season Anthony has hit almost half of his last-second shots.

31.89%

Jordan sails to the rim in the 1987 James Naismith Basketball Hall of Fame Game. He posted 36 points, 4 assists and 4 rebounds. His efficiency rating of 31.89% in the 1987–88 regular season is the best ever recorded.

only at a high level compared to his peers, but as compared to history.

The highest PER ever recorded since 1972–73 was the 31.89 mark Jordan logged in 1987–88 with the Chicago Bulls (measured conventionally, it was a pretty impressive season too, as Jordan averaged 35 points, 5.9 assists, 5.5 rebounds, 3.2 steals and 1.6 blocks, while shooting 53.8 percent from the floor).

In his first MVP year, James came ever-so-close to matching Jordan's mark, as his PER was 31.76, the third best recorded since 1972–73, with only Jordan (who also had a PER of 31.79 in 1990–91) having ever done better. What's interesting is that James' traditional statistics don't seem to rank quite as high as Jordan's, given that he averaged 28.4 points, 7.2 assists and 7.6 rebounds, 1.7 steals and 1.1 blocks while shooting 48.9 percent from the floor. This is where PER is helpful, because it captures the fact that James played fewer minutes than Jordan, 37.7 to 40.4, and the overall pace of play in the league was significantly slower, meaning James had less possessions to garner his statistical totals.

A perfect system? No, Hollinger would say, acknowledging that PER does an injustice to defensive specialists who don't get a lot of blocks or steals (Shane Battier's career PER, for example, is just 13.4); and it fails to capture the impact of rule changes. What would Jordan be able to accomplish in an NBA where defenders weren't permitted to use a hand check on the perimeter? But for fans who want to know how players stack up against each other across eras, they're a lot further along than they ever were before.

The Holy Grail

The impact that more advanced statistical analysis will have on the NBA remains to be seen. Even Morey tends to downplay it. "I don't feel like we can point to anything and say we're better than anybody.

I feel like we're trying to make decisions like everyone else … but I don't think we can say mission accomplished or anything."

The riddle that needs solving most is how to evaluate individual defensive play. Right now the only measures for defensive play are blocks and steals, and while each are useful plays on their own, they can be misleading. A player who leaves his man to block a shot may make the play or may not, but in the process he will almost definitely give the man he was covering an open lane to the offensive glass and a chance at one of the most demoralizing plays and high percentage shots in the game: an offensive rebound and putback. Similarly, steals are exciting to watch, but how about all the easy scores given up by a player who is always gambling in the passing lane, leaving his team vulnerable in behind him? And what about players who don't bite on pump fakes? Or players who don't lose their man by gambling on steals and do otherwise unquantifiable things, like properly rotating or closing out hard on perimeter shooters? Properly evaluating defensive play is what some stat hounds call the Holy Grail.

It's a riddle that will likely be solved at some point, but in the meantime the presence of Morey as an NBA general manager has inspired a generation of fans and followers in a way that Jerry West's career, perhaps the best executive in NBA history, can't quite: West's entree into the front office came on the heels of an exemplary playing career; his eye for talent was justified by the fact that he had talent and had seen first-hand what did and did not work on an NBA floor. Morey is a guy who played high school basketball with an aptitude for math, and thus someone more fans can relate to — hence the Dork Elvis brand of micro-celebrity.

"It's a lot of pressure to put on [Morey] — it's a small sample size — but he's certainly viewed from the outside and not unfairly so, as the leader of this movement, at least in terms of applying it on a team level, and that he became a general manager by way of a different route, based on what he's done with numbers and that he's been able to succeed has been an important message," says Kevin Pelton, who uses a quantitative approach in his writing at *Basketball Prospectus*.

For his part Morey simply believes that the more measures available, the better decisions he can make. "It's almost like you need to take snapshots from all different sides," he says. "You have to look at multiple things before you can be confident a player is contributing. But really it's about making the best marginal choice." And now, as never before, NBA fans have the ability to decide for themselves how good those choices are and why they were made.

Nothing will ever take away from the thrill of watching LeBron James streak down the floor at a speed improbable for a man his size and put the ball through the basket with unrivalled ferocity. That will always be enjoyable. And for serious basketball fans, enjoying that sight while understanding its underlying mechanisms (who's making their teammates better and how? Who's sacrificing individual glory to make the group better?) will make the game that much more engrossing.

The FRANCHISES

Dwight Howard leads the Orlando Magic in a pre-game huddle on December 19, 2009. The Magic beat the Portland Trail Blazers 92–83, with four players posting double-digit point totals and Dwight Howard collecting a double-double. Orlando and Portland split their two-game season series.

ATLANTA
HAWKS

MIKE BIBBY

TEAM ORIGINS: The Hawks, after having moved from both the Iowa-Illinois Tri-cities and Milwaukee in the franchise's first six seasons, abruptly moved from their third home, St. Louis (where they had played since 1955–56), to Atlanta for the 1968–69 season. New owners, real estate developer Thomas Cousins and former Georgia governor Carl Sanders, felt the team could not be profitable in the Midwest. Richie Guerin was retained as the head coach, but the Hawks traded popular point guard Lenny Wilkens when management and Wilkens could not agree on a contract. The Hawks compiled a 48–34 regular-season record in their first year in Atlanta, second in the NBA Western Division. They defeated the San Diego Rockets in the first round of the playoffs but were eliminated by the Lakers in the next round.

GLIMPSES OF GLORY: The Atlanta Hawks have had their share of NBA playoff appearances, competing in the postseason a total of 23 times. In those 23 visits, the Hawks have never advanced to the NBA Finals, and have only been to the Conference Finals twice — both times losing to the Los Angeles Lakers. In 1970, led by NBA great "Pistol Pete" Maravich and center Walt Bellamy, the Hawks won their first of four division championships. Maravich represented the Hawks in the All-Star Game twice: 1973 and 1974.

In the 1980s, the Hawks won two more division championships. In 1980, under coach Hubie Brown, the Hawks finished with a 50–32 record, but were shocked in the playoffs at being ousted in five games by Julius Erving and the Philadelphia 76ers.

In 1987, Dominique Wilkins led the Hawks to a franchise record 57 wins. Wilkins averaged 29 points per game, second only to Michael Jordan. Once again, the Hawks came up short in the playoffs, losing in the second round to Isiah Thomas and the Detriot Pistons.

The Hawks' last division championship was in 1994 — Dominique Wilkins' last year with the team. They posted a 57–25 record that year, but were again clipped in the playoffs, this time losing to Reggie Miller and the Indiana Pacers in the Eastern Conference Semifinals.

2004 DRAFT: "THE JOSHES"

JOSH SMITH
- Drafted 17th overall by Atlanta in 2004
- Youngest player in NBA history to record his 500th block (21-years and 88-days old)
- 2005 Slam Dunk Champion
- Averages 13.6 points per game and 2.6 blocks per game

JOSH CHILDRESS
- Drafted 6th overall by Atlanta in 2004
- Averaged 11.1 points per game and 5.6 rebounds per game
- Featured on the video game cover of ESPN College Hoops 2K5
- Currently plays for the Greek club Olympiacos

PAUL PIERCE

BOSTON
CELTICS

TEAM ORIGINS: The Boston Celtics are one of basketball's iconic franchises. But for a team that is deep-rooted in NBA lore, it had some humble beginnings. In 1946, eleven businessmen who owned either arenas or hockey teams, formed a basketball league named the Basketball Association of America. Walter Brown, who owned the Boston Garden, and was an active executive member of the Boston Bruins hockey team, ran the day-to-day operations of the basketball team. He hired John "Honey" Russell as the team's first head coach, and on November 5, 1946, in front of 4,329 fans, the Celtics lost their first game 57–55 to the Chicago Stags. The franchise's first season (they finished tied for last place with the Toronto Huskies with a 22–38 record) would not reflect the future greatness of the Celtics.

THE GLORY YEARS: The Boston Celtics have won a record 17 NBA championships, including a record eight in a row, from 1959–1966. It was Arnold Jacob "Red" Auerbach, hired in 1950, who eventually transformed the Celtics into one of the NBA's proudest franchises. Prior to the 1956 season, Auerbach acquired center Bill Russell at the draft from the St. Louis Hawks. In the 1956–57 campaign, Russell's rookie season, he helped lead the team to a league-best 44–28 record. The Celtics met the Hawks in the Finals, and although the Celtics were heavily favored, the Hawks took the series to seven games. The Celtics claimed their first of eight straight NBA championships when the Hawks' Bob Pettit missed a buzzer-beater shot in overtime to give Boston a 125–123 victory.

Larry Bird led the Celtics back to glory in the 1980s. A tall, lanky kid from French Lick, Indiana, Bird was drafted sixth overall in 1978 and quickly brought a championship back to Boston, as Bird, Kevin McHale, Robert Parish and the Celtics won it all in 1981. Bird led the Celtics to two more NBA championships in his career: 1984 and 1986, beating the rival Los Angeles Lakers. Twenty-two years later, Kevin Garnett, Ray Allen and Paul Pierce claimed Boston's record-setting 17th championship when they defeated Kobe Bryant and the Los Angeles Lakers in the 2008 NBA Finals.

BATTLE OF THE RUSSELLS (COACHES)

**BILL RUSSELL,
HEAD COACH (1966–69)**

- Won two championships with the Celtics (1968, 1969)
- Led the team to 162–83 record in three years as head coach
- Team record in playoffs (1966–69): 28–18

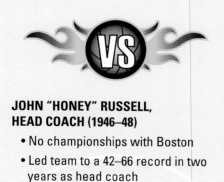

**JOHN "HONEY" RUSSELL,
HEAD COACH (1946–48)**

- No championships with Boston
- Led team to a 42–66 record in two years as head coach
- Team record in playoffs (1946–48): 1–2

CHARLOTTE
BOBCATS

TEAM ORIGINS: In 2002, when the Charlotte Hornets left for New Orleans, Black Entertainment Television CEO Robert L. Johnson seized the opportunity and applied for an expansion team to fill the void in the North Carolina metropolis. On January 10, 2003, he was awarded a team. The name "Bobcats" was chosen out of approximately 1,250 suggestions submitted to the team and the Charlotte Regional Sports Commission. On June 24, 2004, the Bobcats selected Emeka Okafor from the University of Connecticut with the second-overall pick in the draft. Four months later, on November 4, 2004, professional basketball was back in Charlotte, as the Bobcats hosted the Washington Wizards, losing the nail-biter 103–96. The Bobcats finished the season with an 18–64 record.

GLIMPSES OF GLORY: The Bobcats' success has been limited in their short NBA existence, although they have shown some greatness in those six seasons. The first significant moment of greatness was their first draft pick, Emeka Okafor, who won the 2004–05 NBA Rookie of the Year award. As a rookie, Okafor averaged a double-double, with 15.1 points and 10.9 rebounds per game.

On November 24, 2004, led by Emeka Okafor's 22 points and 15 rebounds, the Charlotte Bobcats defeated the defending NBA champions, the Detroit Pistons, 91–89, something no other expansion team has done since the Buffalo Braves defeated the New York Knicks in the 1970–71 season. In their final game of the season, the Bobcats continued to have the Pistons' number, defeating the defending NBA champions again, 97–86, to close out their inaugural season.

GERALD WALLACE

FIRST-EVER DRAFT PICKS
IN CHARLOTTE'S HISTORY

BOBCATS: EMEKA OKAFOR

- Drafted 2nd overall by the Charlotte Bobcats in 2004
- Won the 2004–05 NBA Rookie of the Year and was named to the All-Rookie First Team
- Averaged 13.9 points and 10.6 rebounds per game in five seasons with the Charlotte Bobcats

HORNETS: REX CHAPMAN

- Drafted 8th overall by the Charlotte Hornets in 1988
- Named to the 1988–89 NBA All-Rookie Second Team after averaging 16.9 points per game, third among rookies.
- Averaged 16.7 points per game during his three years with Charlotte

CHICAGO
BULLS

DERRICK ROSE

1987 DRAFT-DAY TRADE: PIPPEN VS. POLYNICE

SCOTTIE PIPPEN

- Drafted 5th overall by the Seattle SuperSonics in 1987 from Central Arkansas State
- Averaged 16.4 points, 2 steals and 6.4 rebounds per game during his career in the NBA
- Seven-time NBA All-Star over his 17-year NBA career

OLDEN POLYNICE

- Drafted 8th overall by the Chicago Bulls in 1987 from the University of Virginia
- Averaged 7.8 points and 6.7 rebounds per game during his NBA career
- Played for five teams (two of them twice) in his 15-year NBA career

TEAM ORIGINS: The Chicago Bulls entered the NBA in 1966–67 under head coach Johnny "Red" Kerr. The Bulls, unlike most expansion franchises who struggle out of the gate, were remarkably successful in their inaugural season. They started by winning their first three games in franchise history, and finished with a 33–48 record, good enough to make the playoffs. Although they were ousted in the first round, the Bulls' organization could hold its head high for posting the best regular-season record by a first-year NBA team.

THE GLORY YEARS: When the Chicago Bulls drafted Michael Jordan in 1984, it was not only history-making for the Bulls, but for the NBA and professional basketball as a whole. His legendary career established the Chicago Bulls as one of the elite teams in the NBA, and would establish the NBA as one of the premier sporting leagues in the world. In his rookie year, Jordan led the Bulls to the playoffs, earned a spot in the All-Star Game and claimed the Rookie of the Year award. He was a legend in the making.

In 1987, Scottie Pippen was drafted by the Seattle SuperSonics and traded at the draft to the Chicago Bulls for Olden Polynice. The pairing of Jordan and Pippen led the Bulls to a 61–21 regular-season record in 1990–91. Chicago swept the defending NBA champions, the Detroit Pistons, in the Eastern Conference Finals that year and faced the Lost Angeles Lakers in the Finals. It was hyped as a battle between two legends, Michael Jordan versus Magic Johnson.

Magic and the Lakers took Game 1 on a last second three-pointer by Sam Perkins. Jordan, Pippen and the Bulls answered by toppling the Lakers in the next four games and capturing the franchise's first NBA championship. The Bulls would repeat the next year, posting a 67–15 record in the regular season and defeating the Portland Trail Blazers in six games in the 1992 NBA Finals. In 1993, Jordan and company claimed a three-peat, when John Paxton's buzzer beater in Game 6 of the NBA Finals sunk Charles Barkley and the Phoenix Suns. After a brief retirement by Jordan in 1994, which included a failed attempt at a professional baseball career, he returned to the Bulls' lineup to lead Chicago to three more NBA titles from 1996 to 1998.

CLEVELAND
CAVALIERS

MO WILLIAMS

TEAM ORIGINS: Bill Fitch not only had a ragtag group of players to work with when he became the Cavaliers' first coach, but for the first seven games of the franchise's history, his team didn't have a home to play in. That's because the Cleveland Arena was booked for the ever-popular Ice Capades. Cavalier fans did not miss much, as the Cavs dropped their first game to their expansion brothers, the Buffalo Braves, 107–92, and continued to lose for most of the season. At one point, Cleveland was a dismal 2–34. By the end of their inaugural season, the Cavaliers had finished with a 15–67 record.

GLIMPSES OF GLORY: In the course of their 35-year history, the Cavaliers have made the playoffs 16 times and the conference finals three times, and despite this, they have never lifted the NBA championship trophy. Their initial playoff appearance, five years after their NBA inception, came in 1976, under Bill Fitch. It was a memorable debut, as they capped their division rivals, the Washington Bullets, in an exciting seven-game, first-round series. Dick Snyder was the hero, eliminating the Bullets, on a bank shot with only four seconds remaining. Next came the storied Boston Celtics, who took the first two games at home. The Cavaliers bounced back taking the next two games in Cleveland, but it was all for naught as the Celtics won the pivotal Game 5, giving them the momentum needed to cap the series off in six games.

In 2003 the Cavaliers selected home-grown superstar LeBron James, from St. Vincent-St. Mary High School in Akron, Ohio, with the first overall pick. James was one of the most highly anticipated rookies in NBA history, and four years after his draft, he led his team to the NBA Finals in 2006–07. That season, Cleveland finished with a 50–32 record. James hushed any critics who wondered about his maturity with a gritty performance in the gruelling Eastern Conference Finals against the experienced Detroit Pistons. Unfortunately, the San Antonio Spurs proved too tough a match for the Cavs and Cleveland was left as NBA runner-up. The playoff run was a big boost to the city and brought back excitement for basketball and hope for the future.

CAVALIER FIRST-ROUND HIGH SCHOOLERS

LEBRON JAMES
- Drafted 1st overall by the Cleveland Cavaliers in 2003
- Won the Rookie of the Year award
- Helped lead team to the 2007 NBA Finals
- 2008–09 NBA MVP

DANNY FERRY
- Drafted second overall by the Los Angeles Clippers in 1989; traded to the Cavaliers for Ron Harper, two first-round picks and a second-round pick
- Averaged 7 points and 2.8 rebounds per game in his 12-year NBA career
- Currently the general manager of the Cleveland Cavaliers

DETROIT
PISTONS

RODNEY STUCKEY

THE PRE-CHICAGO DENNIS RODMANS

DENNIS RODMAN
(Detroit Pistons, 1986–93)

- Won two NBA titles with the Pistons (1989 and 1990)
- Two-time All-Star selection (1990, 1992)
- Defensive Player of the Year (1990, 1991)
- Set a career high on 18.7 rebounds per game in 1991–92 (best in the league)

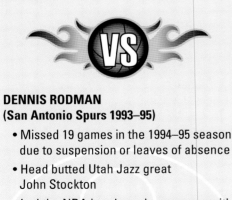

DENNIS RODMAN
(San Antonio Spurs 1993–95)

- Missed 19 games in the 1994–95 season due to suspension or leaves of absence
- Head butted Utah Jazz great John Stockton
- Led the NBA in rebounds per game with 17.3 in 1993–94 and 16.8 in 1994–95

TEAM ORIGINS: Team founder Fred Zollner moved his Pistons team from Fort Wayne, Indiana, to Detroit, Michigan, on September 1, 1957, in order to compete with the larger cities like New York and Philadelphia. Shocking as the move was to the Fort Wayne fan base, the new Detroit Pistons were successful in their first season. George "The Bird" Yardley and Dick McGuire were both named All-Stars and led the Pistons to a 33–39 record in the 1957–58 season. In the playoffs, Detroit beat Cincinnati in the first round, but lost to the St. Louis Hawks in the NBA Western Division Finals, the eventual NBA champions.

THE GLORY YEARS: Led by Isiah Thomas, the 1988–89 Pistons finished the regular season with a 63–19 record. Thomas and Adrian Dantley were the top scorers, both averaging more than 18 points per game, while four other Pistons chipped in more than 13 points per game. The Pistons swept the Boston Celtics and the Milwaukee Bucks in the first two rounds of the playoffs, and then eliminated Michael Jordan and the Chicago Bulls in six games to go to the Finals. The Finals represented revenge for the Pistons, as they downed the Los Angeles Lakers (who had defeated them in the 1988 Finals) in four games.

In the 1989–90 season, the Pistons successfully defended their NBA crown. After posting a 59–23 regular-season record, they swept the Indiana Pacers in the first round, beat the New York Knicks in five games in the conference semifinals, and again beat the Chicago Bulls in the Eastern Conference Finals, this time in seven games. In the Finals, the Pistons manhandled the Portland Trail Blazers and claimed the championship in five games.

There would be a 14-year drought in the Motor City before another championship. Then, in 2003–04, the Pistons cruised through the regular season with a 54–28 record. With an emphasis on tough defense and team play, head coach Larry Brown motivated his relatively unknown team, which included guard Richard Hamilton, center Ben Wallace and point guard Chauncey Billups. The Pistons marched through the Eastern Conference playoffs, defeating Milwaukee in the first round, New Jersey in the semifinals and Indiana in the Eastern Conference Finals before overwhelming Shaquille O'Neal, Kobe Bryant and the Los Angeles Lakers in five games to capture their third NBA championship.

INDIANA
PACERS

DANNY GRANGER

TEAM ORIGINS: Indiana is renowned for its love of high school basketball, as depicted in the 1986 Oscar-nominated film, *Hoosiers.* Ironically, professional basketball did not follow in the same footsteps. After two failed attempts at professional basketball by the NBA (the Indianapolis Olympians in 1953 and the Fort Wayne Pistons in 1957), the ABA decided to take a stab at it in 1967 when eight businessmen pooled together the money for a charter franchise, the Indiana Pacers. Roger Brown was working in a factory in 1967 when the Pacers' first coach, Bob Leonard, approached him to be the first player for the newly born ABA franchise. Little did they both know that Brown would become the legendary swingman who would lead the Pacers to basketball glory and be one of the few Pacers to have his number retired.

THE GLORY YEARS: Success would come quickly for the Pacers. In the 1969–70 season, the Pacers, led by Brown and the 1969 league MVP, center Mel Daniels, stormed their way through the regular season, compiling a 59–25 record. In the playoffs, Indiana continued its dominance, defeating both the Carolina Cougars and the Kentucky Colonels on the way to the ABA Finals. It would take six games, but even the L.A. Stars were no match for the Pacers. In Game 6 Brown racked up 45 points (including seven 3-pointers) en route to a 111–107 victory for the championship. This was the first of three ABA championships for the Pacers, as Brown, Daniels and George McGinnis led the Pacers to back-to-back ABA titles in 1972 and 1973.

Ever since the Pacers joined the NBA for the 1976–77 season, they have not won a championship, but they have come close. Reggie Miller, the 11th overall pick in the 1987 draft, became the face of the Pacers for 18 years. During that time, Miller led the Pacers to the playoffs multiple times, and played his best basketball in the postseason — particularly when he and the Pacers faced off against the New York Knicks. His verbal sparring with film director Spike Lee, a Knicks season ticket holder, is legendary. But more legendary was his 8 points in 11 seconds to win Game 1 of the Eastern Conference Semifinals in 1995. Miller's only NBA Finals appearance came in 2000. Unfortunately, that year Indiana was defeated by Shaquille O'Neal, Kobe Bryant and the Los Angeles Lakers in six games.

COACHES

GEORGE IRVINE
- Coached Pacers from 1984–1986, 1988
- Compiled a record of 54–130 as head coach of the Pacers
- In 1984 led the Pacers to a 22–60 record, their second worst showing in franchise history in both the ABA and NBA
- Was fired midway through the 1988 season after a 6–14 start

LARRY BIRD
- Coached Pacers from 1997–2000
- Compiled a record of 147–67 as head coach of the Pacers
- Led the Pacers to the NBA Finals 2000
- Retired after after his most successful season because of the stress dealing with the day-to-day grind of coaching. He is now the Pacers' GM.

MICHAEL BEASLEY

MIAMI
HEAT

TEAM ORIGINS: The Miami Heat were part of a two-phase league expansion that also included the Orlando Magic, Charlotte Hornets and Minnesota Timberwolves. NBA Hall of Famer Billy Cunningham and movie producer Zev Buffman forked over 32 million dollars to bring the NBA to Miami. In the expansion draft, the Heat drafted Billy Thompson and Jon Sundvold, and with the ninth selection in the NBA draft, the Heat selected center Rony Seikaly from Syracuse University. On November 5, 1988, the Heat played their inaugural game against the Los Angeles Clippers and lost 111–91. The Heat lost the next 17 games, before recording their first victory on December 14, when they defeated the Clippers 89–88. They finished the season with a 15–67 record.

THE GLORY YEARS: In 1995 the Miami brass had had enough and brought in Pat Riley to build a winner. Riley's first order of business was to acquire a franchise player to carry his team. That talent came in the form of seven-foot center Alonzo Mourning. Immediately, Mourning led the Heat to the playoffs and respectability, with four straight division titles, from 1997 to 2000. In 1997, the Heat posted a 55–27 record, and dominated the first two rounds of the playoffs. Unfortunately, Mourning and company met the red-hot Chicago Bulls in the Eastern Conference Finals. Michael Jordan and Scottie Pippen were too much for the Heat, dumping them in five games, on the Bulls' way to Chicago's fifth NBA championship.

In 2003, Miami drafted explosive shooting guard Dwyane Wade out of Marquette University, and in 2004 added future NBA Hall of Fame center Shaquille O'Neal. The 2006 playoffs saw the Heat get a measure of revenge on an old nemesis, the Chicago Bulls, as they ousted the Bulls in six games. Miami went on to defeat the New Jersey Nets and the Detroit Pistons in six games each, to make their first trip to the NBA Finals. There they would face the high-powered offense of Dirk Nowitzki and the Dallas Mavericks. The Mavs took the first two games handily, and the deciding moment of the series came in the last half of the fourth quarter in Game 3, when the Heat rallied from a 13-point deficit to win 98–96. The Heat didn't look back and won the next three games, to claim their first NBA title in team history.

THE MIAMI BIGS

SHAQUILLE O'NEAL

- Won NBA title with the Heat in 2006
- Averaged 18.6 points and 8.7 rebounds per game in three years with Heat
- Quotable: "I'm tired of hearing about money, money, money, money, money. I just want to play the game, drink Pepsi, wear Reebok."

ALONZO MOURNING

- Averaged 15.6 points per game and 8.0 rebounds per game in 10 years with the Heat
- Won NBA title with the Heat in 2006 as Shaq's backup.
- Quotable: "Either it's going to be a great dunk or a great block. I think statistics work in my favor. I don't like getting dunked on."

MILWAUKEE
BUCKS

BRANDON JENNINGS

TEAM ORIGINS: Professional basketball returned to the "cheese state" in 1968, 13 years after the Milwaukee Hawks left for St. Louis. The name "Bucks" was suggested by the winner of the "Name the Team" contest because the buck is spirited, fast, agile and a good jumper. Wisconsin's second attempt at pro basketball proved to be more successful than the first, which lasted all of four seasons. In a coin flip with fellow expansion franchise the Phoenix Suns (by virtue of both teams finishing last in their respective divisions in the 1968–69 season), the Bucks won the rights to the first pick of the 1969 draft. Milwaukee chose Lew Alcindor (later known as Kareem Abdul-Jabbar) out of UCLA, and teamed him with Hall of Fame guard Oscar Robertson, a choice that quickly established success in Milwaukee.

THE GLORY YEARS: For most expansion teams, it takes several years to establish a consistent string of successes. The Bucks were the exception to that rule. In only their second season, they finished with a 56–26 record and made the playoffs, rolling over the Philadelphia 76ers in five games. However, in the second round, the tables were turned on the Bucks, as they suffered a five-game exit at the hands of Willis Reed and the New York Knicks, the eventual 1969–70 NBA champs.

This elimination would only fuel the Bucks in their quest for NBA success. In 1970–71, a young Alcindor, a veteran Oscar Robertson and the Bucks turned the NBA on its head. In the franchise's third year of existence, the Bucks finished with a 66–16 record. Alcindor continued to establish himself as an NBA great by leading the league in scoring, averaging 31.7 points per game and earning him the NBA's Most Valuable Player award. The Bucks dominated the 1971 NBA playoffs, needing only 14 of a possible 21 games to take the championship, the exclamation point on the season being a four-game sweep of the Baltimore Bullets in the Finals. From inception to championship, no other team in modern professional sports history has won a title in a shorter period of time.

A TALE OF TWO INAUGURAL SEASONS

THE MILWAUKEE HAWKS

- Previously known as the Tri-Cities Blackhawks before moving to Milwaukee for the 1951–52 NBA season
- Coached by Doxie Moore, the Hawks finished their inaugural season (1951–52) with a 17–49 record; fifth in the NBA Western Division
- Leading scorer was forward Dick Mehen, who averaged 10.8 points per game

THE MILWAUKEE BUCKS

- Finished their inaugural season (1968–69) with a 27–55 record, seventh in the NBA Eastern Division
- Coached by six-time NBA All-Star Larry Costello
- Leading scorer was guard Flynn Robinson, who averaged 20.3 points per game

NEW JERSEY
NETS

DEVIN HARRIS

TEAM ORIGINS: The New Jersey Nets' franchise (then named the New Jersey Americans) first played basketball in a converted armory in Teaneck, New Jersey, in 1967 — even though they were technically a New York club. The Americans' first head coach was former New York Knicks star, Max Zaslofsky, and in their first professional game the Americans hosted the Pittsburgh Pipers in front of 3,000 fans, with Yankee-great Yogi Berra tossing the jump ball. The team finished with a 36–42 record in its first American Basketball Association season. Before the 1968–69 season, owner Arthur Brown moved the team to New York and changed the name to the "Nets" because it rhymed with other New York professional sports teams, the Mets and Jets. The Nets returned to New Jersey in 1977.

GLIMPSES OF GLORY: Julius "Dr. J" Erving joined the New York Nets in the 1973–74 season, and transformed them into a championship team. In his first season, Erving guided the Nets to a 55–29 record and first place in the Eastern Division. He was the ABA scoring leader and won the league's MVP award. The Nets dominated the playoffs, sweeping the Kentucky Colonels in the Eastern Division and claiming their first ABA championship over Utah in five games. The Nets lost only two games over three best-of-seven playoffs on their run to the championship.

In the ABA's last season, 1975–76, the Nets again posted a 55–29 record. The playoffs, reformatted to deal with the folding of several teams, saw the Nets receive a first-round bye. The San Antonio Spurs, also fresh from a first-round bye, faced the Nets in the second-round semifinals, taking the Nets to seven games. New York prevailed, on the way to their second ABA Finals appearance. In the Finals, the Nets jumped out to a three-games-to-one lead over the Denver Nuggets. The final matchup in ABA history was taken by the Nets in New York, a 112–106 victory, for the championship. The New York Nets became the New Jersey Nets when they merged with the NBA the next season.

The New Jersey Nets' NBA success has been limited. Led by Jason Kidd and Kenyon Martin, the team made the NBA Finals in both 2002 and 2003. Unfortunately, the Nets were defeated by Shaquille O'Neal and the Lakers in four games in 2002, and in 2003 New Jersey lost to Tim Duncan and the San Antonio Spurs in six games.

OWNERS

ARTHUR BROWN (1967–69)

- Forced a playoff game to be played at an arena so decrepit that the ABA declared a forfeit in favor of the visiting team
- Changed the team name from Americans to Nets
- Failed to sign Lew Alcindor (later named Kareem Abdul-Jabbar) when New York held his draft rights

ROY BOE (1969–78)

- Signed Julius "Dr. J" Erving in 1975, who went on to win three ABA MVP awards
- Two ABA championship teams under his ownership (1974 and 1976)
- Helped the Nets join the NBA in 1976
- Sold Erving to the Philadelphia 76ers for $3 million after not being able to settle a contract dispute

NEW YORK
KNICKS

DANILO GALLINARI

TEAM ORIGINS: The New York Knickerbockers were one of the original charter franchises of the Basketball Association of America (BAA). The Knicks, along with the Boston Celtics, are the only two franchises still active from the BAA. On November 1, 1946, the Knicks played the league's first ever game in Toronto, where they defeated the Toronto Huskies 68–66 in front of 7,090 observers. Under head coach Neil Cohalan, the Knicks went on to finish their first season with a 33–27 record before losing to the Philadelphia Warriors in the Eastern Division Semifinals.

THE GLORY YEARS: The Knicks have made 38 playoff appearances, and have reached the NBA Finals eight times, but have only captured two NBA championships.

The 1969–70 season was one for the ages. Future Hall of Famers Willis Reed and Walt Frazier led the Knicks to a 60–22 regular-season record, winning 19 of their first 20 games and 18 in a row. It took the Knicks seven games to beat the Baltimore Bullets in the first round of the playoffs that season, but only five games to dispose of the Milwaukee Bucks in the next round. In the Finals, the Knicks faced the Los Angeles Lakers, led by Wilt Chamberlain and Jerry West. The series was a classic seven-game grinder, which saw the Knicks' Willis Reed suffer a torn thigh muscle in Game 5, only to limp out onto the court in Game 7 to take the tip and boost his teammates' morale. The Knicks beat the Lakers 113–99, with Reed scoring the game's first two baskets.

In 1972–73, the Knicks posted a 57–25 record and advanced to the Finals by eliminating Baltimore in five games and the Boston Celtics in seven games. In the Finals, the Knicks again met the Lakers, and despite dropping Game 1, the Knicks clawed back and swept the next four games to win their second NBA championship.

It was a long drought for the Knicks before they again returned to the NBA Finals. Patrick Ewing, the legendary Knicks center, led the franchise back to the championship series in 1994 — a playoff run that saw the Knicks play in three Game 7s in the last three rounds — losing the title to the Houston Rockets. In 1999, with Ewing on the bench, Larry Johnson carried the team on his back, guiding the Knicks to their eighth NBA Finals appearance. Unfortunately for the Knicks and their fans, the team lost to the San Antonio Spurs 4–1.

COACHES

PAT RILEY (1991–95)
- Guided the Knicks to a 223–105 regular-season record
- Led the Knicks to the 1994 NBA Finals
- Attended Linton High school in Schenectady, New York, where he was a two-sport star in basketball and football

ISIAH THOMAS (2006–08)
- Guided the Knicks to a 52–100 regular season record
- Never made the postseason in his two years as head coach
- Under Thomas' guidance as team president in 2005, the Knicks had the highest payroll in the league and the second worst record

VINCE CARTER

ORLANDO
MAGIC

TEAM ORIGINS: The Orlando Magic's first head coach, Matt Guokas, a former NBA player and basketball broadcaster for the Philadelphia 76ers, led the Magic onto the court in front of a sold-out crowd on November 4, 1989. Powered by veterans Reggie Theus and Scott Skiles, the Magic lost to the New Jersey Nets 111–106.

Unlike most expansion teams, the Magic had a prolific offense, averaging 110.9 points per game; however, they had the worst defense in the league, averaging 119.8 points against per game. The math didn't lie — the Magic finished their first season with a record of 18–64.

GLIMPSES OF GLORY: In 1992 the Magic began to build the foundation of a team that would eventually lead them to the NBA Finals. That year, Orlando selected Shaquille O'Neal out of LSU with the first overall pick. In his rookie season, O'Neal averaged 23.4 points, 13.9 rebounds and 3.53 blocked shots per game to capture the NBA Rookie of the Year award. A year later, the Magic drafted Chris Webber, whom they traded to Golden State, for guard Anfernee "Penny" Hardaway, and three future first-round picks (in 1996, 1998 and 2000).

Together, O'Neal and Hardaway would become one of the best tandems in the NBA. In 1994–95, the Magic finished with a 57–25 record (the best in the Eastern Conference). They won their first playoff series in franchise history by defeating the Boston Celtics in four games in the first round. Orlando continued on to claim its only Eastern Conference title by defeating the Chicago Bulls in six games and the Indiana Pacers in a great seven-game series. The 1995 NBA Finals were a battle of youth versus experience, as future NBA Hall of Famers Clyde Drexler, Hakeem Olajuwon and the Houston Rockets took the young Orlando Magic team to school, sweeping the series. The next season, Shaq signed a monster contract with the Los Angeles Lakers.

Fourteen years later in 2008–09, the Magic would return to the NBA Finals. After finishing with a 59–23 regular-season record, All-Star center Dwight Howard led his team through the playoffs to the NBA Finals. In the Finals the Magic faced a veteran Los Angeles Lakers team led by Kobe Bryant. Kobe and the Lakers were too much for the Magic, who were defeated in five games.

THE PENNYS!

PENNY HARDAWAY
(ORLANDO MAGIC, 1993–99)

- Four-time NBA All-Star (1995–98)
- Went to the NBA Finals in 1995
- Averaged 18.5 points per game
- Starred in the movie *Blue Chips*

PENNY HARDAWAY
(PHOENIX SUNS, 1999–04)

- Averaged 12.3 points per game
- Only played four games in the 2000–01 season
- No All-Star appearances
- Starred in an episode of MTV's *Cribs*

PHILADELPHIA
76ers

ANDRE IGUODALA

TEAM ORIGINS: After the Philadelphia Warriors left for San Francisco in 1961, basketball returned to the City of Brotherly Love in the spring of 1963 when Ike Richman and Irv Kosloff bought the Syracuse Nationals and changed the name to the 76ers. Under head coach and starting center Dolph Schayes, the 76ers finished with a modest record of 34–46 and were eliminated in the first round of the playoffs.

The 1964–65 season was anything but mediocre, as the Philadelphia 76ers added hometown hero and future Hall of Famer Wilt Chamberlain to the roster. Chamberlain made an immediate impact, leading the team in points per game (30.1) and field-goal percentage (52.8). Philadelphia finished with a 40–40 regular-season record and narrowly missed a chance at the NBA Finals, as Chamberlain and company came within two points of defeating the Boston Celtics in Game 7 of the Eastern Conference Finals, losing 110–109.

THE GLORY YEARS: The 1966–67 Philadelphia 76ers are arguably one of the greatest teams in NBA history. Wilt Chamberlain, Billy Walker and Billy Cunningham were the foundation of a team that posted a 68–13 regular-season record and steamrolled through the playoffs. The Sixers defeated the Cincinnati Royals 3–1 in the first round and then eliminated the Boston Celtics in five games in the Eastern Conference Finals. The 76ers overwhelmed the San Francisco Warriors in the NBA Finals, claiming the championship in six games.

The next season, Chamberlain was traded to Los Angeles, and the club spiralled into a state of decline. New ownership took over in 1976, and made an immediate impact by signing Julius "Dr. J" Erving. In 1982, sensing that Erving needed some talent to complement him, the 76ers traded for power forward Moses Malone from the Houston Rockets. Malone and Erving became one of the most lethal combinations in the NBA, leading the 76ers to a 65–17 record in the 1982–83 season. They stormed through the Eastern Conference playoffs, sweeping the New York Knicks in the semifinals and dominating the Milwaukee Bucks in the Conference Finals. In the 1983 NBA Finals, Malone and Erving got the best of Magic Johnson and the Lakers, sweeping the NBA powerhouse and collecting the franchise's second NBA championship.

FIRST ROUNDERS

SHAWN BRADLEY

- Drafted second overall by the Philadelphia 76ers in 1993
- Averaged 9.5 points in three seasons with the 76ers
- Appeared in the movie *Space Jam*
- Retired in 2004; now does charity work

ALLEN IVERSON

- Drafted first overall by the Philadelphia 76ers in 1996
- 7-time NBA All-Star (2000–06); 2001 NBA MVP
- Led 76ers to NBA Finals in 2001
- NBA Rookie of the Year, 1997

TORONTO
RAPTORS

ANDREA BARGNANI

GENERAL MANAGERS

ROB BABCOCK

- Drafted first-round bust Rafael Araujo ahead of All-Star Andre Iguodala
- Traded Vince Carter for two first-round picks, Alonzo Mourning (who never played), Aaron Williams and Eric Williams in arguably the most lopsided trade in team history
- Signed free agent bust Rafer Alston to a six-year, 30-million-dollar deal

BRYAN COLANGELO

- Signed Toronto's franchise player Chris Bosh to a long-term extension in the 2006 off-season
- Discovered and signed international talent such as Andrea Bargnani and Jorge Garbajosa
- Acquired Hedo Turkoglu and Jarrett Jack in the 2009 off-season

TEAM ORIGINS: The NBA made history in 1995 when the league expanded internationally to Canada with two teams: the Toronto Raptors and the Vancouver Grizzlies. Raptors GM and president, former Detroit Pistons great, Isiah Thomas, selected a stubby point guard named Damon Stoudamire out of the University of Arizona with the Raptors first-ever draft pick, seventh overall in the 1995 NBA draft.

Chosen over college standout Ed O'Bannon, the controversial selection of Stoudamire proved to be profitable for the Raptors as he went on to lead the team in points and assists, and was named the NBA's Rookie of the Year. Under head coach Brandon Malone, the Raptors finished their inaugural campaign with a 21–61 record, including a stunning 109–108 upset over the Chicago Bulls, who won the NBA championship that season.

GLIMPSES OF GLORY: In 1999, four years after their inception, the Raptors, led by their budding superstar guard out of the University of North Carolina, Vince Carter, began to taste NBA success. Carter, winner of the 1999 Slam Dunk competition, along with his cousin, point guard Tracy McGrady, led the Raptors to their first playoff appearance. It would be short, however, as the Raptors were swept by the New York Knicks in three games.

Before the 2000–01 season, the Raptors were forced to trade McGrady when the two sides could not agree on a contract extension. Despite the loss, the Raptors finished the season with a franchise best 47–35 record. Once again, they were matched up with the New York Knicks, but this time they triumphed, beating the Knicks in five games to claim their first playoff series win in franchise history. In the next round, Allen Iverson and the Philadelphia 76ers eliminated the Raptors in seven games as Carter's last-second shot for the win in Game 7 rolled off the rim.

WASHINGTON
WIZARDS

JOSH HOWARD

TEAM ORIGINS: After two failed seasons, the Chicago Zephyrs moved to Baltimore with a new name and a new coach in 1963. The name "Bullets" was chosen because the Baltimore team played in an old armory. Future Hall of Famer Walt Bellamy, who was selected with the first overall pick in the 1962 NBA draft placed fourth in NBA scoring in the Bullets' inaugural season, averaging 27 points per game. The Bullets made the in-state move to the Washington area in 1974 and changed their name to the Wizards in 1997 because of the negative connection between bullets and the rise in handgun violence in the Washington, D.C., area.

THE GLORY YEARS: Earl "The Pearl" Monroe led the Baltimore Bullets to a modest 42–40 record in the 1970–71 season, and the Bullets entered the playoffs as clear underdogs. But to the surprise of many, they squeaked out two seven-game victories over the Philadelphia 76ers and the New York Knicks to advance to their first NBA Finals. The long, hard road to the Finals had taken its toll on the Bullets, and Oscar Robertson and the Milwaukee Bucks disposed of the Baltimore club in four straight games.

In 1977–78, after three NBA Finals appearances and three NBA Finals losses, the Bullets finally claimed their championship. Head coach Dick Motta led his Washington Bullets, which included NBA great Elvin "The Big E" Hayes, to NBA glory. Washington again finished with a less than spectacular regular-season record, posting 44 wins and 38 losses; but the Bullets' previous playoff runs throughout the decade would prove invaluable as the team slugged through the playoffs. First, Washington swept the Atlanta Hawks in the first round, then disposed of the San Antonio Spurs in the Eastern Conference Semifinals in six games, and then defeated old rival Philadelphia in the Eastern Conference Finals in six games. In the NBA Finals, the Bullets encountered the Seattle SuperSonics, a team rejuvenated under coach Lenny Wilkens. The series was a seesaw battle throughout, with the Bullets prevailing in Game 7, 105–99.

FRANCHISE PLAYERS

GILBERT ARENAS (2001–)
- Three-time NBA All-Star (2005–07)
- NBA Most Improved Player award (2003)
- Career average of 22.7 points and 5.6 assists per game prior to his 2009–10 suspension
- Cool nickname: Agent Zero

EARL MONROE (1967–72)
- Four-time NBA All-Star (1969, 1971, 1975, 1977)
- Won Rookie of the Year award (1968)
- Career average of 23.7 points and 4.6 assists per game
- Cool nickname: Earl the Pearl

JASON TERRY

DALLAS
MAVERICKS

TEAM ORIGINS: Texas millionaire Donald J. Carter brought basketball back to Dallas in 1980, after the Dallas Chaparrals of the ABA left for San Antonio in 1973. NBA officials awarded him an expansion team for a 12-million-dollar entry fee. Carter decided to start building his franchise by hiring a proven NBA coach — former Coach of the Year, Dick Motta. Motta started by drafting Kiki Vandeweghe with the 11th overall pick in the 1980 draft. However, Vandeweghe refused to sign in Dallas and was traded to the Denver Nuggets for two first-round picks. One of those picks turned out to be Rolando Blackman, who went on to become a franchise great in Dallas. The highlight of the Mavericks' 15–67 inaugural season was a 103–92 upset of their in-state rivals, the San Antonio Spurs.

THE GLORY YEARS: In 1988, under the coaching of John MacLeod, the Mavs surprised everyone by winning 53 games in the regular season and advancing through the first two rounds of the playoffs, before falling to the Los Angeles Lakers in seven games. The next season Dallas made a questionable personnel move trading leading scorer, guard Mark Aguirre, to the Detroit Pistons, and failed to make the playoffs. It would be 13 years before the team would find the consistency needed to become a perennial playoff contender. In 2005 the Mavericks became only the ninth team in NBA history to rebound to win a playoff series after falling to a 0–2 deficit, as they defeated the Houston Rockets in seven games.

In the 2005–06 season, the Mavericks dominated the NBA. After tying a franchise-high 60 victories in the regular season, the Mavericks made quick work of the Memphis Grizzlies in the opening round of the playoffs, sweeping the Grizzlies 4–0. The second round featured power forward Dirk Nowitzki and the Mavericks against the defending NBA champions, the San Antonio Spurs. The Mavericks ground out a seven-game victory over the Spurs, highlighted by Nowitzki's 37-point performance in Game 7. Dallas would go on to face Phoenix and ex-Maverick Steve Nash in the Western Conference Finals. The Mavs ditched Nash and company in six games on their way to their first NBA Finals. Unfortunately, Dwyane Wade and the Miami Heat proved to be too much for the Dallas squad, as the Heat took the championship in six games.

OWNERS

HENRY ROSS PEROT JR (1996–2000)

- Purchased the Mavericks in 1996 from Donald J. Carter
- During his ownership the Mavericks posted a 98–198 record with zero playoff appearances
- Son of former presidential candidate Ross Perot
- Chairman of Perot Systems in Dallas, Texas

MARK CUBAN (2000–)

- Purchased the Mavericks in 2000 from Henry Ross Perot Jr
- In his first two full seasons of ownership the Mavericks posted a 110–54 record with an 8–10 playoff record
- Appeared in WWE's Survivor Series 2003 in an altercation with RAW GM Eric Bischoff and WWE Superstar Randy Orton

DENVER
NUGGETS

CARMELO ANTHONY

TEAM ORIGINS: The Denver Nuggets originated with the NBA in 1949, but folded after only one season, posting a dismal 11–51 record. In 1967, professional basketball made its return to the Mile High City, as the Denver Rockets took to the floor in the American Basketball Association's inaugural year. On October 16, the Rockets, led by head coach Bob Bass had a successful debut defeating the Anaheim Amigos 110–105. Bass' team played to a 45–33 regular-season record in the new league, before being eliminated by the New Orleans Buccaneers in the first round of the playoffs.

GLIMPSES OF GLORY: Before the 1974–75 season, the Denver franchise changed its name from Rockets to Nuggets so as not to conflict with the San Diego (now Houston) Rockets, should the Denver club merge with the NBA. The change brought the team a new look and a winning attitude, going 65–19 that season and making it to the Western Division Finals, where the Nuggets fell in seven games to the Indiana Pacers. Future NBA Hall of Fame coach Larry Brown and first overall pick David Thompson led the Nuggets to a 60–24 record in 1975–76. Brown won the ABA Coach of the Year award and Thompson was named ABA Rookie of the Year. In the first round of the playoffs, the Nuggets knocked off the Kentucky Colonels before facing the powerhouse New York Nets in the ABA Finals. The Nuggets and Nets fought a gruelling series, with the Nuggets conceding to Julius Erving and the Nets 112–106 in Game 6, the final game in ABA history.

In the 1976–77 season the Nuggets made a successful NBA debut, posting a regular season record of 50–32, capturing the Midwest Division title. Thompson led the team in scoring, averaging 25.9 points per game. Complementing him was Dan Issel, who averaged 22.3 points per game. However, the regular-season success did not translate into playoff success, as the Nuggets were eliminated in the Western Conference Semifinals by the eventual NBA champions, the Portland Trail Blazers. In 1985 the Nuggets compiled a 52–30 record and cruised through the playoffs. Hall of Fame forward Alex English led the team, averaging 27.9 points per game. Denver defeated the San Antonio Spurs and the Utah Jazz, before being stopped cold in their tracks by the high-powered Los Angeles Lakers, losing the conference finals in five games.

NUGGETS THIRD OVERALL PICKS

CARMELO ANTHONY

- Drafted third overall by the Denver Nuggets in 2003
- Three-time NBA All-Star (2007, 2008, 2010)
- Won a gold medal with the United States basketball team at the 2008 Olympics

MAHMOUD ABDUL-RAUF

- Drafted third overall by the Denver Nuggets in 1990
- Averaged 16.1 points and 4.1 assists per game in six years with Denver
- Born Chris Wayne Jackson and converted to Islam in 1991
- Famous for refusal to stand for the national anthem (citing Islamic beliefs) and was suspended for one game in 1996 by the NBA

MONTA ELLIS

GOLDEN STATE
WARRIORS

TEAM ORIGINS: The Warriors of Philadelphia left the City of Brotherly Love for the warmer climates of California in 1962. With them came one of basketball's all-time greats, Wilt Chamberlain. The city of San Francisco was blessed to watch the legendary center, and Chamberlain led the league in scoring that first year, averaging 44.8 points and 24.3 rebounds per game in 1962–63, although the team failed to make the playoffs, finishing with a 31–49 record.

THE GLORY YEARS: Throughout their 47-year history in the Bay area, the Golden State Warriors have qualified for the playoffs 16 times, won three conference titles and one NBA championship; and they almost did it all in their second season. Wilt Chamberlain picked up right where he left off in the Warriors' inaugural season, as he again led the NBA in scoring, averaging 36.9 points per game. That season, the much improved Warriors finished with a 48–32 record and their first playoff berth in San Francisco. Golden State went on to win its first Western Conference Finals against the St. Louis Hawks, clipping the Hawks with a 105–95 victory in Game 7. In the Finals, the Boston Celtics proved to be too much for the second-year franchise, as they captured their seventh NBA crown.

The Warriors returned to the NBA Finals in 1967, but again failed to win it all as the team fell to the Philadelphia 76ers in six games. It would be eight more years before Golden State won another Western Conference title and a shot at the NBA title.

In 1975, the Warriors, led by Hall of Famer Rick Barry and head coach Al Attles, met the Chicago Bulls in the Conference Finals, after disposing of the Seattle SuperSonics in six games. The hard-fought series went all the way to Game 7, with a final tooth-and-nail 83–79 victory for the Warriors. Golden State met the Washington Bullets in the NBA Finals, and the third trip to the championship round proved to be the charm. The Warriors took the series in four games and claimed their first championship. Rick Barry was named MVP of the series.

COACHES

DAVE COWENS

- Coached the Warriors for a season and a half (2000–01 to 2001–02) to a 25–80 regular-season record
- In 1977 took a leave of absence from playing for the Boston Celtics to work as a cab driver "to clear his head."
- Career coaching record: 161–191

DON NELSON

- Has coached the Warriors on two separate occasions (1988–1995 and 2006–present)
- Led Golden State to the playoffs five times (1989, 1991, 1992, 1994, 2007)
- Is the winningest coach in NBA history

HOUSTON
ROCKETS

TEAM ORIGINS: Houston received an NBA franchise when the San Diego Rockets moved to the Lone Star State in 1971. Houston's first win at home came on Halloween night, as they beat the Buffalo Braves, 102–87. Elvin "The Big E" Hayes led the Rockets in scoring and rebounds in 1971–72, averaging a double-double: 25.2 points and 14.6 rebounds per game. Tex Winter was the team's first head coach, and he led the team to a 34–48 record.

THE GLORY YEARS: In 1984, the Rockets drafted center Hakeem Olajuwon with the first overall pick. Olajuwon became the face of the Rockets for the next 15 years, leading Houston to the playoffs a remarkable 14 times.

The Rockets' greatest success was in the 1993–94 season. Olajuwon had a career year, averaging 27.3 points and 11.9 rebounds per game and was named the NBA MVP, and the Rockets compiled a 58–24 regular-season record. In the first round of the playoffs, the Rockets rolled past the Portland Trail Blazers in four games. In the semifinals, Charles Barkley and the Phoenix Suns took the Rockets to Game 7, with Houston winning the game 104–94. The 1994 Finals was an epic battle between two of the NBA's best centers in the 90s: Olajuwon versus Patrick Ewing. After facing elimination in Game 5, the Rockets rallied to win the next two games in Houston to capture their first NBA championship. Olajuwon was named the Finals MVP.

In their quest to repeat as NBA champions, the Rockets added future Hall of Famer Clyde Drexler midway through the 1994–95 season. Houston finished with a 47–35 record and faced the Utah Jazz in the opening round of the playoffs — a five-game epic with the Rockets winning the elimination game, 95–91. In the semifinals, they faced the Phoenix Suns, and once again, the Rockets won the series in Game 7, 115–114. In the Conference Finals, the Rockets eliminated their in-state rivals, the San Antonio Spurs in six games. The 1995 Finals saw a veteran Rockets team face the young, up-and-coming Orlando Magic. Experience prevailed, as the Rockets swept the Magic to claim their second NBA championship. For the second year in a row, Olajuwon was named the Finals MVP.

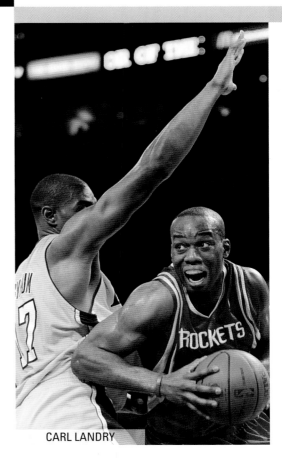

CARL LANDRY

PLAYOFF PERFORMANCES

HAKEEM OLAJUWON
- Two-time NBA Finals MVP (1994, 1995)
- Averaged 25.9 points and 11.2 rebounds per game in 145 playoff games
- Led the Rockets to two NBA titles (1994, 1995)

YAO MING
- Prior to 2010 Ming had led the Rockets to four playoff appearances
- In those appearances the Rockets only advanced to the second round once
- Has an average of 19.8 points and 9.3 rebounds per game in 28 playoff games

BARON DAVIS

LOS ANGELES
CLIPPERS

FIRST OVERALL DRAFT PICKS

DANNY MANNING

- Drafted 1st overall by the Los Angeles Clippers in 1988
- Two-time NBA All-Star (1993, 1994)
- Averaged 19.3 points and 6.5 rebounds per game
- Led Clippers to their first two playoff appearances (1992, 1993)
- Played 14 years in the NBA

MICHAEL OLOWOKANDI

- Drafted 1st overall by the Los Angeles Clippers in 1998
- Averaged 10.1 points and 8.1 rebounds per game
- First player ever to be taken first overall from Pacific University
- Played nine years in the NBA

TEAM ORIGINS: The Los Angeles Clippers' history began, not in sunny California, but in snowy western New York when the NBA awarded an expansion team to the city of Buffalo in 1970. The Buffalo Braves moved to San Diego in 1978, and changed their name to Clippers. After four subpar years in San Diego, the NBA approved a second team for Los Angeles. Clippers' owner Donald Sterling moved his team to downtown Los Angeles, and on November 1, 1984, the team made its debut with a 107–105 victory over the New York Knicks. On March 3, after an unimpressive 22–39 start, head coach Jim Lyman was fired and replaced by Don Chaney. Chaney did not fare much better, as the Clippers finished with a 31–51 record in their debut season.

GLIMPSES OF GLORY: In the city of Los Angeles, the Clippers are dwarfed by their professional basketball brothers, the Los Angeles Lakers, one of the NBA's cornerstone franchises. In the Clippers' time in Los Angeles, they have had glimpses of greatness, but never comparable to their crosstown rivals. Over the course of their 25 years in Los Angeles, the Clippers have qualified for the playoffs only four times.

The Clippers first made the playoffs in 1992, after head coach Larry Brown, who had taken over midway through the season, pushed the team to a 45–37 regular-season record. Despite the midseason turnaround, the Clippers were bounced in the first round of the playoffs in five games by the Utah Jazz. The next year, the Clippers broke even with a 41–41 record and made the playoffs for a second consecutive year. Unfortunately, the Clippers would again be eliminated in the first round, this time by the Houston Rockets.

In 2006, the Clippers made their fourth playoff appearance, and this time they would not see an early exit. Led by All-Star Elton Brand, and complemented by playoff veterans Sam Cassell and Cuttino Mobley, the Clippers finished with their best regular-season record ever (47–35) and a first-round date with the Denver Nuggets. The Clippers jumped out to a 2–0 series lead in Los Angeles before the Nuggets took Game 3 in Denver. The Clippers maintained their composure and took the next two games to win the series in five. It was their first and only playoff series win in franchise history. In the next round, they would be escorted out of the playoffs in six games by the Phoenix Suns.

LOS ANGELES
LAKERS

TEAM ORIGINS: In an attempt to mimic the gate-receipt success of Major League Baseball's Los Angeles Dodgers who had left Brooklyn in 1958, Lakers' owner, Bob Short, moved his basketball team from Minnesota to L.A. in time for the 1960–61 season. With a foundation of promising young players (including future Hall of Famers Jerry West and Elgin Baylor), the Lakers finished second in the Western Division and qualified for the playoffs, making it to the Western Conference Finals before losing Game 7 to the St. Louis Hawks, 105–103.

THE GLORY YEARS: The Lakers are a model of consistency, qualifying for the playoffs 44 times and capturing 10 NBA championships in their 63-year existence (which pre-dates the NBA). The Lakers appeared in seven NBA Finals before finally capturing their first title in 1972, a season that saw them win a record 33 games in a row and finish with 69–13 record. With Elgin Baylor retired, Wilt Chamberlain and Jerry West shouldered the load and defeated the New York Knicks in five games to capture the championship.

The 1980s brought "Showtime" to the West Coast, as head coach Pat Riley led the team to three championships. The first Showtime title (the third for the franchise) came in 1982, when NBA legends Magic Johnson and Kareem Abdul-Jabbar helped the Lakers finish with a 57–25 regular-season record and a run of nine straight playoff wins, before losing Game 2 in the NBA Finals (the Lakers eventually prevailed in six games). Their back-to-back championship seasons in 1987 and 1988 were their last championships of the 20th century.

After luring Shaquille O'Neal from the Orlando Magic in 1996, and trading for the rights to Kobe Bryant in the same year, the Lakers constructed the foundation of a team that dominated the start of the 21st century. Under head coach Phil Jackson (who had led the Chicago Bulls to six NBA championships), the Lakers grabbed the NBA crown three seasons in a row, starting in the 1999–2000 season.

PAU GASOL

LAKER DRAFT GREATS WHO NEVER WON A CHAMPIONSHIP

VLADE DIVAC

- Drafted 26th overall by the Los Angeles Lakers in 1989
- All-Star appearance in 2001
- One of the first European players to establish himself as a solid NBA player
- Averaged 14.3 points per game and 9.9 rebounds per game

ELGIN BAYLOR

- Drafted 1st overall by the Minneapolis Lakers in 1958
- 11-time NBA All-Star
- 1958–59 Rookie of the Year award winner
- Averaged 27.4 points per game and 13.5 rebounds per game
- Inducted into the NBA Hall of Fame in 1977

MEMPHIS
GRIZZLIES

ZACH RANDOLPH

TEAM ORIGINS: The second of two Canadian expansion teams in the mid-1990s, the Vancouver Grizzlies had not fared as well as the Toronto Raptors had, and the result was a move to Memphis for the 2001–02 season. Led by coach Sidney Lowe, the Grizzlies did not impress their Memphis fan base in their inaugural season, compiling a 23–59 record. However, the season was not a complete disaster, as one of the Grizzlies' 23 wins was a six-point victory over the defending NBA champions, the Los Angeles Lakers, 114–108 in Memphis.

GLIMPSES OF GLORY: The Grizzlies struggled in their first two years in Memphis, but during the 2003–04 season, under the guidance of a proven NBA coach, Hubie Brown, Memphis qualified for the playoffs for the first time in franchise history. Led by 7-foot center Pau Gasol and former NBA Rookie of the Year Mike Miller, the Grizzlies achieved a franchise best 50–32 record. By hitting the 50-win mark, the team accomplished something only a handful of NBA teams have done: posting 50 wins after posting 50 losses the previous season. Hubie Brown was awarded the NBA Coach of the Year. In the first round of the playoffs, the Grizzles' inexperience was evident, as the young team was swept in four games by defending NBA Champions, the San Antonio Spurs.

In the next two years, the Grizzlies would post respectable regular-season records, only to continue to disappoint in the postseason. The Grizzlies have yet to win a playoff game, let alone a series, as the club was swept by the Phoenix Suns in 2005 and by the Dallas Mavericks in 2006.

TV COMMENTATORS TURNED HEAD COACHES

HUBIE BROWN

- Television analyst for 12 years with TNT (Turner Network Television)
- For two-and-a-half seasons (2002–04) led the Grizzlies to a 83–85 record and their first playoff appearance
- Nominated for two Sports Grammys (1994 and 1999)

MIKE FRATELLO

- Television analyst for TNT and the YES Network
- For two-and-a-half seasons (2004–06) led the Grizzlies to a 94–77 regular-season record and two playoff appearances
- Fellow play-by-play commentator Marv Albert dubbed him "The Czar of the Telestrator" for his masterful way of diagramming basketball plays on screen

MINNESOTA
TIMBERWOLVES

TEAM ORIGINS: In 1989, the NBA returned to the North Star state after a 30-year hiatus when the Lakers left Minnesota for the warmer climates of California. The name "Timberwolves" was chosen out of 1,284 suggestions in a "Name Your Team" contest, and on November 3, 1989, the newly minted Timberwolves made their NBA debut in Seattle, losing 106–94. Minnesota finished the 1989–90 season with a 22–60 record, besting their expansion brothers the Orlando Magic. Tony Campbell led the team with 23.2 points per game.

THE GLORY YEARS: The Minnesota Timberwolves made their first of eight consecutive playoff appearances in 1997. Forwards Tom Gugliotta and Kevin Garnett represented the Timberwolves in the All-Star Game, and with help from rookie point guard Stephon Marbury, the team finished with a 40–42 record. They were swept by the Houston Rockets in the first round.

The 2003–04 campaign was the best in franchise history. In the off-season, the Timberwolves acquired veterans Latrell Sprewell, Sam Cassell and Michael Olowokandi to complement perennial All-Star Garnett. After a mediocre 9–8 November, the team pulled together and finished with a franchise best 58–24 record, good enough for the Midwest Division title.

More importantly, the Timberwolves gained home-court advantage throughout the playoffs. In their opening round, they wasted no time eliminating the Denver Nuggets in five games. The next round would prove to be a gruelling series, however, as Minnesota faced the battle-tested Sacramento Kings. In Game 7, Garnett showed his clutch defense and blocked a Brad Miller layup attempt with only seconds remaining to give the Timberwolves the victory and their first appearance in the Conference Finals in franchise history. But the seven-game marathon against the Kings proved debilitating for the T-Wolves, and they fell victim to Minnesota's former club, the Los Angeles Lakers, in the Conference Finals, losing in six games. The Timberwolves have not seen postseason action since.

AL JEFFERSON

HIGH SCHOOL SUPERSTARS

KEVIN GARNETT
- Drafted 5th overall by the Minnesota Timberwolves in 1995 from Farragut Career Academy High School in Chicago
- 11-time NBA All-Star
- NBA MVP (2004)
- NBA Defensive Player of the Year (2008)

NDUDI EBI
- Drafted 26th overall by the Minnesota Timberwolves in 2003 from Westbury Christian High School in Houston
- Only played 19 NBA games, averaging 2.1 points per game
- Now plays in Italy for Carife Ferrara

NEW ORLEANS
HORNETS

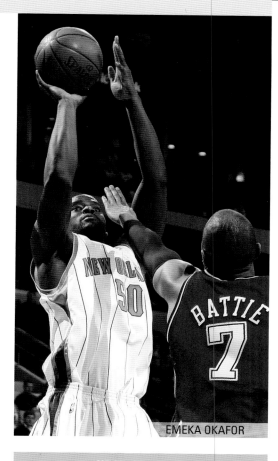

EMEKA OKAFOR

HEAD COACHES

TIM FLOYD

- Coached the Hornets in 2003–04 and recorded a 41–41 record and missed the playoffs
- Overall coaching record in the NBA: 90 wins and 231 losses
- In an interview with the Los Angeles Times was quoted as saying about NBA coaching, "I wasn't very good at it."

BYRON SCOTT

- Has a career record of 305–320 coaching in the NBA, but more importantly, a 32–20 record in the postseason
- Record with the New Orleans Hornets: 156–181 with a 7–5 playoff record
- Won the 2007–08 Coach of the Year award

TEAM ORIGINS: In 2002, the Hornets' franchise left the southern comfort of North Carolina for the raucous lifestyle of Bourbon Street and the city of New Orleans. The Hornets' first game was against the last professional basketball team that had called New Orleans home, the Utah Jazz (New Orleans Jazz 1974–75 to 1978–79). In a successful debut, the Hornets defeated the Jazz, 100–75, the first of 11 consecutive wins at home in their debut season. Coach Paul Silas guided the Hornets to a 47–35 regular season and a playoff berth. The playoff was brief, however, as the Philadelphia 76ers eliminated the Hornets in six games.

GLIMPSES OF GLORY: The Hornets drafted Chris Paul out of Wake Forest University in 2005, and the point guard made an immediate impact. Paul averaged 16.1 points and 7.8 assists per game and captured the 2005–06 NBA Rookie of the Year award.

With Coach Byron Scott, the Hornets would finish 2008 with a 56–26 regular season record to capture their first Southwest Division title in franchise history. Chris Paul soared to elite-player status that year, when he averaged 21.1 points and 11.6 assists per game and made his first All-Star appearance. But it was his performance in the playoffs that cemented his status as a franchise player.

In the playoffs, the Hornets faced a veteran Dallas Mavericks team. New Orleans did not show any signs of being new to the playoffs and defeated the Mavericks in five games. In the next round, they faced four-time NBA champions, the San Antonio Spurs. Many NBA experts felt that the Spurs would dismantle the Hornets, but Chris Paul and company had other ideas. In a long, gruelling, seven-game series, the Hornets gave the Spurs all they could handle. Despite the Hornets leading three games to two, the Spurs battled back to win the series. Chris Paul and forward David West both averaged over 20 points per game in the playoffs, and center Tyson Chandler grabbed an average of 10 rebounds per game.

OKLAHOMA CITY
THUNDER

KEVIN DURANT

TEAM ORIGINS: The state of Oklahoma got its first taste of NBA action when the New Orleans Hornets made Oklahoma City a temporary home during the 2006–07 season, while the city of New Orleans was recovering from the devastation caused by Hurricane Katrina. Consequently, Seattle's owners, who were in the midst of a dispute over a new arena for the team, witnessed how successful professional basketball could be in Oklahoma City. SuperSonics' owner Clay Bennett severed the team's relationship with the city of Seattle, which resulted in a six-day federal trial over the team's lease agreement with KeyArena. On July 3, 2008, a federal judge ruled that Bennett would have to pay $75 million for an immediate termination of the lease. He did, and the team became the Oklahoma City Thunder for the 2008–09 NBA season.

It was 1967 when Seattle was originally awarded an NBA franchise (along with San Diego), and the new team faced the typical struggles of an NBA expansion team. In their first year the SuperSonics recorded a modestly successful 23–59 inaugural record. During the course of their 41-year history in Seattle, the SuperSonics reached the NBA Finals three times and won the NBA Championship in 1979.

THE GLORY YEARS: The late 70s were a great time to be a basketball fan in the Northwest. Coach Bob Hopkins was fired after a 5–17 start in 1977, and former NBA great Lenny Wilkens was hired to take over. Wilkens turned the team around, finishing with a 47–35 regular-season record and a playoff berth. Seattle surprised everyone as they made it all the way to Game 7 of the NBA Finals, defeating the Los Angeles Lakers, the Portland Trail Blazers and the Denver Nuggets to get there. In the Finals, Seattle fought a long, gruelling series against the Washington Bullets, falling at home in Game 7, 105–99.

The next season, Seattle would not be denied NBA glory. Gus "The Wizard" Williams led the team with 19.2 points per game, but it was secondary scoring that made the Sonics successful, as seven players averaged double-digit points. Seattle raced through the regular season with a 52–30 record, first place in the Pacific Division, and rolled through the playoffs in 1979 for a rematch with the Bullets in the Finals. The Sonics destroyed the Bullets in five games to win their first and only NBA championship. Dennis Johnson was named Finals MVP.

INAUGURAL SEASONS

SEATTLE SUPERSONICS, 1967

- Finished with a 23–59 record, 5th in the NBA Western Division
- Coached by Al Bianchi for two seasons (53–111)
- Leading scorer was Mahdi Abdul-Rahman, who averaged 24 points per game

OKLAHOMA CITY THUNDER, 2008

- Finished with a 23–59 record, 5th in the NBA Northwest Division
- Coached by P.J. Carlesimo (1–12) and Scott Brooks (22–47)
- Leading scorer was Kevin Durant, who averaged 25.3 points per game

STEVE NASH

PHOENIX
SUNS

PHOENIX'S BIG DRAFTS

OLIVER MILLER

- Drafted 22nd overall by the Phoenix Suns in 1992
- Height: 6'9"
- Nicknamed "The Big O" because he weighed in at 300 lbs out of college
- Averaged 7.4 points and 5.9 rebounds per game in two seasons with the Suns
- Was cut from the Harlem Globetrotters in 2001 for showing "no appreciation of what it takes mentally and physically to be a Harlem Globetrotter."

AMARE STOUDEMIRE

- Drafted 9th overall by the Phoenix Suns in 2002
- Height: 6'10"
- Rookie of the Year in 2002–03
- Three-time NBA All-Star (2005, 2007, 2008)

TEAM ORIGINS: When Richard Bloch approached NBA Commissioner Walter Kennedy at the prospect of an expansion team in Phoenix, the commissioner looked at him in disbelief and said, "Phoenix? You must be crazy! They will never support pro basketball." Forty years later, it's safe to say the commissioner may have underestimated the market for professional basketball in Arizona. Bloch persisted and with much hesitation, in 1968 the NBA granted him a franchise at a price tag of two million dollars. Johnny "Red" Kerr was hired as the team's first head coach, and he led the Suns to a 16–66 record.

THE GLORY YEARS: In 1976, the Phoenix Suns surprised everyone in basketball when they finished the season 42–40, a remarkable turnaround, given that Phoenix's record was 18–31 at the All-Star break. A large part of this success was Alvan Adams who took home Rookie of the Year honors, averaging 19 points and 9.1 rebounds per game. Adams' and the Suns' remarkable run continued into the playoffs, as Phoenix dumped the Seattle SuperSonics in six games and the defending NBA champions, the Golden State Warriors, in seven. In the NBA Finals against the Boston Celtics, with the series tied at two games, Phoenix forward Garfield Heard hit an 18-foot turn-around buzzer beater to tie the game 112–112 and send the match into its third overtime period. The Celtics went on to win the game in the third overtime, 128–126, and the series in Game 6, but the playoff run would establish Phoenix as a legitimate NBA franchise.

In 1993, the Suns traded for Charles Barkley. Barkley's Suns, which also included Dan Majerle and Kevin Johnson, finished with a 62–20 record, and Barkley was named the NBA MVP. In the playoffs that year, the Suns lost the first two games of the first round best-of-five series to the Los Angeles Lakers. Facing elimination, Barkley rallied the team to three straight wins, marking the first time a team had come back to win a best-of-five series with a two-game deficit. The Suns went on to eliminate the San Antonio Spurs in six games, and then Seattle in an exhausting seven-game series. The Suns took the Chicago Bulls to a seventh and deciding game in the NBA Finals, and with only a couple of seconds left on the clock, Bulls' guard John Paxton hit a three point basket, known in NBA lore as "the shot" to give the Bulls their third NBA championship.

PORTLAND TRAIL
BLAZERS

BRANDON ROY

TEAM ORIGINS: The Portland Trail Blazers were one of three NBA expansion teams, along with the Cleveland Cavaliers and the Buffalo Braves, to make their debut in 1970. On October 15, 1970, the Trail Blazers stepped onto the hardwood and faced off against their expansion brothers from Cleveland. The Blazers were the victor, winning 115–112, on their way to a 29–53 regular season. They had the best record of the three expansion teams in the 1970–71 season.

THE GLORY YEARS: Seven years would pass before the Trail Blazers made their playoff debut, and what a debut it was. Portland's new head coach, Jack Ramsey, turned the Trail Blazers into a winner, going from 37–45 in 1975–76 to 49–33 the next season. Ramsay was helped by the team's acquisition of Maurice Lucas in the ABA dispersal draft and Bill Walton, who had been drafted a couple of years earlier from UCLA. Together, Lucas and Walton led a young and exciting team to a second-place finish in the NBA Pacific Division, but it was in the playoffs that this team would make history.

The Trail Blazers rolled through the first round of the 1976–77 playoffs, defeating the Chicago Bulls in three games, and then continued, defeating the Denver Nuggets in six games. In the Western Conference Finals, the much younger and less-experienced Trail Blazers swept the veteran-laden, Kareem Abdul-Jabbar-led Los Angeles Lakers. In the NBA Finals, Portland faced another tough test — Julius Erving and the Philadelphia 76ers. But the Trail Blazers were up to the task, defeating the 76ers in six games for their first and only NBA championship.

Blazermania would be in full swing after the 1977 championship, and is still strong today. In 1989, the Trail Blazers had another title shot, as future Hall of Famer Clyde Drexler led Portland to a 59–23 regular-season record and a date with the Detroit Pistons in the NBA Finals. Their second time at the dance would not be as successful as their debut, as the Pistons took the title in five games. Two years later, Drexler and company would return to the Finals, this time to be foiled in six games by Michael Jordan and the Chicago Bulls.

COLLEGE CAREERS OF PORTLAND NO. 1 PICKS

GREG ODEN

- Drafted first overall by the Portland Trail Blazers in 2007
- Led Ohio State to the 2007 NCAA Final Four as a freshman
- In 32 games at Ohio State, he averaged 15.7 points and 9.6 rebounds per game
- Missed his entire rookie year with a torn ACL

BILL WALTON

- Drafted first overall by the Portland Trail Blazers in 1974
- Three-time Naismith Men's College Player of the Year
- Part of the legendary 88-game UCLA winning streak from 1971 to 1973, the longest in NCAA history
- Won two NCAA national championships (1972, 1973)

SACRAMENTO
KINGS

TYREKE EVANS

COACHES

RICK ADELMAN (1998–06)

- Record with the Kings: 395–229 in the regular season; 34–35 in the playoffs
- Led the Kings to the 2002 Western Conference Finals
- Coached the Kings to eight consecutive playoff appearances

VS

DICK MOTTA (1989–92)

- Record with the Kings: 48–113 in the regular season
- No playoff appearances during his coaching tenure
- Popularized the phrase "The opera ain't over until the fat lady sings!"

TEAM ORIGINS: The Sacramento Kings trace their history back to 1949 when the club made its debut in Rochester, New York, as the Rochester Royals. Since then, the team has made stops in Kansas City and Cincinnati before settling in the capital of California in 1985. Under the coaching of Phil Jackson, the franchise's first season in Sacramento was a success, as the Kings sold out every home game on their way to a 37–45 record and a spot in the playoffs. However, the Kings' first playoff appearance in California was brief, with the Houston Rockets sweeping them in three games.

THE GLORY YEARS: The Kings' next trip to the playoffs wasn't until 1996, which resulted in a first round, four-game elimination by the Seattle SuperSonics. The Kings returned to the playoffs three years later, a trip that marked the start of an eight-season playoff run. The Kings' most successful playoff drive during this time was in 2002 when the team made it all the way to the Western Conference Finals. That season Sacramento finished with a 61–21 regular-season record, good enough to secure home-court advantage throughout the playoffs. The 2002 Kings were led by two All-Stars: forward Chris Webber — the number-one overall pick in the 1993 NBA draft — who starred as one of the famed "Fab Five" at the University of Michigan that led the Wolverines to the 1993 NCAA Final; and forward Peja Stojakovic from Croatia, whose family fled from war-torn Yugoslavia and settled in Greece where he played basketball for PAOK BC.

In the opening round of the 2002 playoffs, the Kings sent the Utah Jazz home early with a 3–1 series victory. In the next round, Sacramento faced the up-and-coming Dallas Mavericks. Chris Webber and the Kings held Dirk Nowitzki and the Mavericks in check, sending the Mavs back to Texas in five games and catapulting the Kings to the Western Conference Finals where they would meet the mighty Los Angeles Lakers. L.A.'s Shaquille O'Neal and Kobe Bryant, one of the best duos in the history of the game, came up against Sacramento's duo of Webber and Stojakovic. The teams would bump and grind and the two pairs put on a show — it was a modern-day classic. In Game 7, the Kings' point guard Mike Bibby hit two free throws to tie the game at 100, sending it into overtime. However, the Lakers proved to be too much, as point guard Derek Fisher and Shaq would combine for 10 points in overtime, sending the Lakers to their third consecutive NBA Finals.

SAN ANTONIO
SPURS

MANU GINOBILI

TEAM ORIGINS: The San Antonio Spurs' franchise was rescued from oblivion when a group of San Antonio businessmen bought the Dallas Chaparrals of the American Basketball Association and moved them to San Antonio in 1973. The team made an early impact in the ABA by acquiring 21-year-old George "The Iceman" Gervin. With Gervin in the lineup, the club compiled a 45–39 regular-season record and acquired a playoff berth. The Spurs lost to the Indiana Pacers in the first round, but it did not overshadow the team's successful debut.

THE GLORY YEARS: The San Antonio Spurs are one of the most successful professional basketball franchises of all time. In the course of their 37-year history, divided between the ABA and NBA, they have 31 playoff appearances. In 1997, after one of the most frustrating seasons in their history, San Antonio was dealt a little luck, as the franchise won the first-overall selection in the draft lottery. With that pick the Spurs selected Tim Duncan out of Wake Forest University. It was a wise move, as Duncan has led his team to four NBA championships.

Duncan, alongside 10-time All-Star David Robinson, turned San Antonio into an instant contender. In 1998–99, Duncan's second year in the NBA, the Spurs stormed through a lockout-shortened season with a 37–13 record. The Spurs' domination continued all the way to the Finals, where Duncan, Robinson and company pummelled the New York Knicks, taking the championship in five games. Duncan averaged 27.4 points and 14 rebounds during the NBA Finals and was named MVP — his first of three.

Duncan and the Spurs rolled on to three more titles, winning in 2003, 2005 and 2007, and the franchise owes much of its success to Duncan's supporting cast. Point guard Tony Parker was awarded the 2007 Finals MVP and has been named to the All-Star Team three times. Defensive leader Bruce Bowen was elected to the All-Defensive First Team five times during the course of his NBA career. Manu Ginobili, a late second-round pick in 1999, always turns it up for the playoffs, averaging 1.4 points and almost 1 rebound per game better in the playoffs than in the regular season. All of these players were critical in allowing the Spurs to capture three championships in five years.

1987 FIRST-ROUND DRAFT PICKS

DAVID ROBINSON
- Drafted 1st overall by the San Antonio Spurs in 1987
- Averaged 21.6 points and 10.6 rebounds per game in 14 seasons with the Spurs
- 1994–95 NBA MVP
- 1991–92 NBA Defensive Player of the Year
- 10-time All-Star selection

GREG "CADILLAC" ANDERSON
- Drafted 23rd overall by the San Antonio Spurs in 1987
- Averaged 10.1 points and 7.4 rebounds per game in three-and-a-half seasons with the Spurs
- Nicknamed "Cadillac" because he rode his 10-speed bicycle everywhere around campus in college

UTAH
JAZZ

DERON WILLIAMS

BATTLE OF THE BIG MEN

GREG OSTERTAG

- Drafted 28th overall by the Utah Jazz in 1995
- Averaged 4.6 points and 5.5 rebounds per game
- In 89 playoff games averaged 4.2 points and 5.4 rebounds per game
- Became only the second player in NBA history to return to action after donating a kidney to his sister in 2002.

VS

CARLOS BOOZER

- Drafted 34th overall by the Cleveland Cavaliers in 2002
- Two-time NBA All-Star (2007, 2008)
- Averages 17.1 points and 10.1 rebounds per game
- In 34 playoff games has averaged 20.4 points and 12.4 rebounds per game

TEAM ORIGINS: After having limited success on the court, the New Orleans Jazz ownership raised some eyebrows when they moved to the reserved culture of Salt Lake City in 1979. Questions were raised as to whether the NBA's Utah franchise would recapture the hearts of the fans who loved the defunct ABA team, the Utah Stars. In their first season, things looked doubtful. The Jazz, led by head coach Tom Nissalke, posted a dismal 24–58 record.

THE GLORY YEARS: The 1983–84 season saw the Jazz advance to the playoffs for the first time in franchise history. The team was led by guard Darrell "Dr. Dunkenstein" Griffith and swingman Adrian Dantley. After finishing with a 45–37 regular-season record, the Jazz accomplished another franchise milestone by winning their first playoff series, a five-game, first-round affair over the Denver Nuggets. However, they would fall in the second round to the Phoenix Suns. With the help of 1984 first-rounder John Stockton and 1985 first-rounder Karl Malone, the playoffs became a mainstay in Utah for 20 consecutive years. During that time, the Jazz captured six division championships and made six appearances in the Western Conference Finals, winning two of them.

In 1991–92 head coach Jerry Sloan led the dynamic duo and the Jazz to a 55–27 regular-season record, capturing the Midwest Division crown. The Jazz defeated both the Los Angeles Clippers and the Seattle SuperSonics in five games to advance to the Conference Finals. However, Clyde Drexler and the Portland Trail Blazers proved to be too much for the Jazz, as Portland bested Utah in a long, hard-fought, six-game series.

The 1996–97 season was a year to remember. The Jazz became one of the NBA's elite when they posted a 64–18 regular-season record, the best in franchise history. In the playoffs, Utah conquered the city of Los Angeles, defeating the Clippers in the first round and the Lakers in the second round. In the Conference Finals, the Jazz met two-time NBA champs, the Houston Rockets. In Game 6, with only one play remaining, Karl Malone set a pick off a Byron Scott inbound pass and John Stockton buried the winning jumper to send the Jazz to their first NBA Finals. In the Finals, Stockton, Malone and company would lose in six games to Michael Jordan and the Chicago Bulls. The Bulls would be the nemesis for the Jazz the following year, as Chicago again defeated the Jazz in six games to take the crown.

NBA Finals History

1946-47 Finals
Philadelphia Warriors   4
Chicago Stags   1
MVP: N/A

1947–48 Finals
Baltimore Bullets   4
Philadelphia Warriors   2
MVP: N/A

1948–49 Finals
Minneapolis Lakers   4
Washington Capitols   2
MVP: N/A

1949–50 Finals
Minneapolis Lakers   4
Syracuse Nationals   2
MVP: N/A

1950-51 Finals
Rochester Royals   4
New York Knicks   3
MVP: N/A

1951–52 Finals
Minneapolis Lakers   4
New York Knicks   3
MVP: N/A

1952–53 Finals
Minneapolis Lakers   4
New York Knicks   1
MVP: N/A

1953–54 Finals
Minneapolis Lakers   4
Syracuse Nationals   3
MVP: N/A

1954–55 Finals
Syracuse Nationals   4
Fort Wayne Pistons   3
MVP: N/A

1955-56 Finals
Philadelphia Warriors   4
Fort Wayne Pistons   1
MVP: N/A

1956–57 Finals
Boston Celtics   4
St. Louis Hawks   3
MVP: N/A

1957–58 Finals
St. Louis Hawks   4
Boston Celtics   2
MVP: N/A

1958–59 Finals
Boston Celtics   4
Minneapolis Lakers   0
MVP: N/A

1959–60 Finals
Boston Celtics   4
St. Louis Hawks   3
MVP: N/A

1960–61 Finals
Boston Celtics   4
St. Louis Hawks   1
MVP: N/A

1961–62 Finals
Boston Celtics   4
Los Angeles Lakers   3
MVP: N/A

1962–63 Finals
Boston Celtics   4
Los Angeles Lakers   2
MVP: N/A

1963–64 Finals
Boston Celtics   4
San Francisco Warriors   1
MVP: N/A

1964–65 Finals
Boston Celtics   4
Los Angeles Lakers   1
MVP: N/A

1965–66 Finals
Boston Celtics   4
Los Angeles Lakers   3
MVP: N/A

1966–67 Finals
Philadelphia 76ers   4
San Francisco Warriors   2
MVP: N/A

1967–68 Finals
Boston Celtics   4
Los Angeles Lakers   2
MVP: N/A

1968–69 Finals
Boston Celtics   4
Los Angeles Lakers   3
MVP: Jerry West, Los Angeles

1969–70 Finals
New York Knicks   4
Los Angeles Lakers   3
MVP: Willis Reed, New York

1970–71 Finals
Milwaukee Bucks   4
Baltimore Bullets   0
MVP: Kareem Abdul-Jabbar, Milwaukee

1971–72 Finals
Los Angeles Lakers   4
New York Knicks   1
MVP: Wilt Chamberlain, Los Angeles

1972–73 Finals
New York Knicks   4
Los Angeles Lakers   1
MVP: Willis Reed, New York

1973–74 Finals
Boston Celtics   4
Milwaukee Bucks   3
MVP: John Havlicek, Boston

1974–75 Finals
Golden State Warriors   4
Washington Bullets   0
MVP: Rick Barry, Golden State

1975–76 Finals
Boston Celtics   4
Phoenix Suns   2
MVP: Jo Jo White, Boston

1976–77 Finals
Portland Trail Blazers   4
Philadelphia 76ers   2
MVP: Bill Walton, Portland

1977–78 Finals
Washington Bullets   4
Seattle SuperSonics   3
MVP: Wes Unseld, Washington

1978–79 Finals
Seattle SuperSonics   4
Washington Bullets   1
MVP: Dennis Johnson, Seattle

1979–80 Finals
Los Angeles Lakers   4
Philadelphia 76ers   2
MVP: Magic Johnson, Los Angeles

1980–81 Finals
Boston Celtics   4
Houston Rockets   2
MVP: Cedric Maxwell, Boston

1981–82 Finals
Los Angeles Lakers   4
Philadelphia 76ers   2
MVP: Magic Johnson, Los Angeles

1982–83 Finals
Philadelphia 76ers   4
Los Angeles Lakers   0
MVP: Moses Malone, Philadelphia

1983–84 Finals
Boston Celtics   4
Los Angeles Lakers   3
MVP: Larry Bird, Boston

1984–85 Finals
Los Angeles Lakers   4
Boston Celtics   2
MVP: Kareem Abdul-Jabbar, Los Angeles

1985–86 Finals
Boston Celtics   4
Houston Rockets   2
MVP: Larry Bird, Boston

1986–87 Finals
Los Angeles Lakers   4
Boston Celtics   2
MVP: Magic Johnson, Los Angeles

1987–88 Finals
Los Angeles Lakers   4
Detroit Pistons   3
MVP: James Worthy, Los Angeles

1988–89 Finals
Detroit Pistons   4
Los Angeles Lakers   0
MVP: Joe Dumars, Detroit

1989–90 Finals
Detroit Pistons   4
Portland Trail Blazers   1
MVP: Isiah Thomas, Detroit

CREDITS

1990–91 Finals

| Chicago Bulls | 4 |
| Los Angeles Lakers | 1 |

MVP: Michael Jordan, Chicago

1991–92 Finals

| Chicago Bulls | 4 |
| Portland Trail Blazers | 2 |

MVP: Michael Jordan, Chicago

1992–93 Finals

| Chicago Bulls | 4 |
| Phoenix Suns | 2 |

MVP: Michael Jordan, Chicago

1993–94 Finals

| Houston Rockets | 4 |
| New York Knicks | 3 |

MVP: Hakeem Olajuwon, Houston

1994–95 Finals

| Houston Rockets | 4 |
| Orlando Magic | 0 |

MVP: Hakeem Olajuwon, Houston

1995–96 Finals

| Chicago Bulls | 4 |
| Seattle SuperSonics | 2 |

MVP: Michael Jordan, Chicago

1996–97 Finals

| Chicago Bulls | 4 |
| Utah Jazz | 2 |

MVP: Michael Jordan, Chicago

1997–98 Finals

| Chicago Bulls | 4 |
| Utah Jazz | 2 |

MVP: Michael Jordan, Chicago

1998–99 Finals

| San Antonio Spurs | 4 |
| New York Knicks | 1 |

MVP: Tim Pacer, San Antonio

1999–00 Finals

| Los Angeles Lakers | 4 |
| Indiana Pacers | 2 |

MVP: Shaquille O'Neal, Los Angeles

2000–01Finals

| Los Angeles Lakers | 4 |
| Philadelphia 76ers | 1 |

MVP: Shaquille O'Neal, Los Angeles

2001–02 Finals

| Los Angeles Lakers | 4 |
| New Jersey Nets | 0 |

MVP: Shaquille O'Neal, Los Angeles

2002–03 Finals

| San Antonio Spurs | 4 |
| New Jersey Nets | 2 |

MVP: Tim Duncan, San Antonio

2003–04 Finals

| Detroit Pistons | 4 |
| Los Angeles Lakers | 1 |

MVP: Chauncey Billups, Detroit

2004–05 Finals

| San Antonio Spurs | 4 |
| Detroit Pistons | 3 |

MVP: Tim Duncan, San Antonio

2005–06 Finals

| Miami Heat | 4 |
| Dallas Mavericks | 2 |

MVP: Dwyane Wade, Miami

2006–07 Finals

| San Antonio Spurs | 4 |
| Cleveland Cavaliers | 0 |

MVP: Tony Parker, San Antonio

2007–08 Finals

| Boston Celtics | 4 |
| Los Angeles Lakers | 2 |

MVP: Paul Pierce, Boston

2008–09 Finals

| Los Angeles Lakers | 4 |
| Orlando Magic | 1 |

MVP: Kobe Bryant, Los Angeles

2009–10 Finals

| Los Angeles Lakers | 4 |
| Boston Celtics | 3 |

MVP: Kobe Bryant, Los Angeles

DEDICATION

To my family: Avery, Ellis and Faeron; somehow I ended up with a Hall of Fame lineup.

ACKNOWLEDGMENTS

A book like this stands on the shoulders of giants: Were it not for the exploits of Bill, Wilt, Kareem, Dr. J, Michael, Magic, Larry and many more, there would be no book to write. But it also stands on the shoulders — though usually hunched, with their owners typing madly — of those who brought the exploits of the giants to life over the decades.

Television brought basketball stars into our living rooms and basements, and the Internet brings them to our laptops and cell phones. But the quotes, anecdotes, back stories and details that elevate those who elevate for a living are the domain of the reporter: The men and women working for various newspapers, magazines and websites who have measured the ebbing hours of a life well spent by how much time they've spent at a pre-game shoot-around, or waiting out an airport delay, or waiting and wondering how long it will take LeBron James to put his earrings in — the lingering a sure sign that it's time for him to speak.

I'd like to acknowledge the various basketball people I've interviewed and chatted with over the years — too many to mention by name — who filled my head with ideas, stories and knowledge about a game I'd like to think I know well, but could never know well enough. I'd like to acknowledge the greatness of the players who I grew up watching on television, or have been lucky enough to watch in person and talk to afterward. It is always a thrill to see the best do what they do best. And I'd also like to acknowledge Steve Cameron, my editor at Firefly, who proposed the subject and has been diligent, dedicated, skillful and good-humored enough to actually see me see this project through.

But, most importantly, I'd like to acknowledge all the scribes, hacks, beat grunts, feature guys and columnists who put in all those hours, took all those notes, missed all those flights and still churned out all that copy for all of those crazy deadlines so that years later someone like me can read it over and lift their best stuff.

Thanks,

Michael Grange